REGIONAL MONETARY INTEGRATION

This book surveys the prospects for regional monetary integration in various parts of the world. Beginning with a brief review of the theory of optimal currency areas, it goes on to examine the structure and functioning of the European Monetary Union, then turns to the prospects for monetary integration elsewhere in the world – North America, South America, and East Asia. Such cooperation may take the form of full-fledged monetary unions or looser forms of monetary cooperation. The book emphasizes the economic and institutional requirements for successful monetary integration, including the need for a single central bank in the case of a full-fledged monetary union, and the corresponding need for multinational institutions to safeguard its independence and assure its accountability. The book concludes with a chapter on the implications of monetary integration for the United States and the U.S. dollar.

Peter B. Kenen is Adjunct Senior Fellow for International Economics at the Council on Foreign Relations and Walker Professor of Economics and Finance, Emeritus, at Princeton University. Professor Kenen's publications include *The International Economy* (Fourth Edition, 2000, Cambridge University Press), *Economic and Monetary Union in Europe* (1995, Cambridge University Press), *The International Financial Architecture*, and *Exchange Rates and the Monetary System*. He was a member of President Kennedy's Task Force on Foreign Economic Policy and the Economic Advisory Panel of the Federal Reserve Bank of New York. Professor Kenen has served as consultant to the Council of Economic Advisers, the Office of Management and Budget, the Federal Reserve, the U.S. Treasury, and the International Monetary Fund.

Ellen E. Meade is Associate Professor in the Department of Economics at American University, where she has been on the faculty since 2005. Previously, Professor Meade was a Guest Scholar at the Brookings Institution, Senior Research Fellow in the Centre for Economic Performance at the London School of Economics, Senior Economist for the Council of Economic Advisers, and Senior Economist on the staff of the Federal Reserve Board of Governors. Professor Meade has published in the *Economic Journal* (forthcoming), the *Journal of Economic Perspectives*, the *Journal of Economic Literature*, and the *Journal of Money, Credit, and Banking*, among others. She has held affiliations with Chatham House and the American Institute for Contemporary German Studies, been a visiting scholar at the Federal Reserve Bank of St. Louis, and been a consultant to the Bank for International Settlements. In addition, she has taught economics courses at Georgetown University, the Catholic University of Louvain, and the central banks of Bosnia/Herzegovina and Syria.

D0222458

A Council on Foreign Relations Book

Founded in 1921, the Council on Foreign Relations is an independent, national membership organization and a nonpartisan center for scholars dedicated to producing and disseminating ideas so that individual and corporate members, as well as policymakers, journalists, students, and interested citizens in the United States and other countries, can better understand the world and the foreign policy choices facing the United States and other governments. The Council does this by convening meetings; conducting a wide-ranging Studies program; publishing *Foreign Affairs*, the preeminent journal covering international affairs and U.S. foreign policy; maintaining a diverse membership; sponsoring Independent Task Forces; and providing up-to-date information about the world and U.S. foreign policy on the Council's website, CFR.org.

Regional Monetary Integration

PETER B. KENEN

Council on Foreign Relations and Princeton University

ELLEN E. MEADE

American University

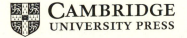

CAMBRIDGE
UNIVERSITY PRESS

CAMBRIDGE UNIVERSITY PRESS
Cambridge, New York, Melbourne, Madrid, Cape Town, Singapore, São Paulo, Delhi

Cambridge University Press
32 Avenue of the Americas, New York, NY 10013-2473, USA

www.cambridge.org
Information on this title: www.cambridge.org/9780521862509

First published 2008

Printed in the United States of America

A catalog record for this publication is available from the British Library.

Library of Congress Cataloging in Publication Data

Kenen, Peter B., 1932–
Regional monetary integration / Peter B. Kenen, Ellen E. Meade.
p. cm.
Includes bibliographical references and index.
ISBN 978-0-521-86250-9 (hardback) – ISBN 978-0-521-71150-0 (pbk.)
1. Monetary unions.   2. Monetary policy.   3. Currency question.
4. International finance.   I. Meade, Ellen E.   II. Title.
HG3894.K46   2008
332.4′5–dc22   2007017768

ISBN   978-0-521-86250-9 hardback
ISBN   978-0-521-71150-0 paperback

To my grandchildren, Zach and Ilan Cohen

and Sela and Asher Kenen

P.B.K.

To my husband, Robert Kahn,

and my sons, Gabriel and

Raphael Kahn

E.E.M.

Contents

Tables, Boxes, and Chart

TABLES

Acronyms

ACU	Asian Currency Unit
ADB	Asian Development Bank
AMF	Asian Monetary Fund
APEC	Asia-Pacific Economic Cooperation (forum)
ASEAN	Association of South East Asian Nations
ASEAN+3	ASEAN members *plus* China, Japan, and the Republic of Korea
BCCB	British Caribbean Currency Board
BLEU	Belgium-Luxembourg Economic Union
CAEMC	Central African Economic and Monetary Community
CAFTA-DR	Central America-Dominican Republic-United States Free Trade Agreement
CAP	Common Agricultural Policy (of the EU)
CFA	Franc of the French colonies of Africa (1945–1958); Franc of the French community of Africa (since 1958)
CMA	Common Monetary Area (in Southern Africa)
CMI	Chiang Mai Initiative
EACB	East African Currency Board
EC	European Communities (also used here to denote the European Economic Community, or Common Market, taken by itself)
ECB	European Central Bank
ECCA	Eastern Caribbean Currency Authority
ECCB	Eastern Caribbean Central Bank
ECCU	Eastern Caribbean Currency Union

ECOFIN	Council of Ministers when attended by Economic and Finance Ministers
ECOWAS	Economic Community of West African States
ECU	European Currency Unit
EMCF	European Monetary Cooperation Fund
EMCP	ECOWAS Monetary Cooperation Programme
EMEAP	Executives' Meeting of East Asia and Pacific Central Banks
EMS	European Monetary System
EMU	European Monetary Union (strictly, Economic and Monetary Union, but commonly used as it is here)
EPU	European Payments Union
ESCB	European System of Central Banks
ESF	Exchange Stabilization Fund
EU	European Union
FOMC	Federal Open Market Committee
GATT	General Agreement on Tariffs and Trade
GCC	Gulf Cooperation Council
G-7	Group of 7 (comprising Canada, France, Germany, Italy, Japan, the United Kingdom, and the United States)
IEO	Independent Evaluation Office (of the International Monetary Fund)
IGC	Intergovernmental Conference (of the EU member states)
IMF	International Monetary Fund
LMU	Latin Monetary Union
MERCOSUR	Mercado Común del Sur (Common Market of the South)
MFG	Manila Framework Group
NAFTA	North American Free Trade Area
NAMU	North American Monetary Union
OECD	Organisation for Economic Cooperation and Development
REMU	Regional Economic Monitoring Unit (of the Asian Development Bank)
SMSA	Standard Metropolitan Statistical Area
SMU	Scandinavian Monetary Union

TEU	Treaty on European Union (i.e., the Maastricht Treaty)
WAEMU	West African Economic and Monetary Union
WAMI	West African Monetary Institute
WAMZ	West African Monetary Zone
WAUA	West African Unit of Account

Acknowledgments

The authors are deeply grateful to the members of the Study Group appointed by the Council on Foreign Relations to assist us in the planning and drafting of this book: David M. Andrews, Caroline Atkinson, Lionel Barber, Zanny Minton Beddoes, David O. Beim, Kenneth J. Bialkin, Benjamin J. Cohen, Stephen S. Cohen, Karen Parker Feld, Richard N. Gardner, Linda S. Goldberg, Morris Goldstein, C. Randall Henning, Yves-Andre Istel, Hendrik J. Kranenburg, Karin M. Lissakers, John H. Makin, David R. Malpass, François Pages, Scott E. Pardee, Hugh T. Patrick, Benn Steil, and Kathleen Stephansen. We are also grateful to the many other people who read and took time to comment on successive versions of the manuscript.

We are especially grateful to Timothy F. Geithner, President and CEO of the Federal Reserve Bank of New York, who chaired the Study Group and helped enormously to synthesize the comments of its members into cohesive advice for the authors.

Ellen Meade expresses her thanks to the Brookings Institution, where she spent the first year of her work on this book, and to the Council on Foreign Relations for financial support, which freed her from some of her teaching during the second year.

The chapter that discusses North America was greatly improved following meetings in Ottawa with Canadian officials and academics. Ellen Meade wishes to thank John Murray and Larry Schembri of the Bank of Canada for their detailed comments, former deputy prime minister John Manley for his insights, and American University's Center for North American Studies for financial support. She also thanks Edwin M.

Truman, Robert Blecker, and Robert Lafrance for detailed comments on an early version of the chapter.

The chapter that discusses East Asia benefited hugely from a full-day seminar convened in Hong Kong in October 2005, by the Asian Office of the Bank for International Settlements and the Hong Kong Institute for Monetary Studies; it was organized by Corrinne Ho of the BIS and Hans Genberg of the Hong Kong Monetary Authority and was attended by officials and academics from several East Asian countries and the Asian Development Bank. The chapter also benefited from discussions in a seminar at the London School of Economics, from a session of the Annual Conference of the Federal Reserve Bank of San Francisco, and from meetings with officials and academics in Singapore, including Khor Ho Ee of the Monetary Authority of Singapore and Professor Ramkishen Rajan of the National University.

We are particularly grateful to two anonymous referees for their insightful comments and to four superb Research Associates at the Council on Foreign Relations, Lindsay Iversen, Nita Colaço, Emma Aller, and Laura Little, for their meticulous research assistance and their help in preparing the final manuscript.

Introduction

There has been a significant regionalization of international trade. In 1990, 37 percent of the foreign trade of Canada, Mexico, and the United States was bilateral trade between pairs of those three countries; by 2004, the figure had risen to nearly 44 percent. In 1990, 29 percent of the foreign trade of thirteen East Asian countries was bilateral trade between pairs of those same countries; by 2004, the figure had risen to 39 percent. (See Table 1.1.) Some but not all of this increase in regional trade reflects the formation of preferential trading arrangements, such as the North American Free Trade Area (NAFTA) and the Association of South East Asian Nations (ASEAN).

This book asks whether we should expect to see an analogous regionalization of the international monetary system over the next one or two decades, the form or forms that it might take, and the potential benefits and costs viewed from the standpoint of the participants. It also asks how regional monetary integration might affect outsiders, including, most important, the United States, because of the key role played by the U.S. dollar in the global monetary system.

Why do we ask these questions now? Over the past several years, a number of countries have given up their national currencies and replaced them either with a multinational monetary union or with a prominent international currency such as the U.S. dollar.

In January 1999, eleven members of the European Union (EU) formed a monetary union, replacing their national currencies with a new single currency, the euro, and creating a new institution, the European Central Bank (ECB), which formulates and implements a single monetary policy

Table 1.1. *Intraregional trade (exports plus imports) as a percentage of total trade, 1990 and 2004*

Country group	1990	2004
Western Hemisphere:		
NAFTA: Canada, Mexico, United States	36.9	43.5
MERCOSUR: Argentina, Brazil, Paraguay, Uruguay	11.0	15.5
MERCOSUR *plus* Chile	13.7	18.6
Africa:		
CAEMC (Central African Economic and Monetary Community): Cameroon, Central African Rep., Chad, Equatorial Guinea, Gabon, Rep. of the Congo	2.8	1.9
WAEMU (West African Economic and Monetary Union): Benin, Burkina Faso, Côte d'Ivoire, Guinea-Bissau, Mali, Niger, Senegal, Togo	11.1	11.2
WAMU (West African Monetary Union): Gambia, Ghana, Guinea, Liberia, Nigeria, Sierra Leone	2.2	2.0
Europe:		
EU-12: Belgium, Denmark, France, Germany, Greece, Ireland, Italy, Luxembourg, Netherlands, Portugal, Spain, United Kingdom	70.7	64.2
East Asia:		
ASEAN: Brunei, Cambodia, Indonesia, Laos, Malaysia, Myanmar, Philippines, Singapore, Thailand, Viet Nam	17.3	22.4
ASEAN *plus* Japan	21.9	25.1
ASEAN *plus* Korea	16.7	21.4
ASEAN *plus* People's Rep. of China	16.0	19.5
ASEAN+3 (ASEAN *plus* Japan, Korea, People's Rep. of China)	29.3	39.0
Memorandum:		
ASEAN *plus* People's Rep. of China *plus* Hong Kong	31.2	31.8
ASEAN+3 *plus* Hong Kong	38.2	47.5

Source: International Monetary Fund, *Direction of Trade Statistics (DOTS)*, 1997 and 2004. There is some double counting in this table. In the NAFTA case, for example, U.S. exports to Canada appear twice, as U.S. exports to Canada and Canadian imports from the United States, and the same double counting of intraregional trade occurs in the measure of each country's total trade. It could be avoided by using a different measure (e.g., intraregional exports as a percentage of total exports), but that would introduce a different bias, because the imbalance between a country's total exports and total imports can change through time, as in the U.S. case.

for the whole euro area. In 2000, Ecuador replaced its own national currency with the U.S. dollar, and El Salvador did the same thing one year later. Such decisions reduce the number of national currencies and can, as these examples illustrate, take two forms: (1) a collective decision by two or more countries to form a full-fledged monetary union, typified by the decision to create the European Monetary Union (EMU);[1] or (2) a unilateral decision by a single country to adopt another country's currency, a decision described hereafter as *de jure* dollarization or euroization, depending on the foreign currency adopted, and typified by the decisions of Ecuador and El Salvador to adopt the U.S. dollar. Both of these tight forms of monetary integration extinguish national currencies; yet, they differ importantly in several ways. The differences and their implications are examined in Chapter 2 but can be summarized succinctly.

The formation of a monetary union involves the creation of a new multinational currency, such as the euro, and its substitution for the members' own national currencies. It also involves the transfer of responsibility for monetary policy to a new supranational institution, such as the ECB.[2] It is thus an ambitious project, politically, institutionally, and

---

[1] Strictly speaking, the acronym EMU stands for Economic and Monetary Union, the more comprehensive project defined by the Maastricht Treaty of 1992, but it is widely used to denote the European Monetary Union, and that is how we use it here. When EMU came into being in 1999, eleven (Austria, Belgium, Finland, France, Germany, Ireland, Italy, Luxembourg, Netherlands, Portugal, and Spain) of the fifteen EU members were able to join immediately, but Greece followed soon thereafter. The three other EU countries (Denmark, Sweden, and the United Kingdom) have not joined EMU. Of the twelve countries that joined the EU in 2004, only Slovenia has qualified for membership and joined EMU at the start of 2007. There are presently 27 members of the EU: Austria, Belgium, Bulgaria, Cyprus, Czech Republic, Denmark, Estonia, Finland, France, Germany, Greece, Hungary, Ireland, Italy, Latvia, Lithuania, Luxembourg, Malta, Netherlands, Poland, Portugal, Romania, Slovak Republic, Slovenia, Spain, Sweden, and the United Kingdom.

[2] It is worth noting at the outset that the formation of a monetary union is not incompatible with adopting the increasingly common combination of a flexible exchange rate and inflation targeting. It can instead be viewed as a decision to adopt that combination at the union level rather than the national level. The euro floats quite freely against outsiders' currencies, and the ECB pursues a monetary policy closely akin to inflation targeting (although purists criticize the asymmetric form of its price objective and the absence of a formal inflation-targeting regime). We will return to these matters at various points in this book.

logistically. The transition to EMU, described in Chapter 3, illustrates this vividly.

The unilateral adoption of another country's currency involves some of the same logistical problems, but it is much simpler, especially when that other currency has been widely used already by the private sector, a practice commonly called *de facto* dollarization.[3] More important, it does not require the creation of a new institution; the responsibility for monetary policy is transferred automatically to an existing central bank – in the case of dollarization, the U.S. Federal Reserve System.[4]

Although EMU is often and rightly described as an integral part of a comprehensive political project, the "ever closer union" of the EU countries, and it could not have come into being without the intimate involvement of the EU's most powerful leaders, François Mitterrand in France and Helmut Kohl in Germany, it is often portrayed as a way to perfect the single market of the EU. Therefore, the advent of EMU aroused a great deal of interest elsewhere, especially in countries belonging to regional trading arrangements. There was discussion in Canada and Mexico of a North American monetary union to complement NAFTA, discussion in Argentina and Brazil of a monetary union to complement MERCOSUR (the Southern Common Market), and discussion in Southeast Asia of a monetary union to complement ASEAN. Furthermore, the members of two other country groups, the Gulf Cooperation Council (GCC) and the Economic Community of West African States (ECOWAS), have committed themselves formally to monetary union, and their plans for reaching it are based on the EMU model.

The motives of a government deciding unilaterally to adopt the dollar or the euro are rather different. It is not concerned to provide a single currency for a single market. It aims instead to immunize its national economy against future currency crises and to import a better monetary policy than it has achieved on its own. If you don't have a national currency, you can't have a currency crisis, nor can you devalue your currency.[5] If you don't have a national central bank, moreover, you can't

---

[3] Angeloni (2004) compares multilateral currency union and unilateral dollarization.
[4] There is another way to achieve this sort of delegation: transforming a country's central bank into a currency board. This is discussed in Chapter 2.
[5] This is the core of the argument for *de jure* dollarization developed by Steil and Litan (2006).

even generate homegrown inflation, and when you banish the risk of homegrown inflation as well as the concomitant risk of a future devaluation, your country's firms and households can borrow at lower long-term interest rates.

This book will ask whether these and other projects are likely to flourish in the years ahead. We will therefore begin in Chapter 2 by reviewing and recasting the analytical framework that economists usually use to weigh the benefits and costs of the two tight forms of monetary integration that we have been describing. The traditional framework needs to be recast because it does not pay enough attention to the implications of international capital mobility, to the size and nature of the members' trade ties to the outside world, or the way in which a single monetary policy alters the impact of various shocks on the member countries of a monetary union. Thereafter, we will complement that analytical approach by tracing in Chapter 3 the way in which the EU countries moved from less rigorous forms of monetary cooperation to a full-fledged monetary union. We will, of course, identify the economic rationale for moving all the way to EMU, but we also will emphasize three unique features of the European story: the commitment to ever-closer union already mentioned; the challenges posed by the impending enlargement of the EU that followed the collapse of the Soviet Union; and the panoply of existing EU institutions that could be assigned key tasks in the creation and subsequent governance of the monetary union. The absence of comparable institutions may be a major obstacle to full-fledged monetary unions elsewhere in the world, although special-purpose bodies might perhaps discharge those duties.[6]

To round out our discussion, we take on three tasks in Chapter 4. First, we look at other monetary unions: some that are defunct, such as the Latin, Scandinavian, and Austro-Hungarian unions; some that exist today, such as the two monetary unions in francophone Africa and the one in the Eastern Caribbean; and some that are now contemplated,

---

[6] Eichengreen (1994) stressed this same point when assessing the likelihood that EMU would have many imitators. Cohen (2003a, 2004a) attaches more importance to the need for political cohesion; in a previous book, however, he foresees dramatic changes in the monetary system, including the spread of *de facto* and *de jure* dollarization, as well as the introduction of privately issued electronic monies that will compete increasingly with national monies, both locally and globally; see Cohen (1998).

such as those that are being designed for the GCC and ECOWAS. These comparisons highlight the problems involved in constructing a durable monetary union, as well as the various ways to solve them. Second, we ask what economists have learned about the comparative merits of fixed and flexible exchange rates. Although that comparison cannot be brought to bear directly on the likely effects of a monetary union or *de jure* dollarization, it can tell us something about the effects of various exchange-rate regimes on inflation rates and real economic growth. Finally, we offer a tentative assessment of economic performance in the EMU countries since the commencement of the monetary union.

Chapters 5 and 6 will examine proposals for monetary unions in three major trading blocs, NAFTA, MERCOSUR, and ASEAN, as well as the larger group of East Asian countries. There, we will use the analytical framework developed in Chapter 2 to weigh the potential costs and benefits of monetary unions in those regions. We will pay particular attention to the trade patterns of the likely participants, a subject that rarely receives the attention it deserves in cost-benefit assessments, and we will address the potentially difficult problem of designing arrangements to manage a monetary union for countries that have different political systems and have not begun to develop common decision-making processes and bodies comparable to those in Europe.

We will conclude that full-fledged monetary unions are not likely to develop in any of those regions in the foreseeable future. There is insufficient political support in Canada and Mexico for the formation of a North American monetary union that would necessarily be dominated by the United States, and there is even less political cohesion in South America, where there are in addition far larger differences in economic policies, as well as a much lower level of intraregional trade. We would not be surprised, however, if smaller countries in Central and South America opted for *de jure* dollarization, although they may wait until they can assess its further effects on economic performance in El Salvador and Ecuador.

We hold the same view with the regard to East Asia, although it is different in many respects from most other regions. Intraregional trade is large and growing fast. Furthermore, most countries in the region display a strong revealed preference for exchange-rate stability, even those that are formally committed to flexible exchange rates. Finally, the East Asian countries are already engaged in loose forms of monetary and financial cooperation. They have created a network of bilateral credit arrangements, the so-called Chiang Mai Initiative, that can be activated to ward off currency crises, and they have begun to promote financial integration, including the development of local-currency bond markets, to reduce the region's reliance on foreign-currency borrowing.

The politics of Asia, however, are far different from those of Europe. Although there are numerous intergovernmental bodies, there are no supranational institutions. Even within ASEAN itself, there is a prohibition against intervention in the internal affairs of its member countries. And there are bitter memories of Japanese aggression going back before World War II. China and Japan are not France and Germany, two countries that put their past conflicts behind them when pursuing monetary integration. It is therefore hard to believe that countries that differ so markedly in their economic and political regimes could readily agree to form a full-fledged monetary union, even one that spanned a subset of the East Asian countries.

There is, nevertheless, a great deal of interest in looser forms of monetary integration by the East Asian countries – in arrangements such as those that the EU adopted two decades before the birth of the euro – and we examine the forms that they might take in the final section of Chapter 6. At that point, indeed, we depart from the stance we adopt in most of this book – assessing the likelihood of monetary integration in various parts of the world – to offer a tentative ranking of the various ways in which the East Asian countries could cooperate more closely in monetary matters.

In short, this book does not predict a rapid transformation of the international monetary landscape. That landscape is likely to change slowly, not only for the reasons already mentioned but for others as well. Very large countries such as China, India, and Brazil are unlikely to constrain their monetary autonomy by entering into monetary unions with their smaller neighbors on terms acceptable to those neighbors. Furthermore, countries that have not experienced much *de facto* dollarization are not very likely to opt for *de jure* dollarization. It is still important, however, to ask how the monetary landscape is most likely to change in the near future, and that is the main subject of our concluding chapter, which examines the implications for the United States.

First and most important, we expect the euro to become more attractive to investors, although we do not expect it to overtake the dollar as the world's leading currency, and a more attractive euro will make it harder for the United States to finance substantial current-account deficits such as those that it has run for the last several years. For the euro to become more attractive, however, economic performance in the euro area will need to improve substantially and the internal arguments over national fiscal policies will need to be resolved. To complicate matters, the Asian countries may opt for exchange-rate arrangements that limit fluctuations in their countries' exchange rates *vis-à-vis* the dollar and the euro, and that could make it harder for the United States to achieve the large depreciation of the dollar that may be needed to reduce the U.S. current-account deficit. Finally, the Asian countries, as well as other country groups, will continue to challenge the preeminent role of the United States in the International Monetary Fund (IMF) and may indeed challenge the paramount role of the IMF itself by creating regional monetary funds. The Japanese sought to create an Asian Monetary Fund in 1997, soon after the start of the Asian currency crisis, but the United States blocked that initiative. Within the next decade, however, the East Asian countries are apt to try again, this time by transforming the Chiang Mai Initiative into something closely resembling a regional monetary fund, and they may go even further by offering India and other South Asian countries membership in that fund.

Let us then summarize the main finding of our book. Although we expect to see some erosion in the dollar's status and in U.S. economic and financial influence in the multilateral arena during the next several years, we do not foresee a dramatic trend toward regional monetary integration over the next two decades.

2

The Forms, Costs, and Benefits
of Currency Consolidation

INTRODUCTION

The two strong forms of monetary integration discussed in the previous chapter, forming a full-fledged monetary union and adopting formally another country's currency, are often described as currency consolidation.[1] That is because they involve a reduction in the number of national currencies. The two arrangements, however, differ in their answers to a fundamental question: Who makes monetary policy? A monetary union assigns that task to a single central bank with shared decision making; *de jure* dollarization assigns it to a foreign central bank – the one that issues the currency replacing the national currency.

Early analytic work on currency consolidation did not even ask this question. It dealt with a rudimentary arrangement, a simple currency union, that bypassed the question completely. We will soon see, however, why we must answer the question when comparing a monetary union and unilateral dollarization.

This chapter, however, has a larger purpose. It surveys the potential benefits and costs of currency consolidation. Does currency consolidation stimulate trade between the two or more countries involved? Does it reduce its members' vulnerability to financial crises? Does it raise or reduce the economic costs of adjusting to various shocks, including both domestic and external shocks?

---

[1] See, e.g., Rogoff (2001).

These are important questions. They can help us assess the strength of the case for EMU, discussed in the next chapter, as well as the actual economic performance of its member countries. They also can help us to decide whether other groups of countries should form monetary unions, and whether certain countries should perhaps opt instead for unilateral dollarization.

We begin, however, by looking back at the early work on the economics of a simple currency union, because it raised a basic issue that must be addressed before we can examine the potential benefits and costs of currency consolidation.

THE ANALYTICS OF A SIMPLE CURRENCY UNION

Suppose that two countries decide to form a simple currency union – an arrangement in which they fix the exchange rate between their countries' currencies without altering the responsibilities or powers of their countries' central banks. When can we say that those countries comprise an *optimum currency area*, in that the constraints imposed by a fixed exchange rate are not injurious to their economies? This question was posed by Robert Mundell more than four decades ago,[2] in a paper that helped earn him the Nobel Prize in Economics, and his answer was used three decades later when economists sought to weigh the benefits and costs of EMU.

Mundell considered two countries, East and West, each with its own central bank, that form a simple currency union by fixing the exchange rate between their currencies rather than changing it from time to time or leaving it to market forces. He also assumed that both countries begin at full employment, that their bilateral trade is balanced, and that there are no capital movements between them.[3] He then introduced a permanent disturbance, a switch in demand between Eastern and Western goods, which we will discuss shortly.

[2] See Mundell (1961).
[3] Writing four decades ago, Mundell was chiefly concerned with stabilizing output and employment. Today, central banks are largely concerned with price stability and, to a lesser degree, overall financial stability. They still monitor output and employment, however, as the size of the "output gap" (the difference between actual and potential output) affects the inflation rate.

Box 2.1. Disturbances and Policy Responses in a Simple Currency Union

A Permanent Increase of Aggregate Demand in the East

This disturbance has three effects

(1) The demand for labor rises in the East
(2) The demand for labor rises in the West but by less than in the East
(3) The East runs a trade deficit with the West

The optimal monetary-policy response:

The Eastern central bank should tighten its monetary policy by enough to choke off the whole increase of aggregate demand in the East; this will return both countries to their starting points.

A Permanent Switch in Demand from Western to Eastern Goods

This disturbance also has three effects

(1) The demand for labor rises in the East
(2) The demand for labor falls in the West
(3) The East runs a trade surplus with the West

The optimal monetary-policy response:

There is none.

A tighter Eastern monetary policy could stabilize the Eastern economy but would worsen matters in the West; an easier Western monetary policy could stabilize the Western economy but would worsen matters in the East.

Both policy responses, moreover, would widen the Eastern trade surplus.

We will start with another disturbance, however, an increase of aggregate demand in one country, because it will help us describe the properties of Mundell's own model, and because we will need it later to highlight an important difference between a monetary union and *de jure* dollarization.

An Increase of Aggregate Demand in the East

Suppose that Eastern households step up their total spending, increasing aggregate demand in the East. This disturbance is asymmetric in origin but will affect both countries. Its effects are summarized in Box 2.1. First, it will raise the demand for Eastern labor, because more workers will be needed to produce more Eastern goods. Second, it will raise Eastern imports from the West and thus raise the demand for Western labor, although the demand for Western labor will rise by less than the demand for Eastern labor, because it reflects only part of the increase of aggregate demand in the East – the part that spills out to the West because of the increase of Eastern imports. Third, the East will run a trade deficit with the West.

These outcomes are unsatisfactory from both countries' points of view; they will experience inflationary pressures coming from their labor markets. Furthermore, the East's trade deficit will be unsustainable unless its central bank has an infinitely large stock of Western currency with which to cover its country's trade deficit and thus maintain the fixed exchange rate (or can borrow Western currency from the Western central bank for as long as it has to cover a trade deficit). Yet there is a simple way to deal with both countries' problems. The Eastern central bank can raise its interest rate to choke off the increase of aggregate demand. That will bring *both* countries back to their starting points – satisfactory levels of employment and balanced trade between them.[4]

A Switch in Demand from Western to Eastern Goods

Suppose instead that Eastern households switch some of their spending from Western to Eastern goods – the case studied by Mundell. This disturbance is strongly asymmetric. Its effects on the Eastern economy are the same as those of the previous disturbance; by raising the demand for Eastern goods, it will raise the demand for Eastern labor. Its effects on the Western economy, however, are different from those of the previous disturbance. By reducing the demand for Western goods, it will reduce the demand for Western labor. Furthermore, the East will run

---

[4] If the Eastern central bank failed to raise its interest rate, the Western central bank could do that, in order to stabilize the Western economy. But this is a second-best solution. It cannot completely stabilize the Eastern economy, because the West will have suffered less inflationary pressure, and it will enlarge the imbalance in the two countries' trade by reducing Western imports.

an unsustainable trade surplus. These effects are also summarized in Box 2.1, which goes on to show why changes in the countries' monetary policies cannot resolve the countries' problems. What, then, can be done? When, as here, the exchange rate is fixed, there are two possibilities.

If wage rates were perfectly flexible, nothing would have to be done. The increase of demand for Eastern labor would raise the Eastern wage rate and thus raise the prices of Eastern goods. The decrease of demand for Western labor would lower the Western wage rate and thus lower the prices of Western goods. Both countries' consumers would then buy fewer Eastern goods and more Western goods, and the adjustment would proceed until it had offset the initial switch in demand from Western to Eastern goods.[5]

If wages rates were rigid, not flexible, but the exchange rate was flexible, the switch in demand from Western to Eastern goods would raise the Western demand for the Eastern currency, which would therefore appreciate, and this would have the same effect as wage-rate flexibility. It would make Eastern goods more expensive for Western consumers and Western goods cheaper for Eastern consumers, reversing the initial switch in demand. This option is foreclosed, however, by the two countries' commitment to a fixed exchange rate.

Is there, then, another way to solve the two countries' problems? Suppose, said Mundell, that workers can move freely between East and West. With a switch in demand from Western to Eastern goods, there will be more jobs in the East and fewer jobs in the West. Hence, workers will move from West to East, resolving the two countries' labor-market problems and ending the imbalance in their trade.[6] Therefore, Mundell concluded that two countries can safely form a currency union – they

---

[5] In effect, the changes in the prices of the two countries' goods would alter the price-adjusted or *real* exchange rate even though the *nominal* exchange rate is fixed.

[6] The labor-market effects are obvious, but the trade-balance effect is not. Here's the explanation: When Western workers move to the East, their demand for Eastern goods is *domesticated*; it ceases to be part of the Western demand for Eastern exports, adding instead to domestic demand in the East. Conversely, their demand for Western goods *is internationalized*; it ceases to be part of domestic demand in the West, adding instead to the Eastern demand for Western exports. So Eastern exports fall and Western exports rise.

may be deemed to constitute an *optimum currency area* – when labor is freely mobile between them.[7]

Restrictions and Extensions

Strongly restrictive assumptions lurk behind Mundell's story. It assumes, for example, that the industries producing Eastern and Western goods are equally labor intensive. And it is utterly unrealistic to assume that workers will move quickly from one country to another, even if there are no border barriers. In a study of interregional adjustment within the United States, Blanchard and Katz showed that migration plays a major role in interregional adjustment, but it takes place gradually:

A negative shock to employment leads initially to an increase in unemployment and a small decline in [labor-market] participation. Over time, the effect on employment increases, but the effect on unemployment and participation disappears after approximately five to seven years. Put another way, a state typically returns to normal after an adverse shock not because employment picks up, but because workers leave the state.[8]

The world is more complicated than Mundell's simple model, and no one would use his model or findings today to make a definitive judgment about the optimality of a currency union or full-fledged monetary union. Nevertheless, this model is the analytical basis for the questions economists usually ask whenever they need to decide whether a pair or group of countries *resembles* an optimum currency area:

(1) Are the countries' apt to suffer large asymmetric shocks, having effects such as those produced by the switch in demand from Western to Eastern goods?
(2) Are their labor markets too rigid to produce the wage-rate changes needed to neutralize asymmetric shocks?

---

[7] Mundell went on to note, however, that this is not the only relevant criterion for judging the optimality of a currency union. A currency union reduces transactions costs and banishes exchange-rate risk, and the resulting benefits may exceed the costs imposed by limitations on labor mobility. If, indeed, those benefits are very large, the whole world might be said to constitute an optimum currency area.

[8] Blanchard and Katz (1992), p. 3.

(3) Do they have high barriers to labor mobility, not only those imposed by their countries' governments but also those imposed by different languages or cultures?

Economists asked these questions about EMU, and we will report their findings.[9] Note right away, however, that Mundell adopted two simplifications that limit the real-world relevance of his findings and of economists' answers to the three questions posed earlier.

First, Mundell dealt with a two-country world. Therefore, he could not ask how those countries' involvement with the outside world could affect the costs of forming a currency union. When looking at national inflation rates in EMU, economists have found that countries that trade heavily with the outside world, such as Ireland, had inflation rates higher than the EMU average when the euro depreciated *vis-à-vis* the currencies of those countries' trading partners.[10] Consider, moreover, the case of Argentina. In 1991, Argentina fixed its currency firmly to the U.S. dollar despite its heavy trade with Brazil and the euro area. Therefore, it encountered serious problems in the late 1990s, when the Brazilian *real* and the euro depreciated sharply *vis-à-vis* the U.S. dollar and thereby depreciated *vis-à-vis* the Argentine peso.

Second, Mundell excluded capital mobility. Goods moved freely between East and West in his two-country model, but bonds and other claims did not. Capital mobility was, of course, more limited in the early 1960s, when Mundell wrote his paper. Yet he did not ignore it in his other

---

[9] When answering the first question, moreover, economists sometimes pose an additional question, which one of us suggested many years ago (Kenen 1969). When countries produce large numbers of goods and industry-specific shifts in demand occur randomly, the shifts in demand will tend to cancel out, reducing their net effects on output, employment, and the trade balance. Therefore, economists also ask whether a country's output is well diversified when assessing the costs to the country of joining a currency union; see, e.g., Bini-Smaghi and Vori (1992) and Krugman (1993). But recent work suggests that industry-specific shocks are less important than country-specific shocks, whereas global shocks have become more important relative to country-specific shocks; see the discussion in Kenen (2002), which surveys at greater length recent research on several issues discussed briefly in this chapter. The relevance of the questions posed in the text has been confirmed by research showing that quantitative answers to those questions help to explain actual differences in countries' exchange-rate policies; see, e.g., Bayoumi and Eichengreen (1998).

[10] See Honohan and Lane (2003, 2004).

early work. In fact, he earned his Nobel Prize partly for his seminal papers on the ways in which capital flows influence macroeconomic behavior and the functioning of monetary and fiscal policies, and he also made a point of particular relevance to a currency union. In a world of very high capital mobility, no single country can conduct an independent monetary policy if it fixes its exchange rate. Whenever its central bank tries to raise interest rates above those in the outside world, it will attract a huge capital inflow, and that will drive down the country's own interest rates until they are no higher than those in the outside world.

Accordingly, the omission of capital mobility limits the relevance of Mundell's findings about the optimality of a currency union. First and most importantly, high capital mobility would prevent his countries' central banks from pursuing independent monetary policies. They would have instead to share a single monetary policy, and we will explain shortly why that is important. Second, the introduction of capital mobility alters the story we told at the beginning of this section. A permanent increase of Eastern aggregate demand cannot be offset neatly, as it was when the Eastern and Western central banks were free to adopt different monetary policies. It will instead have permanent effects on output and employment in one or both of the two countries. In fact, its effects may resemble those of the disturbance that Mundell analyzed – a switch in demand from Western to Eastern goods.

What happens, then, with perfect capital mobility? As there can then be just one monetary policy in a currency union, we have to ask who makes that monetary policy and the nature of its policy domain.

The Crucial Role of the Policy Domain

Suppose that the West decides unilaterally to adopt the Eastern currency and thereby to import the monetary policy of the Eastern central bank. The Eastern central bank, however, does what the Federal Reserve has done despite *de jure* dollarization by other countries. It continues to adhere to a *national* policy domain aimed at the stabilization of the Eastern economy, paying no attention to the Western economy. How will this affect the two countries' economies when the Eastern central bank responds to the disturbances we have been considering?

When there is, again, an increase of aggregate demand in the East, the Eastern central bank will tighten its monetary policy and will therefore raise interest rates in both East and West. Furthermore, it will tighten its monetary policy sufficiently to stabilize the Eastern economy. When it does that, however, it will depress Western output and employment. Recall what we found before. An increase of Eastern aggregate demand affects the Western economy by less than it affects the Eastern economy. Hence, remedial action by the Eastern central bank, if sufficient to stabilize the Eastern economy, will be more than sufficient to stabilize the Western economy and will therefore depress it. The outcome will be second-best from the Western standpoint, compared to the outcome obtained in the absence of capital mobility.[11] In this particular case, of course, the East will run a trade deficit with the West. With perfect capital mobility, however, private investors will finance that deficit by buying Eastern bonds; that is how they equalize the two countries' interest rates and thus transmit from East to West the changes in Eastern monetary policy.

When there is instead a switch in demand from Western to Eastern goods, the Eastern central bank will have again to tighten its monetary policy if it is to stabilize the Eastern economy. But this will exacerbate the situation in the West, where the switch in demand will reduce output and employment, and the tightening of Eastern monetary policy will reduce them further.

---

[11] Alesina and Barro (2002) obtain a similar result using a more sophisticated model. They also show that the West should be able to "bribe" the East to include the Western economy in the policy domain of the Eastern central bank; the resulting gain to the West will exceed the cost to the East. (The cost to the East is the less-than-perfect stabilization of the Eastern economy caused by adding the West to the policy domain of the Eastern central bank – the result obtained below for a full-fledged monetary union.) Advocates of dollarization are, of course, entitled to reply that the second-best outcome obtained in the text may be superior to the best result that the West can obtain on its own, without *de jure* dollarization. The case for dollarization derives in large part from evidence that the central banks of many emerging-market countries have actually destabilized their national economies by pursuing pro-cyclical monetary policies rather than counter-cyclical policies; see, e.g., Alesina, Barro, and Tenreyro (2003). Note, finally, how an increase of Western aggregate demand would affect the Western economy. As output and employment would rise in the East, the Eastern central bank would tighten its monetary policy by enough to stabilize the Eastern economy but not by enough to stabilize the Western economy.

Consider, by contrast, a full-fledged monetary union, much like the one in Europe, in which the East and West create a new supranational central bank, resembling the ECB, and instruct it to stabilize the combination of their two economies – the sum of their outputs or the average of their inflation rates.[12] How would this new central bank combat the disturbances we have been examining?

With an increase of Eastern aggregate demand, output and employment will rise in both countries, but by more in the East than the West. Hence, the *average* increase of output or employment in the whole union will be bigger than that in the West and smaller than that in the East. Therefore, the central bank's policy response will not serve to stabilize *either* country's output. The increase in its interest rate will be too small to stabilize Eastern output, which will therefore be higher than it was to start. But the increase in its interest rate will be too large to stabilize Western output, which will therefore be lower than it was to start. In effect, the central bank's policy response will transform the expenditure-raising shock into one resembling an expenditure-switching shock; output and employment will rise in one country but fall in the other country.

What about the effects of the other disturbance – the switch in demand by one country's consumers from Western to Eastern goods? In this case, of course, there will no change in the total output of the monetary union and no justification for any change in its monetary policy. It cannot even mitigate the impact of the switch.

These results, summarized in Box 2.2, lead us to a strong conclusion. The single monetary policy of a full-fledged monetary union can *never*

---

[12] This is an idealized representation of the policy-making process. The Governing Council of the ECB, its policy-making body, is supposed to focus exclusively on economic conditions and prospects in the euro area as a whole. But there is no way to know whether the members of the Governing Council, especially the heads of the national central banks, are influenced by economic conditions in their own countries, because the ECB does not publish minutes or votes. Meade and Sheets (2005a) and Chappell, McGregor, and Vermilyea (2006) find evidence that votes cast in the Federal Open Market Committee (the U.S. counterpart of the Governing Council) are indeed influenced by regional economic conditions. There also has been research on how best to structure the ECB's Governing Council to yield a monetary policy appropriate for the whole euro area; see Berger (2002), Meade (2003), and the discussion in Chapter 3 of the ECB's policy-making process.

Box 2.2. Disturbances and Policy Responses with
Currency Consolidation

A Permanent Increase of Aggregate Demand in the East

The initial effects of the disturbance are those listed in Box 2.1.

When the West has adopted the Eastern currency and the Eastern central bank stabilizes Eastern output, it will tighten its monetary policy, with these effects:

(1) Eastern output will return to its initial level
(2) Western output will fall below its initial level
(3) The East will run a trade deficit with the West, because Eastern exports will fall below their initial level

When the countries have formed a monetary union, the union's central bank will tighten its monetary policy to stabilize union-wide output, with these effects:

(1) Eastern output will fall but remain above its initial level
(2) Western output will fall below its initial level
(3) The East will still run a trade deficit with the West

A Permanent Switch in Demand from Western to Eastern Goods

The effects of the disturbance are those listed in Box 2.1.
When the West has adopted the Eastern currency and the Eastern central bank stabilizes Eastern output, it will tighten its monetary policy, with these effects:

(1) Eastern output will return to its initial level
(2) Western output will fall further below its initial level
(3) The East will run a smaller trade surplus, because the initial increase of Eastern exports will be partially offset by the fall in Western output

When the countries have formed a monetary union, the union's central bank will not respond to the disturbance, as there has been no change in union-wide output.

fit the needs of any member perfectly. This point has sometimes been made about EMU itself. The monetary policy of the ECB was not tight enough to stabilize the Irish economy in the early years of EMU, and it may have been too tight thereafter to foster economic recovery in Germany and some other EMU countries. The problem, however, is intrinsic to the working of a full-fledged monetary union.

Two final observations before moving on:

(1) Although the supranational central bank of a monetary union cannot completely stabilize Western output when faced with an increase of Eastern aggregate demand, the second-best outcome in the West is better than the one it would face if it adopted the Eastern currency unilaterally and thus imported the monetary policy of the Eastern central bank. As the increase of Eastern output will exceed the increase of average output in the monetary union, the union's central bank will tighten its monetary policy less aggressively than would the Eastern central bank seeking to stabilize Eastern output, and the fall in Western output will therefore be smaller in a monetary union.

(2) The extent of the difference between the two forms of currency consolidation depends on the relative sizes of the countries involved. Suppose that the West is like Luxembourg and the East is like Germany. In a full-fledged monetary union, the two may have the same number of seats on the central bank's governing body. But the small Western economy will weigh less heavily in the union-wide aggregates and averages on which the governing body bases its decisions. If indeed the West is very much smaller than the East, it may well find it hard to choose between a monetary union with the East and the unilateral adoption of the Eastern currency.

THE BENEFITS OF CURRENCY CONSOLIDATION

What can a country gain by entering a monetary union or adopting another country's currency? There are two sorts of benefits – gains in efficiency and gains in credibility.

Efficiency Gains

The most obvious efficiency gain derives from banishing currency conversions. There is no need to go to the foreign-exchange market when buying goods, services, or assets from another country having the same currency. The European Commission estimated that the gains from eliminating foreign-exchange transactions within the EU could amount to as much as 0.4 percent of gross national product.[13] And there is an additional efficiency gain from eliminating currency *translations*. Households, firms, and governments need not adjust periodically the home-currency values of their future cross-border payments and receipts nor adjust the home-currency values of their external debts and claims.

A second efficiency gain derives from greater price transparency. When prices are quoted in a single currency, buyers of goods and services can make price comparisons without having to convert foreign prices into their own countries' currencies. Nor do they have to court the risk that a price comparison made today will be obsolete tomorrow because of an exchange-rate change. Price transparency, in turn, should intensify competition and thus reduce cross-country differences in product prices.[14]

A third efficiency gain derives from the elimination of exchange-rate risk, not only from near-term transactions in goods and services but also from long-term contractual arrangements and from the calculations of future profitability on which major investment decisions are based. Research on the effects of exchange-rate uncertainty has typically found that it depresses the volume of trade but does not do so strongly. Most of that research, however, has dealt mainly with short-term exchange-rate volatility, yet the risk of a near-term exchange-rate change can be hedged in the forward foreign-exchange market.[15] Less work has been done – because it is harder – on the effects of uncertainty about more distant

---

[13] European Commission (1990), p. 68.

[14] See, however, Goldberg and Verboven (2004), who find that the introduction of the euro did not have strong effects on the cross-country dispersion of automobile prices in the euro area.

[15] See, however, Wei (1998), whose findings cast doubt on the role of hedging opportunities in explaining why short-term exchange-rate volatility does not appear to have large trade-depressing effects.

changes in exchange rates, especially their impact on investment decisions by firms producing traded goods. If a firm could be perfectly certain about the amount of foreign currency it would earn in the future by building a new factory to manufacture goods for export, it could readily convert those future earnings into its own currency by selling them in the forward market or taking on foreign-currency debt. But a firm cannot even know with certainty the size of its future foreign-currency receipts because its future foreign sales will themselves depend on future exchange rates.

Recent research suggests, moreover, that the mere existence of separate national currencies has very large trade-depressing effects. In a path-breaking paper, Andrew Rose showed that pairs of countries sharing the same currency trade far more heavily with each other – about three times as much – than other country pairs, and his result has been confirmed by several other studies, although the size of the common-currency effect varies from study to study.[16] Two of those studies deserve special mention because they confront important methodological objections to Rose's original findings.

Rose's data set included a large number of very small countries, and many of his common-currency country pairs likewise involved small countries. Furthermore, his data set excluded the common-currency pairs created by EMU, which was not yet in being at the end of the period covered by his data set. But a paper addressing that omission has found that EMU country pairs trade more intensively with each other than industrial-country pairs having separate currencies – albeit by less than the common-currency pairs in Rose's data set.[17]

Critics of Rose's work also have asked whether his results reflect something other than a common-currency effect: Might they merely reflect the way in which a small country chooses its common-currency partner? One would expect to find large amounts of trade between a small country

---

[16] See Rose (2000, 2004) and Glick and Rose (2002). It should be noted that most of the papers on this subject, including those by Rose, take separate account of short-term exchange-rate volatility and, like others before them, find that it does not have strong trade-depressing effects. Hence, we must view the trade-raising effect of a common currency as being additional to any trade-raising effect of eliminating exchange-rate volatility.

[17] Micco, Stein, and Ordoñez (2003).

and its common-currency partner if the small country adopted the currency of its largest trading partner.[18] The paper addressing this issue uses high-powered methods, but its strategy really amounts to asking a simple question: When two small countries adopt the same large country's currency (e.g., the U.S. dollar), do they trade more intensively with each other than do other country pairs? And the answer, it says, is yes.[19]

Efficiency gains arise in asset markets as well as in goods markets. Two phenomena illustrate this point. First, the long-term interest rates of potential EMU members began to converge in the mid-1990s, when market participants became convinced that EMU would actually happen. Previously, Italy, Portugal, and Spain had to pay interest rates 3 or 4 percentage points higher than France or Germany. Today, most of the interest-rate differences are barely discernible.[20] Second, there was a sudden surge in new issues of euro-denominated debt. New issues of euro-denominated bonds came quickly to exceed the volume of new bond issues that had been forthcoming earlier in the so-called legacy currencies – the ones replaced by the euro in 1999. The bond market, moreover, continues to grow, fed largely by new issues of corporate debt but also new issues of sovereign debt by governments outside Europe.[21]

Although these developments occurred with unexpected speed, and the growth in the bond market was stimulated strongly by some special

---

[18] For evidence to this effect, see Ritschl and Wolf (2003), who studied the currency blocs of the 1930s and found that trade among their members was atypically large even in the 1920s, before formation of the blocs, and that the subsequent creation of the blocs did not greatly raise the amount of trade within them. It must be noted, however, that these blocs were not true common-currency regimes; they were mainly country groups that tied their currencies tightly to gold or to a key currency rather than abandoning their national currencies.

[19] See Tenreyro and Barro (2003) and the summary in Alesina, Barro, and Tenreyro (2003).

[20] This result is commonly ascribed to the elimination of exchange-rate risk. A cynic, however, might interpret it differently. Although the treaty establishing EMU expressly forbids the EU from "bailing out" a government unable to service its debt, it was – and still is – widely believed that this prohibition would be breached if an EU government tottered on the brink of default. We will return to this matter in Chapter 3, when we examine the fiscal dimensions of EMU.

[21] European governments played a role, however, by redenominating their existing bonds and taking other steps to integrate their countries' bond markets; see, e.g., Pagano and von Thadden (2004).

circumstances that need not detain us here, the growth of the bond market was the logical result of the move to EMU. Put yourself in the place of a Belgian investor wondering whether to buy a corporate bond issued by an Italian firm. Before EMU, you had to ask two questions: What will happen to the exchange rate between your own currency, the Belgian franc, and that of the bond issue, the Italian lira? And if the lira depreciated for any reason whatsoever, what might happen to the creditworthiness of the Italian issuer? These concerns receded after the exchange-rate crisis of 1992–93, but the advent of the euro banished them completely, making the bond issues of European firms into closer substitutes, and increasing the depth, breadth, and liquidity of the bond market.[22]

The closer integration of asset markets can have several efficiency-enhancing effects, but one is especially relevant to a monetary union. Because its single monetary policy cannot fit any of its members perfectly, those members and their citizens need other ways to cope with the residual effects of various shocks, and there are two ways to that. Governments can play a role, because fiscal flows adjust automatically to damp down fluctuations in disposable income and help thereby to stabilize household spending. Furthermore, the workings of those built-in stabilizers can at times be reinforced by discretionary changes in taxes or government spending. But households can insure themselves against the effects of various shocks by holding well-diversified portfolios of financial instruments. Several studies have shown that private capital flows play a significant role in smoothing the incomes of regions within individual countries but a smaller role in smoothing the incomes of countries.[23] A monetary union, however, makes countries more like regions,

---

[22] With the advent of the euro, moreover, there was another interesting development. Investment advisors began to suggest that buyers of corporate stocks base their investment decisions on the prospective profitability of European industries, not the comparative economic prospects of European countries.

[23] See Sørensen and Yosha (1998) and Helliwell and McKitrick (1998). Another study finds, however, that regions and countries engaged in substantial risk sharing tend to be more specialized, implying that causation runs in the opposite direction; risk sharing induces more specialization; see Kalemli-Ozcan, Sørensen, and Yosha (1999, 2004). This result implies that a monetary union, by raising capital mobility among its members, may have conflicting effects on the stability of its members' incomes; although

insofar as it integrates their asset markets by banishing exchange-rate risk.[24]

Note finally that some forms of asset-market integration are themselves essential for the functioning of a full-fledged monetary union. If the members' interbank markets are not fully integrated, along with the markets for the financial instruments used by the central bank to implement its single monetary policy, the effects of its monetary policy will not be distributed quickly or uniformly throughout the monetary union.

Trade Integration and Currency Consolidation

Before turning to the credibility gains that can be conferred by currency consolidation, let's first pose a question that bears on the size and durability of the efficiency gains conferred by currency consolidation: Does trade integration – a free trade area, customs union, or fully unified single market – require the adoption of a common currency?

There are, of course, large differences between these forms of trade integration. A customs union is usually more comprehensive than a free trade area; it requires the abolition of *all* tariffs and other trade barriers between its members. Furthermore, it surrounds its members with a common set of tariffs, obviating for the need for complex rules of origin aimed at keeping imports from entering the area *via* the country with the lowest tariff on a particular product.[25] A comprehensive single market, however, like that of the EU, is likely to confer even larger efficiency gains than a customs union, because it permits the free movement of

---

it promotes risk sharing, it also may raise its members' vulnerability to industry-specific shocks by fostering specialization. For a critique of the literature on risk sharing and related issues, see Mélitz (2004).

[24] Putting the point in different terms, a monetary union reduces the strong 'home bias' implicit in many investors' decisions – their manifest preference for domestic assets relative to foreign assets. But it cannot be expected to eliminate home bias, which derives in part from other advantages of holding home-country assets, including, most importantly, readier access to information about the issuers.

[25] On the trade-depressing costs of those rules and other defects of a free trade area, see, e.g., Bhagwati and Panagariya (1996).

labor and capital, not just the free movement of goods. But might a common currency confer even bigger gains? By reducing transactions costs, promoting price transparency, and banishing exchange-rate risk, it must surely enhance the efficiency gains from free trade in goods, services, and assets, and from removing barriers to cross-border movements of workers and firms. The additional gains, moreover, may be multiplicative, not merely additive.

There is, however, another way in which currency consolidation can protect and promote the efficiency gains conferred by trade liberalization. Once countries have liberalized capital flows between their economies, it is extremely hard for them to maintain fixed exchange rates between their countries' currencies, and large exchange-rate changes can then pose a threat to trade integration.

Anticipating the elimination of capital controls within the EU and the resulting intensification of capital mobility, members of the European Monetary System (EMS), the precursor of EMU, tried to "harden" the EMS by agreeing to forgo exchange-rate changes. They feared that expectations of such changes would generate very large capital outflows from weak-currency countries, making it very hard to maintain pegged exchange rates. Their fears were validated in 1992, when the EMS was beset by a major currency crisis. Italy and Britain had to withdraw from the EMS, and their currencies depreciated sharply. Those depreciations and the subsequent devaluations of some other currencies generated strong protectionist pressures in the EU countries that faced intensified competition because of the exchange-rate changes. Those pressures were resisted. A few years later, however, an exchange-rate crisis erupted within MERCOSUR, when the Brazilian *real* was set free to float, and Argentina imposed new trade restrictions on its imports from Brazil.[26]

These episodes involved large, abrupt exchange-rate changes, resulting from failed attempts to maintain fixed exchange rates. Smaller, more gradual changes in flexible exchange rates are less apt to generate protectionist pressures disruptive of regional trade agreements. A free trade area or customs union may not require a single currency if its members

---

[26] On both of these episodes, see Fernandez-Arias, Panizza, and Stein (2004); also Eichengreen (1998), who reaches the same conclusion as the next paragraph in the text.

do not seek to keep their exchange rates fixed. But a more comprehensive single market in goods and assets may be exposed to protectionist pressures unless its members move to a common currency.

Credibility Gains

One obvious benefit of currency consolidation was mentioned in Chapter 1. A country that does not have its own currency cannot suffer a currency crisis – unless, of course, it imprudently adopts the currency of a country that is itself crisis-prone or joins a monetary union that is likewise crisis-prone. This benefit is strongly stressed by advocates of *de jure* dollarization, who also emphasize another benefit. It is a way for a country to import a monetary policy better than its own.

We have seen that the monetary policy of a full-fledged monetary union cannot be perfectly optimal for each of its members individually, and the monetary policy of a foreign central bank is likely to be even less optimal for a country adopting its currency unilaterally. Nevertheless, those monetary policies may be far better than a homegrown policy. Too often, national monetary policies have been made to serve their countries' fiscal needs – the government's need to finance a budget deficit and, in extreme cases, the need to inflate away the government's debt. Such policies often have led to chronically high inflation, even to hyperinflation. Even when this has not happened, moreover, central banks that have tried repeatedly to stimulate output and employment have merely generated inflation instead.[27]

Some governments may be unwilling to forgo access to captive financing, and no one can force them to do so. Others may be well intentioned, but they cannot credibly commit themselves – or their successors – without trying visibly to tie their own hands.

There are, of course, several ways to do that, but some are more robust than others. A government can grant operational independence to its central bank, but could someday rescind it. That is why some governments

---

[27] This was the risk identified by Kydland and Prescott (1977) and Barro and Gordon (1983) in their widely cited papers on the intrinsic time-inconsistency of a discretionary monetary policy.

have imbedded the commitment to central-bank independence in their countries' constitutions and, in the case of EMU, in the treaty establishing the European Union. Others, including Mexico, have not yet gone that far, but their central banks enjoy *de facto* independence, and they have used it to set for themselves the aim of reducing domestic inflation. In fact, the combination of inflation targeting with exchange-rate flexibility is the regime favored by many economists, especially for large and medium-sized countries.[28] A number of countries, however, continue to peg their exchange rates and have thus bound their central banks to the pursuit of monetary policies consistent with the maintenance of their pegged exchange rates. In a world with high capital mobility, however, a mere commitment to a pegged exchange rate cannot be perfectly credible. Pegged rates are too vulnerable to speculative attacks, whether or not justified by economic fundamentals.

This became painfully clear in the late 1990s, when many countries with fixed or quasi-fixed exchange rates had to abandon them in favor of greater exchange-rate flexibility. In fact, the official community came close to endorsing the so-called two-corner view: Governments rejecting exchange-rate flexibility must fix their exchange rates firmly; adjustable or "soft" pegs are no longer viable.[29] Thus, the finance ministers of the G-7 countries made this statement in their report to the 1999 Köln Summit:

> Some emerging economies have sought to achieve exchange rate stability by adopting peg regimes against a single currency or a basket of currencies, often in the same region, of countries with which they have the closest trade and investment links. Countries choosing fixed rates must be willing, as necessary, to subordinate other policies to that of fixing the exchange rate. If countries choose fixed rates, recent history suggests that arrangements institutionalizing that policy can be useful to sustaining a credible commitment to fixed rates.[30]

And the ministers went on to declare that the international community should not provide large-scale financial assistance to a country trying to defend a fixed rate " ... unless the rate is judged to be sustainable and certain conditions have been met, such as where the exchange rate

---

[28] We will say more about this policy prescription in Chapter 5.
[29] Eichengreen (1994) was among the first to take this view; for a qualified restatement, see Fischer (2001).
[30] G-7 (1999), para. 30b.

policy is backed by a strong and credible commitment with supporting arrangements, and by consistent domestic policies."[31]

What sorts of "supporting arrangements" can "institutionalize" a commitment to a fixed exchange rate?

Currency Boards and Dollarization

The most obvious candidate at the time was a currency-board regime of the sort adopted by Argentina in 1991. A currency board is obliged to hold foreign-currency assets at least as large as its monetary liabilities, and it must stand ready to swap home for foreign currency, and *vice versa*, at an irrevocably fixed price – one peso for one dollar in the Argentine case. As a currency board cannot vary its monetary liabilities at its discretion by buying or selling home-currency assets, such as government bonds, it cannot conduct an independent monetary policy.[32] Therefore, a currency board replaces a homegrown monetary policy with that of another country – the United States, in the Argentine case.

Currency boards were established initially in several British colonies to provide sound backing for the colonies' own currencies, but they were replaced by central banks after the colonies gained their independence.[33] Hong Kong adopted a currency-board regime in 1983 to restore

---

[31] G-7 (1999), para. 33b.

[32] There are, in fact, two more constraints on the discretion enjoyed by a currency board, both of them stemming from the fact that it cannot acquire home-currency assets to alter its own monetary liabilities. First, it cannot serve as a lender of last resort to the banking system. Second, it cannot neutralize the monetary effects of its foreign-currency transactions.

[33] But the countries of the Eastern Caribbean Currency Union have adhered to a currency-board regime since 1965, and two other currency boards have been around for decades – one in Djibouti, established in 1949, and one in Brunei Darussalem, established in 1967. On the history and structure of various currency boards and an assessment of their effects on economic performance, see Ghosh, Gulde, and Wolf (2000); also Baliño and Enoch (1997). It is worth noting an important difference between the colonial currency boards and their modern counterparts. The main monetary liabilities of the colonial boards were local-currency banknotes held by the public. The monetary liabilities of their modern counterparts also include deposit liabilities to the banking system – the cash reserves that banks must hold as fractional backing for the checking and saving deposits they owe to the public. Hence, a "run" on a modern currency board can cause an implosion of the banking system and a massive contraction of credit.

confidence in its own currency when it became clear that China would eventually reclaim sovereignty over Hong Kong. Estonia and Lithuania adopted currency boards in the early 1990s, soon after they gained their independence, and two more currency boards were created in 1997, in Bulgaria and Bosnia-Herzegovina.[34]

The Argentine arrangement was not a "pure" currency-board regime. In 1995, for example, Argentina was hard hit by a speculative attack in the wake of a Mexican currency crisis. The central bank suffered a large fall in its foreign-currency holdings, and Argentine banks experienced a corresponding fall in their peso deposits with the central bank and were thus under pressure to cut back their lending. To relieve the pressure on the banks, the central bank relaxed the rules of the currency-board regime. It reduced the reserve requirements of the country's banks – the fraction of the banks' deposit liabilities they had to "back" by holding deposits with the central bank.[35] Five years later, moreover, Argentina abandoned its currency-board regime after several events conspired against it: the sharp depreciation of the Brazilian *real*; a rapid build up of government debt due in part to the profligate spending of the provincial governments; and an ill-timed proposal by the country's finance minister, Domingo Cavallo, to switch from a dollar peg to a more flexible basket peg.[36]

Other countries' currency boards also have engaged in unorthodox practices. In 1998, for example, the Hong Kong Monetary Authority bought huge amounts of corporate stock to combat massive speculation against the Hong Kong dollar conducted in roundabout fashion *via* the Hong Kong stock market.[37] In fact, Steve Hanke, an ardent advocate of currency boards, argues that very few currency boards truly deserve the

---

[34] The two Baltic countries, moreover, have euro-based currency boards and can therefore count on a seamless transition to membership in EMU.

[35] Under the Argentine regime, moreover, a fraction of the central bank's liabilities were backed by peso-denominated bonds, not foreign-currency assets, but this deviation from orthodoxy did not play a major role in the ultimate collapse of the regime.

[36] A brief but balanced account of the Argentine crisis is provided by the IMF's Independent Evaluation Office (IEO 2004, ch. 1). Cavallo's proposal was sound analytically; by pegging the peso to the U.S. dollar, Argentina had exposed itself to the effects of fluctuations in the dollar exchange rates of its major trading partners, including Brazil and the euro area. He made his proposal, however, at a time when peso holders had begun to doubt the viability of the dollar peg and were thus poised to flee the peso.

[37] Goodhart and Lu (2003) describe this episode in detail.

name because they have engaged in unorthodox practices.[38] To which, of course, there is an answer: Some of the present-day currency boards have been long-lived precisely because they have taken unusual steps to cope with unusual problems.

Nevertheless, attention has shifted to a more durable way of importing another country's monetary policy – *de jure* dollarization.

There are two important differences between a currency-board regime and *de jure* dollarization. First, a country having a currency board retains its foreign-currency reserves and continues thereafter to earn interest on them. A country replacing its currency with the dollar, euro, or some other foreign currency must use some or all of its foreign-currency reserves to buy the foreign-currency banknotes it needs to buy back its own banknotes, and it thus loses interest income.[39] Second, it may be harder to exit from *de jure* dollarization than from a currency-board regime. A simple decree may suffice to abolish a currency-board regime. But the reintroduction of a national currency requires preparation; new national banknotes must be printed and distributed to the country's banks before they can be issued to the public. If, as is likely, the public notices these preparations and fears that the new national currency will be devalued or allowed to depreciate, there may be massive withdrawals from the banking system, as households and firms transfer their dollars or euros to other countries' banks.

There is, however, a strong similarity between the two regimes. Under both regimes, a country ties itself to a single foreign currency, typically the dollar or euro. This is not problematic for a country that trades mainly with the issuer of that currency. It is problematic, however, for a country that trades heavily with third countries. If those other countries'

---

[38] See Hanke (2002).

[39] This loss of *seigniorage* has as its counterpart a reduction in the government debt of the foreign country whose currency is being adopted; it is able to buy back some of its interest-bearing debt by printing the banknotes needed by the country adopting its currency. It has indeed been suggested that the United States should promote *de jure* dollarization by transferring the interest saving to dollarizing countries. Legislation authorizing transfers of that sort was introduced by Senator Connie Mack (The International Monetary Stability Act of 1999) but it did not reach the Senate floor (see Box 5.1 for additional detail). On the potential benefits and costs of *de jure* dollarization viewed from the U.S. standpoint, see Cohen (2004b).

currencies depreciate sharply *vis-à-vis* the dollar or euro, a country tied
to the dollar or euro may experience serious problems – falling exports,
rising imports, and a recession in its tradable-goods sector. That's what
happened to Argentina, and it was the reason for Cavallo's proposal that
Argentina switch from a dollar parity for the peso to a parity based on a
basket of foreign currencies. But his earlier decision to establish a dollar-
based currency board reflected in part the extent of *de facto* dollarization
that had taken hold in Argentina during the years of high inflation that
preceded his decision. When one foreign currency is widely used within a
country, it is the obvious substitute for the domestic currency even when
it is not the optimal substitute, based on the structure of the country's
foreign trade.

Note, finally, that these two regimes cannot prevent a government from
running budget deficits and borrowing to cover them. They can prevent
the monetization of debt, but they cannot prevent the creation of debt.
They may indeed tempt a government to go on a spending spree, because
the adoption of another country's currency is likely to give it low-cost
access to long-term credit, not only from foreigners but from its citizens
as well. Argentina and Panama provide examples. Argentina borrowed
heavily in the final years of its currency-board regime, and it had eventually to default on its debt. Panama has been fully dollarized for decades.
Nevertheless, it has been a chronic client of the IMF, largely because of its
fiscal problems.[40] A monetary union, however, is also exposed to the risk
of large-scale government borrowing, which is why the treaty creating
EMU contained limitations on deficits and debt.

THE COSTS OF CURRENCY CONSOLIDATION

There are two obvious costs to currency consolidation. The first is the one
imposed by forgoing local control over the conduct of monetary policy.
The second is the one imposed by forgoing the use of exchange-rate
changes.

---

[40] During the thirty years ending in 2000, Panama had IMF-supported programs in twenty
years, although some of them were precautionary programs and half of the available
funds were not used; see IEO (2002).

The cost of forgoing control over monetary policy was discussed at the start of this chapter. We saw why a country that joins a monetary union or adopts the currency of another country cannot conduct an independent monetary policy and why an imported monetary policy cannot be perfectly suitable, whether it is set by the supranational central bank of a monetary union or by the foreign central bank that issues the currency adopted unilaterally by the country. We also saw that membership in a monetary union may be better from this standpoint than unilateral dollarization, because of the difference in the policy domains of the relevant central banks, although the difference may be inconsequential for a small country weighing the choice between the two forms of currency consolidation. Finally, we saw that the cost of currency consolidation depends, importantly, on the quality of a country's homegrown monetary policy. In some cases, the second-best monetary policy imported by joining a monetary union or adopting unilaterally some other country's currency may be far superior to a homegrown policy.

The cost of forgoing exchange-rate changes, whether produced by market forces or by periodic changes in pegged rates, depends on the sorts of shocks to which a country is exposed and the optimality of exchange-rate changes as responses to those shocks. Let's look more closely at these matters.

The Role of Exchange-Rate Changes

Recall what we saw earlier, when considering a simple currency union and the effects of a switch in spending from Western to Eastern goods, which reduced the demand for Western labor and raised the demand for Eastern labor. If wages were perfectly flexible, they would fall in the West, reducing the prices of Western goods, and would rise in the East, raising the prices of Eastern goods. Hence, those changes would offset the switch in spending; both countries' consumers would buy fewer Eastern goods and more Western goods. There would thus be no need for workers to move from West to East or for a change in the exchange rate connecting the two countries' currencies. When wages are rigid, however, a depreciation or devaluation of the Western currency can substitute for changes in wages. It will make Eastern goods more expensive for Western consumers and Western goods cheaper for Eastern consumers. There-fore, an exchange-rate change is an optimal response to an expenditure-switching shock or, more precisely the best available response, absent adequate wage flexibility or cross-border labor mobility.[41]

When assessing the cost of currency consolidation, then, we need to answer the three questions posed earlier in this chapter: Are the countries involved apt to suffer large asymmetric shocks of the sort represented here by an expenditure-switching shock? Are their labor markets insufficiently flexible for them to rely on wage-rate changes to neutralize those shocks? Do they display too little labor mobility to compensate fully for wage rigidity?

There were many attempts to answer the question about shocks during the runup to EMU, and they took three forms. Some studies sought to measure the cross-country co-variation of the shocks affecting various European countries. Other studies pursued that same aim by examining the degree of industrial diversification in European countries or decom-posing output shocks into country-specific shocks and industry-specific shocks. And a third group of studies sought to predict how EMU itself might modify its members' vulnerability to various sorts of shocks.

Early work on the measurement of shocks looked at the cross-country co-variation of changes in aggregate output or the real exchange rate (i.e., the exchange rate adjusted for relative price levels).[42] These are endoge-nous variables, however, and their cross-country covariation depends not only on the covariation of the truly exogenous shocks but also on the responses to them, including policy responses, and on the thickness of

---

[41] In a world without capital mobility, moreover, the effects of a once-for-all devaluation of a pegged exchange rate need not be very different from the effects of relying on market forces to bring about the necessary change in the exchange rate, as the switch in demand from Western to Eastern goods will cause a market-determined rate to move in the right direction and, eventually, by the right amount. When changing a pegged rate, of course, a government risks making a wrong-sized change – devaluing by too little or too much. But the market also can make a wrong-sized change and is indeed likely to do so temporarily if consumers do not respond immediately to an exchange-rate change. Matters become more complicated, however, with the introduction of capital mobility, because short-run movements in market-determined exchange rates are then heavily influenced by capital flows, and these in turn are influenced by asset-holders' expectations about future exchange rates.

[42] For a survey and critique of this early work, see Bayoumi and Eichengreen (1999).

the channels through which they travel from one country to another. To deal with this and other problems, Bayoumi and Eichengreen adopted a technique devised by Blanchard and Quah,[43] which allowed them to disentangle exogenous shocks and separate two types: supply shocks, which have permanent output effects, and demand shocks, which do not. Their results are replicated in Table 2.1, which lists the correlations of the shocks hitting various EU countries with those hitting Germany, and also lists the correlations of the shocks hitting U.S. regions with those hitting the Mid-East region.[44]

There do not seem to be large differences in the variability of the shocks, measured by their standard deviations; European supply shocks appear to vary somewhat more than U.S. supply shocks, but European demand shocks appear to vary somewhat less than U.S. demand shocks. Yet the interregional correlations for both sorts of shocks are lower on average for the European countries than for the U.S. regions, suggesting that Europe was further from being an optimum currency area than was the United States in the period under study and could therefore incur the costs of forming a monetary union and abjuring the use of changes in nominal exchange rates to offset asymmetric shocks.

The earliest work of the second type, on domestic diversification, appeared in two papers, one by Lorenzo Bini-Smaghi and Silvia Vori,

---

[43] Blanchard and Quah (1989).

[44] Although the strategy adopted by Bayoumi and Eichengreen is clearly superior to those adopted earlier, it does not solve two problems: (1) It does not distinguish decisively between changes in output produced by truly exogenous shocks and changes reflecting the transmission of shocks from one country or region to another. (2) It takes no explicit account of the difference between the monetary-policy regime in the United States and the regime in Europe. The United States constitutes a full-fledged monetary union, and we have already shown that the monetary policy of such a union tends to transform an expenditure-changing shock into something resembling an expenditure-switching shock, as output rises in the country or region where the shock originates, and output tends to fall elsewhere; in other words, it tends to raise the frequency with which outputs are negatively correlated. During part of the period covered by Table 2.1, however, most of the European countries listed in that table belonged to the EMS, which had a monetary-policy regime resembling the one prevailing under unilateral dollarization. The German Bundesbank set monetary policy for the whole EMS, but it had a national policy domain. Hence, an output-raising shock necessarily elicited a policy response by the Bundesbank, but the sizes and signs of the resulting output changes depended on the origin of the shock – whether in Germany or in some other member country of the EMS.

Table 2.1. *Shocks to European countries and to U.S. regions*
(Blanchard-Quah shock extraction)

Country or region	Standard deviations		Correlations[1]	
	Supply shocks	Demand shocks	Supply shocks	Demand shocks
Belgium	1.5	1.6	0.61	0.33
Denmark	1.7	2.1	0.59	0.39
France	1.2	1.2	0.54	0.35
Germany	1.7	1.4	–	–
Greece	0.3	1.6	0.14	0.19
Ireland	2.1	3.4	−0.06	−0.08
Italy	2.2	2.0	0.23	0.17
Netherlands	1.7	1.5	0.59	0.17
Portugal	2.9	2.8	0.21	0.21
Spain	2.2	1.5	0.31	−0.07
United Kingdom	2.6	1.6	0.11	0.16
European Average	1.8	1.9	0.33	0.18
Mid-East	1.2	1.9	–	–
New England	1.4	2.5	0.86	0.79
Great Lakes	1.3	3.3	0.81	0.60
Plains	1.6	2.2	0.30	0.51
South East	1.1	1.8	0.66	0.50
South West	1.9	1.8	−0.12	0.13
Mountain	1.8	1.5	0.18	−0.28
Far West	1.3	1.7	0.52	0.33
U.S. Average	1.5	2.1	0.46	0.37

[1] With Germany in the case of European countries and with the Mid-East region in the case of U.S. regions.

Source: Adapted from Tamin Bayoumi and Barry Eichengreen (1993), "Shocking Aspects of European Integration," in F. Torres and F. Giavazzi, eds. *Adjustment and Growth in the European Monetary Union*. Cambridge: Cambridge University Press, pp. 193–229, Tables 7-4 and 7-6.

and the other by Paul Krugman.[45] Both studies found that European countries are less specialized than U.S. regions and, by implication, less vulnerable to industry-specific shocks. But Krugman went on to warn that the joint effects of EMU and the European single market might lead to greater specialization. Thus far, moreover, empirical work supports

[45] Bini-Smaghi and Vori (1992) and Krugman (1993).

his conjecture. Here are the main findings of a major research project on trends in the location of European industries:

Most European countries showed significant convergence of their industrial structure during the 1970s, but this trend was reversed in the early 1980s. There has been substantial divergence from the early 1980s onward, as countries have become more different... from most of their EU partners. The most dramatic changes in industry structure have been the expansion of relatively high technology and high skill industry in Ireland and in Finland. However, the specialization process has occurred more generally, with nearly all countries showing increasing differences from the early 1980s onward.[46]

Others believe, however, that monetary union will promote intra-industry specialization, not interindustry specialization, and will thereby reduce its members' vulnerability to asymmetric shocks, and Frankel and Rose have sought to show that this is already happening in Europe.[47] Working with data for twenty-one industrial countries, they find that the degree of economic integration, measured by the size of the trade links between pairs of countries, is strongly associated with the size of the time-series correlation between their output fluctuations. They conclude that countries joining a monetary union may, with time, satisfy more fully some of the criteria normally used to define an optimum currency area, because they will become more closely integrated.

This inference is debatable. It rests on two strong suppositions: (1) that economic openness, measured by the size of the trade links between pairs of countries, is an appropriate index of economic integration; and (2) that the pair-wise correlation between output fluctuations is an appropriate index of the similarity in the shocks afflicting a pair of countries. That correlation, however depends on several features of the country pair at issue, not only the characteristics of the shocks afflicting them but also their policy responses to them and the thickness of the channels through which the effects of shocks travel from country to country. Frankel and Rose are fully aware of these complications. Nevertheless, they interpret their findings as showing that countries become more similar as a result of

---

[46] Midelfart-Knarvik et al. (2000), p. 1.
[47] Frankel and Rose (1998).

integration and that the shocks afflicting them become more symmetric, reducing the cost of membership in a monetary union.

With the passage of time, we will learn more about the effects of monetary union on the nature and size of the shocks affecting its members – whether it raises or lowers their vulnerability to asymmetric shocks. And we also may be able to answer a more important question – whether a monetary union will catalyze reforms that raise the flexibility of labor markets and reduce the barriers to labor mobility.[48] Thus far, however, the Single European Act appears to have been the more important catalyst for reform; it mandated the transformation of the EU from a customs union into a single market for goods, services, capital, and labor. It can likewise be argued that EU accession has done more to foster reform in the Central European countries than will their admission to the monetary union.

Other Costs and Caveats

We have already mentioned two other effects of currency consolidation – the change in the domain of monetary policy, and the interest-income loss suffered by a country that opts for unilateral dollarization. We have seen that a member of a monetary union or a country that adopts another country's currency has to import a monetary policy different than one ideally suited to its particular needs. This will, of course, be costly for a country that had a homegrown monetary policy with which it was well satisfied. The case of Germany comes to mind, where there was very strong opposition to EMU, because it would replace the "stability oriented" monetary policy of the Bundesbank with that of the new and unfamiliar European Central Bank. In many other cases, however, the substitution of a union-wide or foreign country's monetary policy may be beneficial, because too many countries' homegrown policies have been

---

[48] Padoan (2002) emphasizes this possibility and Eichengreen (2001a) makes an analogous point about the effects of *de jure* dollarization. The debate about dollarization, he says, has focused too heavily on the conventional questions posed in this chapter; it should instead focus on ways in which dollarization might foster financial and fiscal stability, as well as labor-market reform. If it has no first-order effect of that sort, it is "largely irrelevant" to the problems of crisis-prone emerging-market countries.

ill-suited to their needs. We also have seen that a country adopting another country's currency must use some or all of its foreign-currency reserves to buy that country's currency and will then lose the interest income furnished by those reserve holdings.

There is, however, another effect of *de jure* dollarization. A country adopting another country's currency loses its lender of last resort – the institution capable of rescuing its banks if their depositors lose confidence in them and try to withdraw their funds. A "run" can start because of fears about the soundness of a single bank, but it can spread to other banks if the first bank is unable to repay its depositors. Advocates of *de jure* dollarization respond to this concern by saying that banks which are basically sound, such as the affiliates of large foreign banks, should be able to borrow abroad when they have no local lender of last resort. In the Argentine case, however, there was a run on the banks, including the local affiliates of foreign banks, and they could not borrow abroad, not even from their parents, because of the uncertainties created by the crisis and by the government's responses to it.[49]

COMPARED TO WHAT?

We have made several sorts of comparisons in this chapter. At times, we have compared a full-fledged monetary union with unilateral dollarization. When making that comparison, moreover, we have typically assumed that a country on its own can conduct a sensible monetary policy, although we have often portrayed unilateral dollarization as a way for a country to import a monetary policy better than its homegrown monetary policy. At other times, we have compared currency consolidation

---

[49] See, e.g., Edwards (2002). This problem need not arise in a full-fledged monetary union. But Europe has adopted a federal structure, in which the national central banks survive and retain a significant amount of operational autonomy. Therefore, some have wondered how quickly and decisively the European regime would respond to an incipient banking crisis, and their doubts are reinforced by another feature of that same regime. The ECB is not directly involved in the prudential supervision of the banking system and may thus lack the information required to decide whether an individual bank faces a liquidity problem and is thus deserving of financial support or faces a genuine solvency problem and should be restructured or shut down. We will return to these matters in Chapter 3.

with the use of exchange-rate changes to cope with various shocks. That was the comparison made by Mundell and is the one implicit in much subsequent research on the characteristics of an optimum currency area. For that same reason, incidentally, economists may have wasted time and effort by trying so hard to decide on the eve of EMU whether Europe was close to being an optimum currency area. The twelve members of EMU began with system of pegged exchange rates, the EMS, and had already ruled out exchange-rate flexibility as being deleterious to deep integration – the creation of a comprehensive single market for goods, services, capital, and labor. They had therefore to choose between a rather fragile EMS and some sort of EMU.

It is impossible conceptually to meld all these comparisons into a single ranking of monetary systems, partly for reasons already mentioned. It may be very hard, perhaps impossible, for some countries to pursue a prudent monetary policy; they may therefore be better off with the imperfect fit of an imported monetary policy. And it may be impossible for a group of countries to achieve deep integration without adopting a common currency to eliminate currency conversions and the risks arising from exchange-rate uncertainty.

It is not our aim, however, to rank regimes abstractly. It is rather to predict as best we can the choices that countries are likely to make in the years ahead and their implications for the form and functioning of the international monetary system. To that end, we turn next to EMU, the most prominent monetary union today. We ask why and how it was created and what it can teach us about the institutional and political arrangements that may be needed to govern a full-fledged monetary union.

3

The European Monetary Union

INTRODUCTION

The European Monetary Union is without question the most ambitious project of its type. A group of highly developed countries with sophisticated monetary systems managed by some of the world's best-known central banks agreed to substitute a single European currency for their own national currencies and to subordinate their own countries' central banks to a new institution – the European Central Bank.

Why and how did this happen? Economists and political scientists have given many reasons. Some of them have focused on problems internal to the EU itself – the threat to the stability of the EMS posed by the adoption of the Single European Act, which required the ending of all capital controls in 1990. Once that had happened, it was argued, the EMS would face the risk of massive speculation against its weakest currencies. The freeing of capital movements, it was said, would force the EU countries to choose between a "retreat" to greater exchange-rate flexibility or an "advance" to full-fledged monetary union.[1]

Politics also played a role in the decision to move to EMU. A single European currency could challenge the hegemony of the U.S. dollar and give a larger role to the EU in managing the world's monetary system. There had for years been discontent, especially in Europe, with U.S. dominance of the international monetary system, what Charles de Gaulle had once described as the "exorbitant privilege" of the United States – its

---

[1] See, e.g., Padoa-Schioppa (1988).

freedom to finance its balance-of-payments deficits in its own national currency. There was, in addition, discontent with U.S. economic policies – the belief that the United States was exporting homegrown inflation to Europe. That was indeed one of the reasons cited obliquely by President Giscard d'Estaing of France and Chancellor Kohl of Germany when they called for the creation of the EMS in 1978.[2]

Yet the actual decision to move on to EMU had other causes, too. The collapse of the Soviet Union and the likelihood that several Central European countries would soon seek to join the EU posed a unique challenge. The "deepening" of the EU would be made more difficult once many more countries had joined. Yet the "widening" of the EU could not be postponed for long; it was essential to secure the economic and political stability of its Eastern neighbors. There was, moreover, some concern that the unification of Germany might dilute its commitment to the EU itself, turning it inward and eastward.

Although we allude to some of these matters later in this chapter, we will focus on three questions: How was it decided to move to EMU? What are its main aims and features, including the fiscal constraints it imposes on its members? And is it reproducible elsewhere in the world or is it inextricably bound into the institutional framework of the EU itself? We defer to the next chapter, however, an assessment of economic performance in the euro area – the ultimate test of the success of the entire project.

THE ANTECEDENTS OF EMU

In 1957, six European countries adopted the Treaty of Rome, creating what was called the European Economic Community (EC),[3] a customs union abolishing tariffs on trade between the member countries

---

[2] On the catalytic role of transatlantic rivalry, see Henning (1998); on the corresponding role of transpacific rivalry, see Henning (2005).

[3] A purist would use EEC to denote the European Economic Community and would reserve EC for the collectivity of three Communities: the European Economic Community or Common Market, the European Coal and Steel Community, and the European Atomic Energy Community, as well as their institutional incarnations, a single Commission and single Council of Ministers. But EC is used here to cover both regimes and to distinguish them from the European Union (EU) created by the Maastricht Treaty.

and surrounding them with a common external tariff. This started the process that led in 1991 to adoption of the Treaty on European Union, also known as the Maastricht Treaty, in which the EC countries committed themselves to three ambitious goals: implementation of a common foreign and security policy, close cooperation on justice and home affairs, and formation of an economic and monetary union, "ultimately including a single currency."[4] Box 3.1 describes the institutional structure of the EU, which does not differ greatly from that of the EC.

From the Rome Treaty to the EMS

Monetary cooperation in Europe began long before the creation of the EC.[5] It started in 1950 with the creation of the European Payments Union (EPU), which liberalized trade in Western Europe by replacing a cumbersome network of bilateral payments arrangements with a single, multilateral arrangement and provided a framework for achieving currency convertibility, an objective reached in 1958. Monetary cooperation, however, was conducted within the framework of the worldwide Bretton Woods System administered by the International Monetary Fund (IMF). Under that regime, each government had to adopt a pegged exchange rate for its currency, defined in terms of gold or the U.S. dollar. A government could change its exchange-rate peg with IMF approval, but only when it had a "fundamental disequilibrium" in its balance of payments. Nevertheless, the Rome Treaty committed the EC countries to treat their exchange rates as a matter of "common concern," and they took steps to formalize that commitment. In 1958, they established a Monetary Committee to monitor economic and financial conditions; in 1964, they established the Committee of Central Bank Governors, a body that would play a major role in designing EMU. In 1969, moreover, the EC governments agreed in

---

[4] The text of the treaty was approved at Maastricht in 1991, signed in 1992, and came into force in 1993, after ratification by every member country. When the treaty was approved, the EU had twelve members, but three more joined soon thereafter, ten more joined in 2004, and two more joined in 2007. Only thirteen countries, however, belong to the monetary union (the most recent entrant, Slovenia, joined in 2007).

[5] The brief history that follows draws on Kenen (1995).

Box 3.1. The Institutions of the EU and Their Role in the Governance of EMU

The *European Council* brings together the heads of state or government of the EU countries and the President of the Commission. It sets policy goals and guidelines; it also appoints the President of the ECB and the other members of the ECB's Executive Board, acting on recommendations made by the Council of Ministers.

The *European Commission* is the executive body of the EU but also has the exclusive right to initiate EU legislation by making proposals or recommendations to the Council of Ministers. The Commission enforces EU law and can bring a member state before the European Court of Justice in the event of noncompliance. It also represents the EU internationally. The Commission makes decisions by majority voting. At present, each member state nominates a Commissioner, and the President is chosen by the European Council, but the further growth of EU membership will introduce rotation. A new Commission is chosen at five-year intervals, and its whole membership must be approved by the European Parliament, which can also dismiss the whole Commission.

The *Council of Ministers* represents the member states. It adopts legislation but shares that power with the European Parliament. It coordinates the economic policies of the member countries, defines and implements the common foreign policy of the EU, and must approve international agreements negotiated by the Commission. Legislation involving taxation and certain other matters must be adopted unanimously; in other cases, a simple or qualified majority suffices. A qualified majority obtains if a majority of member states votes "yes" (in some cases, a two-thirds majority), if 73.9 percent of the total votes are cast in favor, and if the "yes" votes represent at least 62 percent of the EU's population. The votes cast by individual countries vary with their size: Germany, France, Italy, and the United Kingdom have twenty-nine votes each, whereas Cyprus, Estonia, Latvia, Luxembourg, and Slovenia have only four, and Malta has just three. The Council meets in several incarnations, the Council of Economic and Finance Ministers (ECOFIN) being the most relevant for EMU. There is also a less formal body, the *Eurogroup*, comprising the Economic and Finance Ministers of the thirteen euro area countries.

The *European Parliament* is elected directly by the citizens of the EU countries and shares legislative authority with the Council of Ministers, except in the limited number of matters reserved entirely to the Council. If the two bodies disagree, a conciliation committee is formed to seek agreement, but the Parliament must ratify that agreement; otherwise, the legislation is not adopted.

The *European Court of Justice* hears cases brought by the Commission, by national governments, or by individual citizens of EU countries. It has twenty-seven members, one from each EU country, but need not hear cases in plenary session. The Court has rarely been involved in matters pertaining to EMU, but the Commission brought one case concerning implementation of the Stability and Growth Pact.

Note: These are the institutional arrangements that prevailed in 2007, reflecting the provisions of the Maastricht, Nice, and Amsterdam Treaties.

principle to form an economic and monetary union, and they appointed Pierre Werner, prime minister and finance minister of Luxembourg, to chair a group of experts that would propose a plan. Their report was completed in 1970 and called for complete monetary union by 1980.

The Werner Report envisaged a three-stage process. The first stage would focus on the coordination of monetary and fiscal policies. Although governments would still formulate their national policies, adherence to EC guidelines would foster policy coordination and thereby obviate the need for large exchange-rate changes in the second stage. That second stage would see the narrowing of exchange-rate fluctuations and the creation of a fund for monetary cooperation to provide short-term credit to EC countries having balance-of-payments problems. The third stage would see the irreversible fixing of exchange rates, the abolition of all capital controls, and the creation of a unified central banking system to take over the conduct of monetary policy.[6] By that time, moreover, the size and financing of national budgets would be decided at the EC level by a new body responsible to the European Parliament.

---

[6] Gros and Thygesen (1999) point out, however, that the Werner Report said very little about institutional matters, and one can safely say that this central banking system would not have enjoyed the policy-making autonomy conferred on the ECB by the Maastricht Treaty.

The EC governments endorsed the strategy proposed by the Werner Report and implemented some of its recommendations. In March 1972, exchange-rate fluctuations were reduced by limiting the swings in bilateral exchange rates to a $2\frac{1}{4}$ percent band. This arrangement was known as the "snake in the tunnel" because the whole band could undulate within the wider $4\frac{1}{2}$ percent band established for dollar exchange rates by the Smithsonian Agreement of 1971 – the attempt to reform the Bretton Woods System after the Nixon administration had sought to devalue the dollar.[7] In 1973, however, the Bretton Woods System collapsed completely, abolishing the tunnel and allowing the snake to undulate freely, but the resulting changes in exchange rates *vis-à-vis* the dollar were too costly for some EC countries, and they left the snake, allowing their currencies to float independently.

The EC adopted two other proposals made by the Werner Report – the creation of a European Monetary Cooperation Fund (EMCF), and the promulgation of EC guidelines to foster the convergence of national policies. But policy divergence, not convergence, was occurring everywhere after the huge jump in oil prices that followed the Arab-Israel war of 1973. Inflation rates were rising but at different speeds, as were unemployment rates. When, therefore, the EC countries looked again at monetary cooperation in the late 1970s, they abandoned the plan proposed by the Werner Report, responding instead to a call by Chancellor Schmidt of Germany and President Giscard D'Estaing of France to pursue a less ambitious goal: creating a "zone of monetary stability" within the EC by establishing a European Monetary System (EMS).

The two leaders' motives were different but mutually compatible. Schmidt was deeply dissatisfied with the policies of the Carter administration in the United States, especially its failure to combat inflation, and he feared that the resulting weakness of the dollar would cause the deutsche

---

[7] The decision to narrow the band for bilateral rates reflected concern that large changes in those rates could alter substantially the prices received by various countries' farmers under the EC's Common Agricultural Policy (CAP); for an explanation, see Gros and Thygesen (1999), pp. 11–12. There may not seem to be a huge difference between a $2\frac{1}{4}$ percent band and a $4\frac{1}{2}$ percent band. The latter, however, applied to dollar exchange rates. If, then, the French franc was at the top of its dollar band and the Italian lira at the bottom, a switch in their positions *vis-à-vis* the dollar would alter the bilateral franc-lira rate by more than 8 percent.

mark to appreciate, not only *vis-à-vis* the dollar but also against other EC currencies. Giscard D'Estaing was animated by a familiar French predilection for fixed exchange rates but did not want France to rejoin the snake, because it had not functioned symmetrically enough.[8] The Schmidt-Giscard initiative was endorsed by the EC governments in 1978, the main features of the EMS were then defined by the Council of Ministers, and it came into being early in 1979.

From the EMS to EMU

The EMS was meant to be more flexible and symmetrical than the Bretton Woods System, which had been based mainly on the U.S. dollar. Each country participating in the exchange-rate mechanism of the EMS had to keep the exchange rate for its currency within a band defined by a grid of central rates for the various pairs of participating currencies. When an exchange rate reached the edge of its band, both countries involved were supposed to intervene on the foreign-exchange market to keep the rate from moving further. But they had unlimited access to short-term credit from the EMCF whenever they required a partner country's currency for that intervention. The central rates could be revised with the consent of all concerned, and there were twelve such realignments before 1992, when the EMS experienced a major crisis. Eight EC countries joined the exchange-rate mechanism initially, and others joined thereafter.[9]

A European Currency Unit (ECU) was meant to play a major role in the EMS. It was defined as a basket of EC currencies and was the accounting

---

[8] See Ludlow (1982) on the two leaders' views and the EMS negotiations; also Fratianni and von Hagen (1992) and Gros and Thygesen (1999). Although the EC central banks helped to design the EMS, they were wary of the plan. The Bundesbank, in particular, insisted on changes that made the EMS less symmetrical, and it also sought assurances from the German government that the Bundesbank would not be bound by the rules of the EMS if adherence to those rules conflicted with the Bundesbank's pursuit of price stability. Its reservations were set out in the so-called Emminger letter, which the Bundesbank invoked in September 1992 and that played a role in triggering the EMS crisis of 1992–93; see Kenen (1995), ch. 7.

[9] Italy and the United Kingdom were forced to drop out at the start of the 1992 crisis, and though Italy rejoined thereafter, in time to qualify for membership in EMU, the United Kingdom did not. Hence, the pound continues to float *vis-à-vis* all currencies, including the euro.

unit of the EMS. But it played a bigger role in financial markets than in the EMS itself, and it also played a role in the Maastricht Treaty, which was drafted on the supposition that the ECU would be transformed into the new currency of the monetary union. The euro did not get its present name until 1995, when it was decided to rechristen the ECU.

Most of the early exchange-rate realignments in the EMS reflected its members' attempts to offset inherited cost and price disparities, as well as the new disparities produced by the different ways in which the EC countries responded to the oil shock of 1979. This first phase ended abruptly, however, in March 1983, when the Mitterand government in France abandoned headlong economic expansion in favor of rigorous stabilization. There was another realignment at that point, but very few thereafter. In fact, the EMS began to resemble a fixed-rate regime, as France, Italy, and other EC countries sought to "borrow credibility" from the Bundesbank by committing themselves firmly to exchange-rate stability and using that commitment as the rationale for pursuing domestic policies aimed at combating inflation. Some even began to think again about monetary union.

The case for taking that big step was supported by two considerations, both linked to the adoption in 1986 of the Single European Act, which committed the EC to forging unified markets for goods, services, capital, and labor by the end of 1992.

First, the adoption of the Single European Act lent strength to the belief long held by many Europeans that closely integrated national economies like those of the EC had more to gain from exchange-rate stability than from occasional realignments. In fact, the potential benefits of the single market could not be captured fully without banishing exchange-rate risk and the costs of using separate national currencies.[10]

Second, the creation of the single market required the ending of all capital controls, and the EC had decided that this should be accomplished by mid-1990. Once those controls were gone, however, doubts about the fixity of EMS exchange rates could generate speculative capital flows

---

[10] This view was set out strongly in the Commission's subsequent statement of the case for EMU aptly titled *One Market, One Money* (European Commission, 1990), but the case has since been strengthened by the findings of Rose (2000) and others, discussed in Chapter 2.

large enough to *force* exchange-rate realignments or, at least, to interfere with the normal conduct of monetary policy. This point was made persuasively by Tommaso Padoa-Schioppa, who warned against trying to pursue full capital mobility, fixed exchange rates, and separate national monetary policies. "In the long run," he wrote, "the only solution to the inconsistency is to complement the internal market with a monetary union."[11]

Third, the EMS had proven to be less symmetric than its founders had intended. It was helpful to import credibility from the Bundesbank, but mimicking the Bundesbank's monetary policy could be very costly to other countries whenever economic conditions in those countries differed from conditions prevailing in Germany. When the dollar was weak, moreover, the deutsche mark was correspondingly strong – too strong to suit the needs of some other EC countries – and this problem was amplified by the reunification of Germany. When the German budget deficit began to grow in the wake of reunification, the Bundesbank tightened its monetary policy. Its partners, however, did not face the same problem; some of them, indeed, faced recessions. In short, the policy domain of the Bundesbank was national, not European, and a full-fledged monetary union began therefore to seem attractive by contrast with the asymmetric EMS.

These views were reflected in a memorandum that the French finance minister, Edouard Balladur, addressed to his counterparts in early 1988. He criticized the asymmetric features of the EMS and asked that his colleagues contemplate far-reaching reforms, including a monetary union. Somewhat surprisingly, his German counterpart, Hans-Dietrich Genscher, responded by proposing the creation of a European central bank.[12] The end result was the appointment of a committee chaired by Jacques Delors, President of the European Commission, and its members included the governors of the twelve EC central banks. Its task was not

---

[11] Padoa-Schioppa (1988), p. 376. It should be noted, however, that the growth of capital flows during the 1980s and 1990s might have destabilized the EMS even without the abolition of all capital controls.

[12] On these memoranda and subsequent contributions, see Gros and Thygesen (1999), pp. 396–400; also Dyson and Featherstone (1999), especially pp. 159–66 and pp. 326–34.

to advocate monetary union but rather to devise a plan and a way to implement it.[13]

The Delors Report

The Delors Report listed three requirements for monetary union: the full convertibility of the EC currencies, the integration of financial markets, and the irrevocable locking of exchange rates. The first two, it noted, had already been achieved by the EC countries. By meeting the third, the EC would become a single currency area, but it should adopt a new single currency as soon as possible after exchange rates had been locked.[14]

Like the Werner Committee before it, moreover, the Delors Committee proposed that the EC countries create a new institution to formulate and execute monetary policy, but it said much more about the structure and mandate of that institution. The European System of Central Banks (ESCB) would comprise a central institution, having its own balance sheet, and the national central banks of the EC countries. The Council of the ESCB would formulate monetary policy and manage the EC's exchange-rate policy, and it would be independent of instructions from national governments and from EC institutions.

The ESCB would be committed to maintaining price stability but would also support "the general economic policy set at the Community level" insofar as it could do so without jeopardizing price stability. The ESCB also would be responsible for the maintenance of a properly functioning payment system, and it would participate in the coordination of banking supervision.[15]

Most of these recommendations found their way into the Maastricht Treaty. But the responsibility for exchange-rate policy was divided

---

[13] The inclusion of the central bank governors influenced strongly the content of the Delors Report, notably its emphatic endorsement of central bank independence, and a subsequent decision to ask that the central bank governors draft a statute for the ESCB and ECB reinforced their influence. Very few changes were made in their draft before it was appended as a protocol to the Maastricht Treaty, and the treaty itself reproduced key provisions of the statute. On the role and influence of the central bank governors, see Andrews (2003).

[14] Committee for the Study of Economic and Monetary Union (1989), para. 23. This document is cited hereafter as Delors Report (1989).

[15] Delors Report (1989), para. 32.

awkwardly between the Council of Ministers and the ESCB, and the ECB's involvement in bank supervision was sharply circumscribed.

The Delors Report also dealt with fiscal policy. National policies would have to be coordinated to achieve a mix of fiscal and monetary policies appropriate for internal balance and for the Community to play its part in the international adjustment process.[16] But mere coordination would not be enough. Binding rules would be needed to limit national budget deficits; the ESCB would be barred from lending directly to national governments; and there would be limits on government borrowing in foreign currencies.[17] These recommendations also found their way into the Maastricht Treaty, apart from the one about limits on foreign-currency borrowing.

The emphasis on price stability, the strong endorsement of central bank independence, and the emphasis on fiscal rectitude are often attributed to the role played by the central bank governors in the preparation of the Delors Report.[18] Yet they really reflected the evolution of academic and official views about the role and conduct of monetary policy in the years between the Werner and Delors Reports.[19] When the latter was written, however, several EC central banks were still taking instructions from their finance ministries or from other governmental bodies. The Bank of England did not achieve operational independence until 1997, and some of the other EC central banks were not granted independence until their governments *had* to grant it in order for their countries to qualify for EMU.

It should be noted, moreover, that the ECB is more independent than most other central banks. Because the Statute of the ECB and ESCB is annexed to the Maastricht Treaty, it cannot be amended without the unanimous consent of the EU governments, whereas the constitutions of

---

[16] Delors Report (1989), para. 30.

[17] Delors Report (1989), para. 30.

[18] Thereafter, moreover, they were charged with drafting a statute for the ESCB and ECB, and very few changes were made in their draft before it was appended as a protocol to the Maastricht Treaty. The main changes, mentioned below, had to do with exchange-rate policy and the (limited) role of the ESCB in bank supervision. On the role of the central bank governors, see Andrews (2003).

[19] See, e.g., McNamara (1998). For a discussion of the evolution in central bank independence, see Crowe and Meade (2007).

many other central banks are embodied in ordinary legislation, which can be amended by their countries' legislatures. And though the Maastricht Treaty instructs the ECB to treat price stability as its "primary objective," it does not tell the ECB how to define price stability.[20]

The Delors Report also dealt with the transition to EMU, proposing a three-stage process. The first stage would feature preparatory steps, including the design of a framework for policy surveillance and coordination. For fiscal policies, in particular, coordination would require "concerted budgetary action" by the EC countries. Furthermore, all of the EC currencies would enter the exchange rate mechanism of the EMS, and every effort would be made to avoid more exchange-rate realignments.[21]

The second stage would introduce major innovations. Precise rules would be used to limit national budget deficits (although they would not be binding until the third stage). The ESCB would be established and begin to move from coordinating national monetary policies to the design and implementation of a single monetary policy. The Delors Committee recognized the problems involved in making this gradual transition, and the matter was revisited during the debate in the runup to Maastricht about the role of the European Monetary Institute (EMI), the body that would oversee the transition to EMU.[22] It was eventually agreed that the responsibility for monetary policy is inherently indivisible and should therefore reside with the national central banks until the start of the third stage, when the ECB would take over the conduct of monetary policy.

The third stage would begin with the irrevocable locking of exchange rates. Furthermore, foreign-exchange reserves would be transferred to the ECB, in order for it to conduct intervention *vis-à-vis* third currencies "in accordance with Community exchange rate policy."[23] At some point

---

[20] The distinction at issue, between "goal" independence and "instrument" independence is discussed at length by Debelle and Fischer (1994).

[21] Delors Report (1989), para. 51.

[22] The EMI was led by Alexandre Lamfalussy, who deserves enormous credit for bringing EMU into being. One main task of the EMI was to design and test the large-value payment system (TARGET) needed to link the banking systems of the EU countries; on this and related matters, see Padoa-Schioppa (2004a), ch. 6.

[23] Delors Report (1989), para. 60.

in the third stage, moreover, a new single currency would replace the members' national currencies.

In June 1989, the Madrid Summit received the Delors Report and took the first step toward EMU, deciding that the first stage would start in July 1990. In December 1989, the Strasbourg Summit agreed to convene an intergovernmental conference (IGC) in December 1990 to work on the subsequent stages. And in June 1990, the Dublin Summit decided to convene *two* IGCs, one on economic and monetary union and one on political union, and these took place in parallel. The results were combined in the Maastricht Treaty, hence its formal name: The Treaty on European Union.

There was not much disagreement in the IGC on EMU about the structure and powers of the ECB – not even about the proposed constraints on national fiscal policies. It was clear to all participants that the design of EMU would have to satisfy German concerns. The ECB would have to resemble the Bundesbank; it would have to be protected from political interference and would have to pursue price stability. There was much more debate about the transition to the third stage – the start of full-fledged monetary union. Would country membership be automatic? Could a country opt out – or drop out after joining? And when would the third stage start? We will return to these questions.

MONETARY POLICY IN EMU

The Structure and Tasks of the Eurosystem

The Eurosystem set up by the Maastricht Treaty comprises the ECB and the national central banks of the countries that have adopted the euro.[24] Its organization is described in Box 3.2, which compares it to its U.S. counterpart, the Federal Reserve System.

---

[24] The term ESCB used in the Delors Report and the Maastricht Treaty is now used exclusively to denote the ECB and the national central banks of *all* the EU countries (whether or not the country is a member of EMU). The term is still needed because the countries that have not adopted the euro have certain limited rights and duties; see Articles 45–48 of the Statute.

Box 3.2. Comparison of the Eurosystem and the U.S. Federal Reserve System

	Eurosystem	Federal Reserve System
Institutional structure	Independent central bank with federated structure	Independent central bank with federated structure
	European Central Bank (ECB) in Frankfurt	Board of Governors in Washington, DC
	National central banks (NCBs) in thirteen member states	Federal Reserve Banks in twelve Districts
Appointment of officials	Six Executive Board members appointed by the member states to nonrenewable eight-year terms	Seven Governors appointed by U.S. President to nonrenewable fourteen-year terms, subject to Senate confirmation
	Governors of thirteen national central banks appointed domestically to terms no shorter than five years pursuant to national legislation	Presidents of twelve Federal Reserve Banks appointed by Banks' Boards of Directors to renewable five-year terms, subject to approval by Board of Governors
Responsibilities of board	Current business and administration of the ECB	Supervises operations of Federal Reserve Banks
	Oversees the cross-border (TARGET) payment system	Approves changes in reserve requirements
		Approves changes in discount rate
		Supervises and regulates U.S. banking system
		Oversees domestic payment system
		Administers consumer credit legislation
Legislative mandate or goal	Primary objective is to maintain price stability	To promote effectively the goals of maximum employment, stable prices, and moderate long-term interest rates
Monetary-policy body	Nineteen-member Governing Council comprising six members of	Twelve-member Federal Open Market Committee (FOMC) comprising seven

	Executive Board and thirteen NCB governors, each with one vote (but country groups will be introduced when the number of EMU members totals sixteen)	Board members, President of NY Federal Reserve Bank, and four other Bank Presidents (on rotating basis), each with one vote
Monetary-policy operations	Decentralized, executed by each NCB in its own national financial market	Centralized, carried out by the NY Federal Reserve Bank in the U.S. financial market
Foreign-exchange intervention	By the Eurosystem at its discretion, but subject to "general orientations" if adopted by Council of Ministers	By the Board of Governors in coordination with and at the request of the U.S. Treasury

The ECB is managed by its Executive Board, composed of the President and Vice President of the ECB and four other members, all of whom are chosen by the European Council (i.e., the heads of state or government) on the recommendation of the Council of Ministers, which must first consult the European Parliament and the ECB's Governing Council. Members of the Executive Board serve for staggered eight-year terms and cannot be reappointed.[25]

The six members of the Executive Board and the governors of the national central banks serve on the Governing Council, which is the main policy-making body of the Eurosystem.[26] The Governing Council meets twice each month, but it normally devotes only one such meeting to monetary policy. Decisions are taken by simple majority vote, with

---

[25] Although there is no *de jure* requirement that members of the Executive Board come from certain countries, there would seem to be a *de facto* requirement. Francesco Giavazzi and Charles Wyplosz have noted that each of the four largest countries in the euro area (France, Germany, Italy, and Spain) appear to have a permanent claim to a seat on the Executive Board; see Giavazzi and Wyplosz (2006).

[26] The President of the Council of Ministers and a member of the European Commission may participate in the deliberations of the Governing Council but may not vote. (The President of the Council of Ministers, however, may submit a motion for consideration by the Governing Council.) The President of the ECB may likewise attend meetings of the Council of Ministers when it discusses matters relating to the work of the Eurosystem.

the President casting the deciding vote.[27] Governing Council members have said repeatedly, however, that they take decisions about monetary policy by consensus rather than by formal voting. As building a consensus requires more time than securing a simple majority, it may slow the adjustment of the Eurosystem's monetary policy. Whether this is true or not, decision making by the Governing Council is apt to be affected by the impending enlargement of EMU, which will eventually include the ten newest EU members. To limit the effects of this widening on decision making, the ECB proposed a reform of voting rights that was then adopted by the European Council, and it will take effect as soon as the Eurosystem has more than fifteen members.[28] Under the revised voting scheme, the six members of the Executive Board will continue to have one vote each, but the number of votes cast by the national central banks will be capped at fifteen, and voting rights will rotate across countries according to a predetermined scheme.[29]

The Governing Council announces its decisions about monetary policy right after its monthly meeting on monetary policy, and the President typically engages in a question and answer session with journalists. Unlike the Bank of England and Federal Reserve, which publish detailed nonattributed minutes shortly after each policy meeting and reveal how each official voted, the Governing Council publishes neither minutes nor votes. The absence of published information on its deliberations, together with its somewhat opaque strategy for pursuing price stability, discussed below, have generated criticism that the Eurosystem is not sufficiently transparent about its decision making.[30] Although the identification of individuals and their votes could expose members of the Governing Council to political pressure and should therefore be avoided, the publication of nonattributed minutes would serve to enhance transparency without subjecting policy makers to national pressures.

The ECB transmits an annual report to the European Parliament, the Council of Ministers, and the European Commission, and the Parliament

---

[27] The rare exceptions to this rule are listed in Article 10 of the Statute.

[28] This reform was adopted by the Council in March 2003 and amends Article 10.2 of the Statute.

[29] The rotation allocates a set number of votes across three different country groups. Meade (2003) provides additional detail and a critique of the reform.

[30] Blinder et al. (2001) offer a complete account of the transparency and communications practices of central banks in the major industrial countries.

may then hold a general debate on the report. The President of the ECB and other members of the Executive Board also may appear before the relevant committees of the Parliament, at the request of the Parliament or on their own initiative. The ECB is thus accountable to the Parliament in much the same way that the Board of Governors of the Federal Reserve System is accountable to the U.S. Congress. The Congress, however, can issue instructions to the Federal Reserve System by amending the Federal Reserve Act, but the European Parliament has no such power. In fact, the ECB – being a supranational institution created by treaty – is thoroughly insulated from any attempt to influence its policies:

> When exercising the powers and carrying out the tasks and duties conferred upon them by this Treaty and the Statute..., neither the ECB nor a national central bank, nor any member of their decision-making bodies shall seek or take instructions from Community institutions or bodies, from any government of a Member State or from any other body. The Community institutions and bodies and the governments of the Member States undertake to respect this principle, and not to seek to influence the members of the decision-making bodies of the ECB or of the national central banks in the performance of their tasks.[31]

Furthermore, the member countries of the EU must make sure that their national laws, including the statutes of their central banks, are fully compatible with this and other provisions of the Maastricht Treaty.

The treaty spells out the powers and duties of the ECB. The "primary objective" of the ECB is price stability. It is also instructed, however, to "support the general economic policies in the Community" insofar as it can do that without prejudice to price stability.[32] To these ends, it is instructed to define and implement the monetary policy of the Community, to conduct foreign-exchange operations consistent with the provisions of Article 111 (discussed later), to hold and manage the foreign reserves of the Member States, and to promote the smooth operation of the payment system.[33]

---

[31] Treaty on European Union (hereafter TEU), Article 108.
[32] TEU, Article 105(1). This language resembles the wording of the Delors Report, but with one change – the substitution of "policies in the Community" for "policy set at the Community level." This change was proposed by the United Kingdom with the apparent aim of encouraging the ECB to support the economic policies of its member countries, not merely policies set at the Community level.
[33] TEU, Article 105(2).

The treaty also instructs the ECB to contribute to the "smooth conduct of policies pursued by the competent authorities relating to the prudential supervision of credit institutions and the stability of the financial system," and it can be assigned specific tasks pertaining to prudential supervision, but not unless the Council of Ministers decides unanimously to confer those tasks upon it.[34] Thus far, however, the Council has not assigned such tasks to the ECB.[35] The treaty stops short of giving the ECB the duty and power to serve as a lender of last resort, which would require it to accommodate a need for central-bank money arising from illiquidity in the banking system.[36] Instead, the national central banks are expected to serve as lenders of last resort to their own countries' banks, subject to the general understanding that such operations should not undermine the monetary policy of the ECB.[37]

Because it lacks lender-of-last-resort powers, the ECB differs from the Federal Reserve and other major central banks that have broad powers to maintain financial-market stability. Garry Schinasi describes the ECB as the "ultimate 'narrow' central bank" in that it has a mandate to maintain price stability but only a limited role in maintaining financial stability, which is confined to oversight of the payment systems.[38] It should be noted, however, that a central bank serving as a lender of last resort typically functions in conjunction with a centralized fiscal authority, which

---

[34] TEU, Articles 105(5) and (6).

[35] It should be noted, however, that a common supervisory system for the euro area would require a major reorganization of present arrangements, which are determined separately in each EU country.

[36] Traditionally, a lender of last resort provides short-term financing to an illiquid (but not insolvent) bank in order to reinforce confidence in the banking system and prevent a banking crisis. In practice, however, it is difficult to distinguish illiquidity from insolvency, and an individual bank may be so large that its failure would threaten the whole banking system. Humphrey (1992) offers a detailed discussion of lender-of-last-resort powers. If made too generous or reliable, lender-of-last-resort funding can encourage banks to engage in excessively risky behavior. This "moral hazard" problem was the primary reason for German refusal to let the Bundesbank serve as a lender of last resort, and German views undoubtedly influenced the decision to deny the ECB explicit authority to take on this task. For a thorough discussion of the lender-of-last-resort role and financial stability, in general and as it pertains to EMU, see Schinasi (2006).

[37] European Central Bank (2000a) provides a detailed discussion of the framework for banking supervision in the euro area.

[38] Schinasi (2003).

ultimately stands behind any rescue operation, and there is no single fiscal authority standing behind the ECB. It may therefore be sensible, at least in the short term, for the national central banks to serve as the lenders of last resort.[39] We cannot really know, however, how the Eurosystem would deal with a banking or financial crisis affecting the whole euro area.

Article 111 of the Maastricht Treaty, mentioned above, pertains to exchange-rate policy for the euro. Its first part deals with a problem that has not yet arisen and need not detain us – concluding a formal international agreement on an exchange-rate regime that would link the euro to other countries' currencies. Its second part deals with the world we know now. Absent any formal international agreement involving the euro, "the Council of Ministers, acting by a qualified majority on a recommendation from the Commission and after consulting the ECB or on a recommendation from the ECB, may formulate general orientations for exchange-rate policy in relation to these currencies." But those general orientations must not prejudice the maintenance of price stability.[40]

The ECB's Monetary Policy Strategy

In October 1998, shortly before the start of EMU, the Governing Council announced that "three main elements" would guide its decisions about monetary policy: a precise definition of the treaty's price-stability objective and a "two pillar" strategy for achieving that objective.[41] The Governing Council defined price stability as an annual increase in the euro area consumer price index of less than 2 percent over the medium term.[42]

---

[39] Goodhart (2002) makes this argument.

[40] TEU, Article 111(2). The treaty, however, does not say who will decide whether a particular exchange-rate policy is prejudicial to price stability, whereas the antecedent of this particular caveat, the Emminger letter, gave the Bundesbank that power; see note 8. As the guardian of price stability, however, the ECB would probably have the last word.

[41] See European Central Bank (1999, 2000b), European Commission (2004a), and Issing et al. (2001).

[42] In the run-up to EMU, the European statistical agency, Eurostat, working with its national counterparts, constructed an index of consumer prices for each EU country based on a common set of goods and services, so that it could be used to track inflation across the euro area. Although the resulting index, the Harmonized Index of Consumer Prices, or HICP, covers identical goods and services, each country's HICP uses national

The first pillar involved an assessment of developments in monetary aggregates and included a numerical reference value for money growth (defined as an annual increase in a broad monetary aggregate, M3, of 4.5 percent). The second pillar involved a "broadly based assessment of the outlook for price developments and the risks to price stability . . . using a wide range of economic indicators."[43]

At the time that it erected its two pillars, the ECB was concerned with bridging the credibility gap posed by handing the conduct of monetary policy to a new, untested institution:

Building credibility is particularly important for the ECB at the outset of Stage Three since it is a new institution. . . . [The national central banks] that are components of the Eurosystem have, over the years, built up a strong reputation for maintaining price stability.[44]

The European predecessor of the ECB, the German Bundesbank, had served as "anchor" central bank in the EMS, had a long-established reputation for fighting inflation, and had used a money-growth target as a guide to policy making. The first of the two pillars, then, was meant to connect the ECB to its most credible predecessor and thereby provide a firm anchor for inflation expectations. Nevertheless, the targeting of monetary aggregates had long since ceased to be the preferred guide for policy among central banks. As for the Bundesbank itself, although it had relied on monetary targeting for many years, it had missed its target more than half the time.[45]

At the same time, however, the ECB was concerned about the several sources of uncertainty that were quite likely to arise with the move to monetary union; it had "particular concern . . . [about] the way in which the transition to Stage Three of EMU will affect economic behavior, institutional structure and statistical series in the euro area."[46] The second

---

weights to construct a consumption basket reflecting its own households' preferences. Cecchetti and Wynne (2003) provide a thorough discussion of the measurement issues involved.

[43] European Central Bank (1999), p. 49. Jaeger (2003) provides a detailed discussion and analysis of the ECB's first pillar.

[44] European Central Bank (1999), p. 44.

[45] Kole and Meade (1995) review industrial-country experience with monetary targeting and focus in particular on the Bundesbank.

[46] European Central Bank (1999), p. 44.

pillar, then, gave it leeway to consult all of the available economic and financial data before coming to a policy decision.

Almost from the outset, the ECB's policy-making regime was besieged by criticism. Its definition of price stability, an inflation rate below 2 percent, was seen to be ambiguous and asymmetric, largely because it had no lower bound. Critics urged the ECB to adopt an explicit value or range for targeted inflation, in order to indicate clearly that the ECB would not tolerate deflation. Furthermore, the ECB's first pillar was seen as being obsolete – an artifact of an earlier era in which several central banks had used monetary targets. Calling it the "poison pillar," Begg et al. argued that the rationale for using it – providing continuity with the Bundesbank – would weaken over time.[47] The ECB was therefore urged to merge its two pillars and thereby take account of all of the relevant information, including the behavior of monetary aggregates. Going even further, Lars Svenssen recommended that the ECB move directly to an inflation-targeting framework of the sort employed in New Zealand, Sweden, and the United Kingdom.[48]

In May 2003, after a lengthy evaluation, the Governing Council announced some small but important clarifications and revisions of its policy-making strategy. With regard to price stability, the Council indicated that it was aiming for inflation "below, but close to, 2 percent,"[49] thus helping to alleviate concerns that it might tolerate deflation.[50] The Council also reversed the ordering of the two pillars and relabeled them as "economic analysis" and "monetary analysis" so as to differentiate their functions. This reform effectively downgraded the importance of the monetary aggregates, and the Council underscored the change in their role by saying that it would now monitor a wide range of monetary statistics and no longer announce a numerical reference value for M3 growth. Commenting on the new roles of the two pillars, the ECB noted that "monetary analysis mainly serves as a means of cross-checking, from a medium to long-term perspective, the short to medium-term indications

---

[47] Begg et al. (2002).
[48] Svensson (2002a, 2002b, 2003a).
[49] European Central Bank (2003), p. 79.
[50] Svensson (2003b) still argued, however, that the ECB's definition of price stability is not precise enough.

coming from economic analysis."[51] Galí et al. and others agreed that these refinements helped to align the ECB's rhetoric with its behavior but said that there was still ample room for improvement.[52]

The Implementation of Monetary Policy

Although decisions about monetary policy are centralized in the Governing Council, monetary-policy operations are decentralized; they are undertaken by the national central banks in their own financial markets. The national central banks implement monetary policy through weekly open-market operations, mainly in the form of repurchase agreements (repos) conducted at an interest rate set by the Governing Council. Two standing facilities are available to banks, a marginal lending facility that banks can use to obtain additional liquidity at a penalty interest rate, and a deposit facility that banks can use to earn interest on excess liquidity but at an interest rate lower than the repo rate. The interest rates on these standing facilities put a ceiling and floor, respectively, on short-term market interest rates.

All of the liquidity provided by the national central banks to their countries' commercial banks is furnished on a collateralized basis; the ECB and the national central banks designate lists of assets eligible for use as collateral.[53] Late in 2005, however, the ECB introduced an important change in its rules regarding collateral. Concerned by the large size and long duration of the fiscal deficits of some member countries and the failure to enforce the fiscal sanctions discussed later in this chapter, the ECB announced that it would cease to accept as collateral securities issued by national governments if those governments' credit ratings dropped below A–. Were that to happen to large debtors such as Greece and Italy, their debt instruments would become far less attractive to banks throughout the euro area.

The monetary-policy operations of the Eurosystem do not affect the balance sheet of the ECB; they affect the balance sheets of the national

---

[51] European Central Bank (2003), p. 87.
[52] Galí et al. (2004).
[53] European Central Bank (2005a) provides additional detail on the monetary-policy operations and procedures of the Eurosystem; Bartolini and Prati (2003) discuss key differences between the operating procedures of the Eurosystem and the Federal Reserve.

central banks.[54] The effects of the Eurosystem's monetary policy are thus transmitted to the commercial banks of the euro area *via* the banks' cash balances with their national central banks. There is an interbank market in the euro area, much like the Federal Funds market in the United States. A commercial bank can use that market to borrow or lend in order to adjust its cash position with the national central bank of the country in which the bank is located.

An integrated interbank money market of this sort, with a common short-term interest rate, is indeed essential for the successful transmission of monetary policy throughout a monetary union. In the case of the Eurosystem, however, the integration of its members' money markets posed a challenge because of the decentralized nature of its operations. Yet there was a relatively rapid convergence of interest rates in the member countries' overnight markets. It occurred within three weeks after the euro was introduced,[55] thanks to the smooth functioning of TARGET, the large-value payment system which settles interbank payments crossing its members' national borders.[56]

The Integration of Capital Markets

The integration of bond and equity markets across the EMU countries did not occur instantaneously but has advanced substantially. Before 1999, the Council of Ministers had decided that, from the start of the monetary union, all of the members' new government debt would be issued in euros, and all of their outstanding debt would be redenominated in euros and reconventioned to conform to a common technical standard. These decisions reflected competition among national governments to win benchmark status for their own countries' bonds, as well as their

---

[54] The ECB does have its own balance sheet; its assets include the foreign-exchange reserves called up from the national central banks in accordance with Article 30 of the Statute. The ECB is empowered to use those reserves for intervention on the foreign-exchange markets. The income of the national central banks deriving from their monetary operations is pooled at the end of each financial year and then redistributed to them in proportion to their paid-up capital contributions.

[55] See Gaspar and Hartmann (2005).

[56] TARGET connects the real-time gross settlement payment systems of the member countries *via* an interlinking mechanism operated by the ECB; for more on the structure and functioning of TARGET, see European Central Bank (2004).

desire to produce an integrated market that could compete in size and breadth with the market for U.S. government securities. Thanks to these changes, the bonds of different governments became easier to compare and more readily substitutable.

The integration of the markets for government debt had a powerful spillover effect on the markets for corporate debt. It generated a dramatic growth in issuance, in secondary market trading, and in competition among underwriters.[57] At the same time, a market emerged for lower-rated corporate debt. The resulting growth in the issuance and trading of corporate debt may have redefined home bias; investors now show a generalized preference for euro-denominated assets, rather than assets issued by firms in their home countries.[58] It may be too early to know, however, whether the issuance of corporate debt will reduce the traditional reliance on bank lending by European firms.[59] Finally, equity issuance in the euro area has grown substantially, and total stock-market capitalization is roughly equal to 60 percent of euro-area GDP, more than double its size a decade ago. Nevertheless, new equity issues remain far less important as a source of corporate financing than in the United States.

The Impact of the ECB's Monetary Policy

When the ECB adjusts short-term interest rates, how does it affect economic activity in the euro area? Understanding the answer to this question – how the transmission mechanism operates – is critically important for ECB officials who need to know how their decisions will affect the euro area in the aggregate and whether their effects will differ across countries. Microeconomic research has looked at the effects of changes in monetary policy on bank lending, bank interest rates, and financial markets broadly. Macroeconomic research has used econometric models to examine the effects of changes in monetary policy on the components of aggregate demand.

---

[57] Pagano and von Thadden (2004), p. 2.
[58] Baele et al. (2004).
[59] See Hartmann et al. (2003) for a discussion. It is important to note that the integration of credit markets across EMU countries has not paralleled the integration in capital markets.

Because the creation of the monetary union was a major regime change and because many studies of the transmission mechanism are based on data from the pre-1999 period, it is too early to describe precisely the new "equilibrium" transmission mechanism. Yet studies have already found some cross-country convergence in the transmission mechanism during the mid- to late 1990s, indicating that preparations for EMU and expectations about the performance of the euro yielded effects even prior to the start of EMU.[60] Macroeconomic evidence suggests that investment is the most interest-sensitive component of aggregate demand in the euro area, whereas consumption is the main interest-sensitive component in the United States.[61]

So, how successful has the ECB been with its monetary policy? The answer depends on how we measure success. Annual inflation, which was well below 2 percent at the start of the monetary union, was somewhat higher than 2 percent for some time thereafter. Nevertheless, some observers still applaud the ECB, because actual inflation typically was held within a narrow range, from 2 to $2\frac{1}{2}$ percent, even as others chastised it for failing to meet its stated target.[62] Measures of expectations, however, indicate that market participants trust the ECB to honor its commitment to keep inflation at or close to 2 percent. Yet when success is measured by looking more broadly at economic performance, the ECB's track record looks less satisfactory. We defer this larger question to Chapter 4, where we will examine economic performance under a variety of exchange-rate arrangements.

The Currency of the Realm

The design and distribution of the euro banknotes and coins proved to be one of the more contentious aspects of EMU. This is not particularly surprising, given the role that physical currency, adorned with historical figures and landmarks, plays as a visible symbol of national identity.

---

[60] See, for example, Angeloni et al. (2003a) and Massmann and Mitchell (2003), both of which rely on pre-1999 data to look at the euro-area transmission mechanism.

[61] Angeloni et al. (2003b) compare in detail the difference in output responses of the U.S. and euro-area economies.

[62] Compare Charles Goodhart's comments in House of Lords (2002–03) with Galí et al. (2004).

It was decided early on that new banknotes and coins would not be introduced at the start of EMU; instead, the members' national currencies would continue to circulate for three years thereafter. That provided ample time to design the banknotes and coins and their security features, to conduct the printing and minting operations, and to work out the logistics of the actual changeover to the new physical currency and the simultaneous retirement of the old national notes and coins.

It was at first suggested that one side of each euro banknote should show some well-known national feature of the particular country in which it was issued, but that idea was rejected. It was instead decided that all of the banknotes should be identical and that the architectural features displayed should be generic rather than actual structures. This decision greatly facilitated the production of the banknotes, which involved nine paper mills, fifteen printing plants, and scores of employees across the euro area, and it also avoided the need to guard against the use of controversial landmarks, such as the German Reichstag. National symbols were permitted to grace the backs of euro coins, but it took time to agree on the shapes of the coins out of concern for the needs of the blind, and time to agree on their metallic content because of concerns about allergies to nickel. In the end, the replacement of the legacy currencies with the physical euro took place without a hitch, but the issues involved underscore the importance of seemingly small details for the success of a monetary union.

FISCAL POLICY IN EMU

There are three ways in which fiscal policy can complement or complicate monetary policy, but a single member of a monetary union may not take full account of them when setting its fiscal policy to meet its own national needs.

Why National Fiscal Policies Matter

First, the mix of fiscal and monetary policies can affect the foreign-currency value of the union's currency. Recall what happened in the United States during the early 1980s, when the Federal Reserve pursued a tight monetary policy and the Reagan administration ran a big budget deficit; the combination drove up interest rates, and the dollar appreciated strongly. The Delors Report made no mention of this episode, but its members may have had the episode in mind when stressing the need for Europe to play an appropriate role in the international adjustment process and thus the need for policy coordination to manage the policy mix.

Second, fiscal policy has a role to play in maintaining macroeconomic stability within a monetary union – to offset country-specific shocks or deal with the feature of a monetary union noted in Chapter 2, the fact that the union's single monetary policy cannot fit all of its members perfectly unless they face identical expenditure-changing shocks. Each country can, of course, rely on the automatic stabilizers built into its own fiscal system. Whenever economic activity contracts, tax payments fall automatically, whereas transfer payments rise, and these changes in fiscal flows cushion the impact of a slump. Conversely, tax payments rise and transfer payments fall whenever economic activity expands. These built-in stabilizers, however, are rarely strong enough to maintain or restore economic stability, and there may be a need to go further – to cut taxes when the economy slumps severely and raise them when it grows too fast. Yet politics can get in the way of symmetrical stabilization. When tax revenues rise in prosperous times, governments may spend them or use them to cut tax rates, rather than pay down debt in anticipation of the next recession and the budget deficit it is likely to produce. There is, therefore, the risk that government debt will grow over the whole business cycle.[63]

---

[63] This tendency is mitigated, however, in a large multiregional economy such as that of the United States, where the federal fiscal system functions in ways that soften the impact of shocks affecting individual regions asymmetrically. When one region suffers a slump while another enjoys a boom, households and firms in the former will make smaller tax payments to the federal government, those in the latter will make larger tax payments, and there may thus be little net impact on the federal budget. This phenomenon was noted by Ingram (1959), emphasized later in Kenen (1969), and inspired a pathbreaking empirical paper by Sala-i-Martin and Sachs (1992), who found that a region's tax payments to the U.S. federal government fall by 34 cents whenever its per capita income falls by one dollar. Their paper was criticized by von Hagen (1992) for failing to disentangle the effects of cyclical fluctuations from those of a different phenomenon – the fact that high-income regions normally pay more taxes than

Third, the deficits and debt of a single country may affect other countries, especially when they have fixed exchange rates or a single currency, as well as integrated capital markets. An increase in one country's long-term interest rate as a result of an increase of government borrowing could drive up interest rates in other countries, crowding out investment in those countries and raising the cost of servicing their governments' own debts.[64] Furthermore, a highly indebted government may be unable to service its debt and may even be seen to be courting insolvency well before it gets there. The union's central bank may then be forced to come to the aid of banks and other financial institutions that hold that government's debt.

These concerns explain why the Delors Report called for strict limits on national budget deficits and why limits on debt stocks, as well as budget deficits, found their way into the Maastricht Treaty.

The Fiscal Provisions of the Maastricht Treaty

The Maastricht Treaty contains two safeguards against the various ways in which fiscal policies can impinge on the functioning of the monetary union. First, it contains a "no bail-out clause," which insulates the EU from any liability incurred by a member state, and it also insulates each member state from any liability incurred by another member state.[65] Second, it contains an "excessive deficit procedure" aimed at limiting budget deficits and holding down government debt. Article 104 of the

---

low-income regions. Work by others, however, taking account of von Hagen's critique, came up with significant cyclical effects; see the discussion in Kenen (1995), pp. 89–90. It must nevertheless be noted that the EU budget is quite small and is financed by agreed contributions from the EU governments, not by taxes on households or firms. Hence, it cannot help to stabilize output and income in the EU as a whole, nor offset asymmetric shocks by making automatic transfers between member countries.

[64] Although the possibility of interest-rate spillovers was emphasized heavily in the early debate about the Maastricht Treaty, they are unlikely to be large. A country running a big budget deficit may experience an increase in its own long-term interest rate, but other countries' interest rates may not be affected unless financial markets come to believe that the ECB will behave perversely – that it will accommodate the big budget deficit.

[65] TEU, Article 103. This clause does not cover the ECB explicitly, but it is more likely to acquire public-sector obligations as assets rather than as liabilities.

treaty begins with a binding commitment, then lists two criteria by which to judge compliance with it.[66]

Member States shall avoid excessive government deficits. The Commission shall monitor the development of the budgetary situation and of the stock of government debt in the Member States with a view to identifying gross errors. In particular it shall examine compliance with budget discipline on the basis of the following two criteria:
(a) whether the ratio of the planned or actual government deficit to gross domestic product exceeds a reference value [3 percent of GDP], unless either the ratio has declined substantially and continuously and has reached a level that comes close to the reference value; or, alternatively, the excess over the reference value is only exceptional and temporary and the deficit remains close to the reference value;
(b) whether the ratio of government debt to gross domestic product exceeds a reference value [60 percent of GDP], unless the ratio is sufficiently diminishing and approaching the reference value at a satisfactory pace....

If the Commission finds that a government is running or may run an excessive deficit, it will inform the Council of Ministers, which will make a formal finding, and if the Council decides that the deficit is excessive, it will make confidential recommendations to the government concerned. If, thereafter, the Council concludes that the government has not taken adequate action, it may publish its recommendations, and if that step does not suffice, it may request that the government adopt measures that the Council judges to be necessary to rectify the situation. If, finally, the government fails to comply with that request, the Council may impose certain penalties. It can, for example, require the government to make a non-interest-bearing deposit of an "appropriate" size until it has corrected its deficit and, as a last resort, convert the deposit into a fine.

The Stability and Growth Pact

Many economists criticized these provisions. They argued, in particular, that *ex ante* limitations on deficits and debts are not the best way to insulate the monetary policy of the ECB from the potential problems

---

[66] The bracketed numbers in the text are those contained in a protocol to the treaty.

posed by large government debts.[67] But others, including Theo Waigel, the German finance minister, feared that the excessive deficit procedure might not provide enough protection against fiscal folly.[68] Therefore, he proposed additional measures, and these are now known collectively as *The Stability and Growth Pact*. It has three parts:

A resolution adopted by the European Council commits the EU governments to aim at budgets "close to balance or in surplus" over the medium term, so that cyclical fluctuations will not cause excessive budget deficits, and it calls for the correction of excessive deficits "as quickly as possible," usually within one year. It also urges the Council of Ministers to make vigorous use of the financial sanctions listed in the treaty.

Legislation adopted thereafter by the Council of Ministers requires the euro-area governments to take additional steps in the third stage of EMU. Each government must prepare a *stability program* describing the measures it will take to keep its budget close to balance. Each government must also publish its program and update it annually, and the Council of Ministers must review the program, asking whether it is based on realistic assumptions and whether it provides a safety margin adequate to guard against an excessive deficit.

Finally, the Council adopted legislation to speed up the implementation of the excessive deficit procedure, define the size of the financial sanctions (which can be as large as half of one percent of a country's GDP), and set the speed with which a deposit turns into an outright fine when a government fails to correct an excessive deficit.

Assessing Compliance with the Fiscal Rules

Table 3.1 shows that few EMU members have had budgets "close to balance or in surplus" over the period since the introduction of the euro. Most of them, indeed, have run budget deficits in recent years, with

---

[67] See, e.g., Begg et al. (1991), Wyplosz (1991), Buiter, Corsetti, and Roubini (1993), and Eichengreen (2005). For recent critiques that take account of actual fiscal performance, see Buti et al. (2003), Fatàs et al. (2003), von Hagen (2003), and European Commission (2004a). For a defense of the fiscal rules and a critique of the reforms adopted in 2005 and described later, see Buti (2006).

[68] Waigel was concerned in part to reassure domestic opponents of EMU; see Collignon and Schwarzer (2003), pp. 178–81. On German public opinion and EMU, see Nölling (1993), pp. 136–38.

Table 3.1. *Government deficits and debt as percentages of gross national product*

Country	1999	2000	2001	2002	2003	2004	2005	2006*	2007*
Government Deficit									
Austria	−2.4	−1.6	0.3	−0.5	−1.5	−1.1	−1.5	−1.9	−1.4
Belgium	−0.4	0.1	0.6	0.0	0.1	0.0	0.1	−0.3	−0.9
Finland	2.2	7.1	5.2	4.1	2.5	2.3	2.6	2.8	2.5
France	−1.8	−1.4	−1.5	−3.2	−4.2	−3.7	−2.9	−3.0	−3.1
Germany	−1.5	1.3	−2.8	−3.7	−4.0	−3.7	−3.3	−3.1	−2.5
Greece	−1.8	−2.0	−3.6	−4.9	−5.8	−6.9	−4.5	−3.0	−3.6
Ireland	2.3	4.4	0.9	−0.4	0.2	1.5	1.0	0.1	−0.4
Italy	−1.8	−0.7	−3.0	−2.9	−3.4	−3.4	−4.1	−4.1	−4.5
Luxembourg	3.7	6.3	6.2	2.0	0.2	−1.1	−1.9	−1.8	−1.5
Netherlands	0.7	2.2	−0.1	−2.0	−3.1	−1.9	−0.3	−1.2	−0.7
Portugal	−2.9	−2.9	−4.4	−2.9	−2.9	−3.2	−6.0	−5.0	−4.9
Spain	−1.2	−0.9	−0.5	−0.3	0.0	−0.1	1.1	0.9	0.4
Government Debt									
Austria	67.5	67.0	67.1	66.0	64.4	63.6	62.9	62.4	61.6
Belgium	114.8	109.1	108.0	103.2	98.5	94.7	93.3	89.8	87.0
Finland	47.0	44.6	43.8	41.3	44.3	44.3	41.1	39.7	38.3
France	58.5	57.2	57.0	58.2	62.4	64.4	66.8	66.9	67.0
Germany	61.2	60.2	59.4	60.3	63.8	65.5	67.7	68.9	69.2
Greece	105.2	106.2	114.8	110.7	107.8	108.5	107.5	105.0	102.1
Ireland	48.6	38.4	35.8	32.1	31.1	29.4	27.6	27.2	27.0
Italy	115.5	111.2	110.7	105.5	104.2	103.8	106.4	107.4	107.7
Luxembourg	6.0	5.5	7.2	6.5	6.3	6.6	6.2	7.9	8.2
Netherlands	63.1	55.9	52.9	50.5	51.9	52.6	52.9	51.2	50.3
Portugal	54.3	53.3	55.9	55.5	57.0	58.7	63.9	68.4	70.6
Spain	63.1	61.2	57.8	52.5	48.9	46.4	43.2	40.0	37.9

* Forecast.

Source: Data for 1999 through 2001 from Eurostat and European Commission (2004a), "EMU after 5 Years," *European Economy Special Report 1* (and not strictly comparable with those for subsequent years); data for 2002 through 2007 from European Commission Spring Economic Forecasts, 2006–2007, *European Economy*, 2006 (2).

France, Germany, Greece, Italy, and Portugal running deficits larger than 3 percent of GDP in no fewer than three of the five most recent years, 2002 through 2006. Although some of this fiscal deterioration reflects the slowdown of economic activity in the euro area, the Commission ascribes part of it to discretionary measures.[69] It also notes, however, that fiscal policies have been responsive to debt levels, and this effect is manifest in Table 3.1. Some of the high-debt countries have run fairly small budget deficits, and all but two that had debt ratios higher than 60 percent in 1999 reduced their debt ratios thereafter. Most of the reductions were rather small, however, and some of the countries with lower debt ratios reduced them even further.[70] In short, the data give little support to the hypothesis cited above, that debt ratios are bound to rise through time because governments are prone to "give away" cyclical surpluses rather than pay down debt. More important, a major econometric study found that the fiscal rules have not prevented the EU countries from following countercyclical fiscal policies.[71]

Some EU countries have been found formally to have excessive deficits, but these were typically corrected before the governments involved came close to facing financial sanctions. In 2002, however, France and Germany, began to run large deficits and ran the risk of being told how to reduce their deficits. Had they failed to comply, they would have faced financial sanctions. Therefore, they persuaded the Council to "suspend" the excessive deficit procedure, triggering much criticism and a rash of proposals for reforming the fiscal rules of EMU. Some of those proposals were eminently sensible; the Commission, for example, suggested that the time limit for ending an excessive deficit should take account of country-specific conditions.[72] Others, however, were blatantly self-serving; some governments even suggested that certain sorts of government spending

---

[69] European Commission (2004a).

[70] Some of the fall in debt ratios, however, reflected reductions in the governments' debt-service payments resulting from lower interest rates, rather than reductions in discretionary spending.

[71] Gali and Perotti (2003). It also should be noted that large budget deficits and high or rising debt levels have not greatly affected long-term interest rates. There is, indeed, no compelling evidence that the general level of long-term rates rose when the two largest euro-area countries, France and Germany, started to run large budget deficits in 2002.

[72] European Commission (2004b).

be excluded from their budget deficits, such as their contributions to the EU budget, their spending on research and development, and, in the German case, the continuing costs of reunification.

The Council of Ministers debated these proposals at a marathon meeting in March 2005 and agreed on recommendations that were then approved by the European Council. Henceforth, more attention will be paid to debt sustainability, countries with low debt levels will be given more time to reach the medium-term objective of budgets "close to balance or in surplus," and countries experiencing abnormally low growth rates rather than deep recessions need not be deemed to have excessive budget deficits. Furthermore, implementation of the excessive deficit procedure will take into account the level of public investment, spending on research and development, and the up-front costs of structural reforms that have long-term cost-saving effects.[73] Finally, implementation will also take into account government spending aimed at achieving "European policy goals, notably the unification of Europe" (an oblique but obvious reference to the costs of German reunification).

The Council of Ministers was careful to note that sanctions can still be imposed on a country that fails to correct an excessive deficit, but it made that much less likely, emphasizing instead a different way to deal with the problem:

> The Council underlines that the purpose of the excessive deficit procedure is to assist rather than to punish, and therefore to provide incentives for Member States to pursue budgetary discipline, through enhanced surveillance, peer support and peer pressure. Moreover, policy errors should be clearly distinguished from forecast errors in the implementation of the excessive deficit procedure.[74]

In effect, it assured France and Germany that they would not face fines if they failed to correct their excessive deficits within the next couple of years.[75]

---

[73] For an elegant defense of this recommendation, see Beetsma and Debrun (2004).

[74] European Council (2005), Annex II, para. 3.

[75] In March 2006, however, the Council of Ministers took note of Germany's commitment to reduce its budget deficit below 3 percent of GDP by 2007, although it required the German government to make interim reports on its progress and to continue reducing its "structural" deficit even after ending its excessive deficit. It remains to be seen, however, what action the Council will take with respect to the three other countries (Greece, Italy, and Portugal) that have run or are expected to run large budget deficits.

STARTING THE MONETARY UNION

Recall the three questions posed earlier in this chapter: Would membership in the monetary union be open automatically to all EU countries? Could a country opt out or drop out later? And when would the monetary union begin?

There was not much debate about the first question. For as long as anyone can remember, as far back indeed as the Werner Report, German officials and academics argued that monetary union should be the last step in a process involving the prior economic convergence of the EU countries. It was therefore decided at Maastricht that membership in EMU would not be automatic. Instead, each country would have first to satisfy the four "convergence criteria" set out in Box 3.3.[76]

Many questions were raised about these criteria. Why must a country prove that it can defend its exchange rate in order to enter a monetary union in which it will have no exchange rate of its own? Why must it reduce its national inflation rate when, upon entering EMU, all of its members' inflation rates were expected to converge to the same inflation rate – the one imposed by the monetary policy of the ECB? And why should its long-term interest rate be treated as an indicator of durable convergence? It is, of course, a forward-looking variable, conveying information about market participants' expectations. But it may be heavily influenced by their expectations about a country's chances of entering EMU, and that is what actually happened; recall how rapidly interest rates converged in 1998, as soon as markets learned which countries would enter EMU.

Some academics, moreover, criticized the whole notion of prior convergence. Rudiger Dornbusch, for example, wanted EMU to start without waiting for convergence, and he urged two key countries, France and Germany, to move immediately to monetary union. A two-speed Europe, he maintained, would be better than a no-speed Europe, and that is what might happen if EMU were delayed.[77] But German views on this and

[76] The same convergence criteria will be used to judge when the ten new EU members are ready to join the monetary union, a decision to which we have taken strong exception; see Kenen and Meade (2004). One of those countries, Slovenia, has already met the convergence criteria, but others are still far from doing so.

[77] Dornbusch (1990). Swoboda (1991) took a similar position, and the Commission also favored a short transition, fearing that the EMS might be fragile; see Italianer (1993).

Box 3.3. The Convergence Criteria in the Maastricht Treaty

Article 121 of the Maastricht Treaty lists four convergence criteria by which to judge the readiness of an individual EU country for participation in the monetary union, and they are explained in a protocol to the treaty:

1. *Achieving a high degree of price stability,* which the protocol defines to mean

   ...an average rate of inflation, observed over a period one year before the examination, that does not exceed by more than 1½ percentage points that of, at most, the three best performing Member States in terms of price stability.

2. *Achieving a sustainable financial position,* which the protocol defines to mean that

   ...at the time of the examination, the Member State is not the subject of a Council decision...that an excessive deficit exists.

3. *Maintaining the country's exchange rate within the normal EMS band,* which the protocol defines to mean that

   ...the Member State has respected the normal fluctuation margins...without severe tensions for at least the last two years before the examination. In particular, the Member State shall not have devalued its currency's bilateral central rate against any other Member State's currency on its own initiative for the same period.

4. *Achieving a long-term interest rate indicative of durable convergence and of the country's participation in the EMS,* which the protocol defines to mean that

   ...over a period of one year before the examination a Member State has an average nominal long-term interest rate that does not exceed by more than two percentage points that of, at most, the three best performing Member States in terms of price stability.

---

other matters could not be ignored without putting the whole project at risk.

There was, of course, less danger of putting the project at risk by allowing individual countries to opt out, and that possibility was entertained in a draft of the treaty prepared by the Dutch government shortly before the Maastricht meeting. It said that no EU country would be required to join the monetary union if its national parliament "does not feel able to approve of the irrevocable fixing of its currency" (i.e., participation in the monetary union). The draft was meant to deal with two countries' reservations – those of Denmark and the United Kingdom. It was soon recognized, however, that other countries' parliaments, including the German Bundestag, might have similar reservations, and that could scuttle EMU. Accordingly, the Danish and British cases were handled in an *ad hoc* way by appending protocols to the treaty exempting Denmark and Britain from participation.[78] What about opting out after having joined? The treaty did not offer a way out. It treated EMU membership as an obligation of EU membership, and there is no exit from the EU itself.[79]

At one point in the bargaining about EMU, however, it seemed that EMU might be delayed indefinitely. The penultimate draft of the treaty set out this procedure: Once the Council of Ministers had decided which EU countries had fulfilled the necessary conditions for participation, it would submit to the European Council and European Parliament its

[78] Sweden was not yet a member of the EU and obtained no such exemption when it joined, but it has devised an exemption of its own by declining to enter the exchange-rate mechanism of the residual EMS, now known as ERM II, and thus failing to fulfill one of the convergence criteria.

[79] A theoretical paper by Fuchs and Lippi (2006) raises an interesting point. It shows that a monetary union with voluntary membership may have trouble basing its monetary policy on economic conditions in the union as a whole, which is what the ECB is supposed to do. A credible threat of exit by a member country might force the union's policy-making body to pay attention to economic conditions in that particular country and, by implication, in every other country. Hence, the permanence of EMU membership may be deemed to underpin the policy-making framework of the ECB. Yet Italy's poor economic performance, including a large appreciation of its real exchange rate *vis-à-vis* Germany and other EMU members, has led to a simmering debate in Italy about leaving EMU, legally or otherwise, and reintroducing a new national currency. Any such move, however, would surely lead to sharp a depreciation of that new currency. There is, in addition, an unresolved question on which lawyers disagree. Would Italy be free to redenominate its public debt? Normally, a country introducing a new national currency is entitled to do that. The euro, however, is not Italy's own currency; it is a multinational currency, and any attempt to replace Italy's euro-denominated debt with domestic-currency debt could perhaps be challenged by the holders of that debt, including the citizens of Italy itself. We return to the economic issues involved at the end of Chapter 4, where we examine the overall impact of EMU on economic performance in its member countries.

opinion concerning a starting date. Taking account of that opinion and that of the Parliament, the European Council would then decide whether to start the third stage. Failing a decision to start the third stage, the whole procedure would be repeated at least once every two years. This is what an EMU enthusiast said after reading that draft of the treaty:

> We began with a plan for monetary union – the Delors Report. We wound up with a set of rules for deciding in the future whether to establish a monetary union. Instead of charting a pathway to EMU, the conference has laid out an obstacle course. Worse yet, the finish line may not stand still. It can drift freely into the next century.[80]

But that was not the end of the matter, because the Italian and French governments came up with a different plan.[81] The procedure would start as before, with the European Council receiving opinions from the Council of Ministers and European Parliament. The European Council would then ascertain whether a majority of EU countries was ready to enter EMU and whether it was appropriate to start the third stage. If so, it would set the starting date. But then the innovation: If no starting date had been set by the end of 1997, the third stage would start automatically on January 1, 1999, whether or not a majority of member countries had qualified for entry. And that is what actually happened.

POLITICS, ECONOMICS, AND EMU

What was the fundamental rationale for EMU? Was it political or economic? The best answer, we believe, is "some of both."

Monetary union would not have been achieved without the strong backing of key European leaders, notably François Mitterrand and Helmut Kohl, and their support derived from their commitment to the larger European project, born of their predecessors' realization that the future prosperity of Europe required the economic reconstruction of Germany but that the future peace of Europe required that Germany be

---

[80] Quoted in Kenen (1995), p. 26.
[81] See Dyson and Featherstone (1999), pp. 251, 447, and especially p. 518.

bound into a community of democratic states. In Helmut Kohl's own words:

With the introduction of the euro, the European Union will grow even closer together as an establishment of peace and freedom. The notion of freedom is and remains the driving force of European integration.[82]

But just as the threat from the Soviet Union lent urgency to the economic recovery of Germany, so too did the collapse of the Soviet Union lend new urgency to European integration. Recall what we said at the start of this chapter. With the crumbling of the Berlin Wall and the emergence of newly independent countries in Central and Eastern Europe, Europeans worried about the implications. Would Germany be wholly preoccupied with the challenges posed by reunification? Would it begin to pay more attention to its Eastern neighbors than to its Western partners? Should Europe put widening before deepening by looking to the integration of the newly independent countries before seeking closer integration, or might an early widening of the EU complicate subsequent deepening by making it harder to reach agreement within a more heterogeneous Europe?

The decision of the Dublin Summit in June 1990 to hold two Intergovernmental Conferences – one on monetary union and one on political union – answered these questions decisively. It put deepening first. But that does not tell the whole story. We have seen that the move to monetary union was already under way. It began with the Balladur memorandum, which questioned the long-run viability of the EMS. No one asked at that stage whether Europe resembled an optimum currency area – an issue discussed in Chapter 2. In fact, economists did not even start to raise that question until the ink was dry on the Maastricht Treaty. Furthermore, Europe had already rejected the counterfactual implicit in that question – abandoning the EMS in favor of floating exchange rates – and had reaffirmed its rejection of that option when, in 1987, it adopted the

---

[82] Kohl (1997). Compare his view with that of Martin Feldstein, writing a few months later: "Instead of increasing intra-European harmony and global peace, the shift to EMU and the political integration that would follow it would be more likely to lead to increased conflicts within Europe and between Europe and the United States." See Feldstein (1997), p. 60.

Basel-Nyborg Agreements, which aimed at making the EMS resemble a system of fixed exchange rates.

The story told by this chapter, however, raises another question: How would the European countries have designed a monetary union if they had not already created the institutions that are given important EMU-related tasks in the Maastricht Treaty – the Commission, the Council of Ministers, the European Council, and the European Parliament? The answer can perhaps be found by looking at other monetary unions, past and present, to ask how they came into being and how they dealt with the questions that, in the European case, involved the institutions of the European Union.

4

Monetary Arrangements and Economic Performance

INTRODUCTION

Before looking at the merits and likelihood of additional monetary integration in the Western Hemisphere and in East Asia, we turn our attention in this chapter to other monetary unions and ask how they have differed from EMU constitutionally and operationally. After that, we take on another important issue by examining the implications of monetary integration for economic performance, both in general and in the euro area.

Our discussion of EMU in Chapter 3 stressed the many ways in which EMU is embedded in the institutional framework of the European Union. Some of those features may be unique to the European case, but other monetary unions, even those without comparable institutions, must deal with most of the questions that faced the architects of EMU. How is the union organized? How does a particular country qualify for membership? How is the union's monetary policy determined? Are the union's operations centralized or decentralized? And what, if anything, does monetary union imply for other policies of the member countries? Some of the monetary unions we highlight were not full-fledged monetary unions as we defined them in Chapter 1, because the countries involved did not share a single currency or hand over authority for monetary policy to a supranational central bank.[1] Thus, our review of monetary unions

---

[1] According to Gandolfo (1992, p. 765), "there is no precise and generally accepted definition of 'monetary union' in the economic literature." Hawkins and Masson (2003)

past and present will show that only a few of them share features with EMU, although the EMU model has been important for the design of two prospective monetary unions, in western Africa and the Middle East.

Thereafter, we seek to answer another important question: What do we know about the effects of monetary and exchange-rate regimes on economic performance, specifically on inflation, growth in real per capita GDP, and the volatility of growth? To answer this question, we must look first at two ways of classifying countries – one based on governments' own descriptions of their exchange-rate regimes and the other based on actual exchange-rate behavior, because there are numerous differences between them. We have then to see whether there are discernible differences among countries with different regimes and with different levels of income or development. The evidence suggests decisively that fixing the exchange rate by adopting a hard pegged regime such as a monetary union or dollarization generally results in lower inflation. However, the evidence with regard to growth in real per capita GDP and the volatility of growth is mixed, and we are unable to arrive at a consistent answer here.

Finally, we review the specifics of economic performance since the start of EMU.

PAST AND PRESENT MONETARY UNIONS

The circulation of monies for use in transactions beyond national borders dates back very far: to Athens in the fifth century BCE. Thereafter, the Roman Empire's solidus coin and the Moslem world's dinar coin, specie monies whose metallic content was stable for centuries, circulated widely, from the Middle Ages.[2] Many of the monetary arrangements of the nineteenth century also arose from trading relationships in which one country's specie coins were presented as payment in another country. These monetary arrangements governed the standards of issuance and rules of circulation of the specie coins.

We begin our discussion of historical monetary unions with four major nineteenth-century arrangements – the Zollverein, the Latin Monetary

---

use the same precise and narrow definition that we do, whereas Cohen (1993, 2003a) and Graboyes (1990) adopt a much broader definition.

[2] See Dwyer and Lothian (2004).

Union, the Scandinavian Monetary Union, and the Austro-Hungarian
Monetary Union – all of which were tied to specie. We then provide a
brief description of an important twentieth-century monetary arrangement, the Belgium-Luxembourg Economic Union, which dissolved in
1999 when its members joined EMU. Finally, we discuss some monetary arrangements that have their roots in colonial ties: the East African
Currency Board, the Common Monetary Area or Rand Zone, the East
Caribbean Currency Union, and the CFA Franc Zone. Currency boards
also were widespread in the British and French colonies prior to political
independence. Although we do not dwell on them at length, as they do not
involve currency consolidation,[3] we will say something about those currency boards that linked a set of colonies together *via* a common currency
or the combination of a common currency and a shared central bank.

Nineteenth-Century Monetary Arrangements

The Zollverein, the Latin Monetary Union, and the Scandinavian Monetary Union were agreements between countries or states in a federation
to exchange specie-based coins and to set specie requirements or standards for the minting of those coins. Although they are frequently called
monetary unions, it would perhaps be better to call them exchange-rate
unions or common currency-standard areas.[4]

The Zollverein grew out of the Deutscher Bund established in 1815;
the Bund was a federation of thirty-five independent German states and
four independent cities.[5] By agreement, there were no restrictions on the
internal migration of labor and capital. In 1834, twenty-six of the states
formed a customs union (Zollverein) and adopted a common external

---

[3] A currency board constrains the monetary policy of a single country by requiring that
the monetary liabilities of that institution be fully backed by holdings of an anchor
currency but does not substitute that anchor currency for the local currency. That is
why it does not involve currency consolidation. Hanke, Jonung, and Schuler (1993)
provide a long list of currency boards; see Appendix C, pp. 172–80.

[4] We owe these descriptions to Cohen (2003b) and Flandreau (2003), respectively. Flandreau (2003, p. 113) argues as we do, that it is wrong to term the nineteenth-century
arrangements "unions," because the treaties that created them "never sought to pool
national monetary sovereignties under a common central bank."

[5] See de Vanssay (2002) for more detail.

tariff.[6] The Treaty creating the customs union specifically requested that the states "take action in order to bring their coinage systems on to a common standard."[7] The money supplies of the states were composed primarily of gold and silver coins, with each state setting its own rules regarding denomination, purity, weight, and coinage fee.[8] The Zollverein monetary union, which dates from 1837, was established by a series of agreements that set standards for the minting of silver coins and the harmonization of coinage fees. There were effectively two monetary areas within this arrangement: the northern states adopted a common coin known as the thaler, and the southern states adopted the gulden. The thaler and gulden did not exchange at par, but at a ratio that was regulated by agreement.[9] The states were left free to mint unstandardized gold coins until 1857, but under the terms of Austria's accession to the monetary union, gold coins were outlawed.[10] (Austria withdrew from the monetary union in 1866 following its defeat in the Austro-Prussian war.) With the political unification of Germany under Prussian leadership after the Austro-Prussian war, a new gold-backed coin, the mark, was introduced throughout Germany in 1871, and the Reichsbank was established several years later as the national central bank. Thus, the exchange-rate union or common standard area that had linked the independent German states came to an end with political unification.[11]

---

[6] The largest of these states was the Kingdom of Prussia, which represented more than 50 percent of the federation's population.

[7] Article 14 of the Zollverein Treaty quoted in de Vanssay (2002), p. 32.

[8] As each state monopolized the coinage of money, it charged a coinage fee (seignorage) that was generally between 3 and 6 percent of the coin's value; see de Vanssay (2002), p. 32.

[9] Thalers exchanged for guldens at the rate of 1:1.75.

[10] Austria's silver coin was known as the Austrian gulden.

[11] Scholars disagree as to whether the German monetary union followed the formation of the Zolverein and therefore predated political unification or began in the 1870s with political unification. Cohen (2003b), de Vanssay (2002), and Graboyes (1990) take the first view; Bordo and Jonung (2003) and Flandreau (2003) take the second. But there can be no dispute about a more important point: The monetary union that followed German political unification reflected the development of a national monetary policy and was not a monetary union in our sense, because it did not involve the linking of sovereign states. We omit other nineteenth-century monetary unions that pre- or postdated political unification in Italy, Switzerland, and the United States. Bordo and Jonung (2003) and Flandreau (2003) discuss these cases.

The Latin Monetary Union (LMU) linking Belgium, France, Italy, and Switzerland was established by an international treaty in 1865. Greece adhered to the treaty from 1868 and joined the union formally in 1876. The LMU countries had a history of accepting each other's coins as means of payment going back to the early 1800s; it was based on the mutual acceptance of the French bimetallic system that set the fineness of gold and silver coins at 90 percent, fixed the relative values of gold and silver at 15.5:1, and established the franc as the unit of account. Smaller-value "subsidiary" silver coins also circulated, but these were debased in the mid-1800s by Italy and Switzerland in order to gain seigniorage revenue. This experience led to the adoption of a treaty to formalize the monetary arrangement. The LMU was intended to set common standards for the issuance of coins and to specify the obligations of central banks with respect to acceptance of the other members' coins. Each country could mint unlimited quantities of the large-value gold and silver coins,[12] which were legal tender throughout the monetary area, and participating countries were required to accept these coins at par without limit. The treaty also set formal limits on the quantity of subsidiary coins that could be minted, imposed a standard of 83.5 percent silver fineness for those coins, and limited each central bank's obligation to accept them.[13] The treaty did not regulate the issuance or acceptance of paper money.

In the early 1870s, the price of silver fell on world markets, but the relative parities between gold and silver remained unchanged within the union. Therefore, countries melted down their gold coins for export and began flooding the market with newly minted silver coins.[14] A conference was subsequently convened in 1874 at which member countries agreed to restrict the supply of new silver coins (and the LMU was said to adopt a "limping gold standard"). During World War I, increased government spending resulted in an overissuance of subsidiary coins; convertibility was suspended in 1920; and the union was formally disbanded in 1927.

---

[12] The large-value coins were those greater than five francs in value.

[13] The limit on the issuance of subsidiary coins was set at six francs per person, and the reciprocal acceptance of those coins was set at fifty francs per transaction. See de Cecco (1992), pp. 58–59.

[14] According to Bordo and Jonung (2003), Italy financed its deficit by exporting newly minted silver coins.

Substantial trade flows between Denmark, Norway, and Sweden in the 1860s resulted in an accumulation of foreign coins that were accepted for payment. The weights and denominations of the national coins were not standardized, and negotiations began in 1862 to reach a common standard. The result of these negotiations, the Scandinavian Monetary Union (SMU), began with two members, Sweden and Denmark, in 1873, but Norway joined in 1875.[15] The SMU was based on a decimal gold standard for a new currency, the krona. Each country could mint unlimited quantities of gold krona coins, as well as subsidiary coins (which were silver and copper with 80 percent fineness). The coins were legal tender in all three countries, and each central bank was obligated to accept at par unlimited amounts of the other members' currencies. Unlike the Zollverein or LMU, the member central banks also accepted paper drafts at par from their counterparts, and the official agreement was eventually extended to formalize this practice. Marcello de Cecco argues that the SMU was the most successful of the nineteenth-century monetary unions because the acceptability of paper drafts minimized the need for gold transfers and exchange rates remained fixed.[16] The SMU suffered strains at the outbreak of World War I, and its member suspended the convertibility of banknotes in 1914. By the mid-1920s, legal tender status was restricted to the currency of the issuer, and the union ceased functioning.[17]

The dual monarchy in Austria and Hungary that was created with the Compromise of 1867 is not uniformly regarded among scholars as a monetary union. At issue is the relative independence of the two states within the federation. One economic historian, Marc Flandreau, argues that the Compromise was:[18]

...a comprehensive agreement which carefully delineated political and economic rights and obligations. . . . It recognized that the two parts of the monarchy were distinct political entities, and defined the domains where the two countries

---

[15] At the time, Norway and Sweden were linked by a formal political union, but Bordo and Jonung (2003) argue that each of them had substantial *de facto* independence.

[16] See de Cecco (1992). By 1905, bilateral exchange rates for the member countries' currencies were no longer quoted.

[17] According to de Vanssay (2002, p. 37), the 1872 Convention that formed the legal basis for the SMU has never been formally revoked.

[18] Flandreau (2003), pp. 117–18.

were fully sovereign, and those where sovereignty was shared. Among the latter we find the common market and trade policy, the common currency, a common army, a common diplomacy and foreign representatives. Among the former were the right for each part to have its own parliament, government electoral system, laws and budgets. Thus, the dual monarchy can be called a *de facto* monetary union.

Going further, Flandreau contends that the dual monarchy provides the closest historical parallel to EMU. The Compromise of 1867 established the empire of Austria and the kingdom of Hungary with completely separate fiscal authorities and a joint obligation to service the common debt.[19] Initially, Hungary agreed not to establish a central bank, to cede the making of monetary policy to the Austrian central bank and to accept responsibility for the florin banknotes already in circulation.[20] In 1878, the central bank was reorganized as the Austro-Hungarian Bank. It had offices in both countries, the governor was nominated jointly, decision making was shared, and seignorage revenue was divided.[21] Under a monetary reform in 1892, undertaken in order to stabilize the external value of the currency, the silver florin was retired and replaced with the gold crown. After the adoption of the gold standard, the currency was stable until 1914, when excessive government spending prior to World War I undermined the monetary regime. Although the Austro-Hungarian monetary union effectively ended at this point, the central bank did not disband until 1922.[22]

Table 4.1 lays out the key features of the monetary arrangements reviewed in this chapter. As the table makes clear, with the exception of the Austro-Hungarian monetary union, few nineteenth-century arrangements resembled EMU, our present-day prototype, but several twentieth-century unions resemble it more closely.

---

[19] Common debt had been issued before 1867. See Flandreau (2003) for a description of contributions to the common budget and debt service.

[20] The florin was based on a silver standard.

[21] Flandreau (2003) dates the commencement of the monetary union from 1867, whereas the National Bank of Austria (2005) dates it from 1878.

[22] Flandreau (2003) dates the end of the Austro-Hungarian monetary union from 1914, while the National Bank of Austria (2005) dates it from the dissolution of the central bank in 1922.

Table 4.1. *Past and present monetary unions*

Monetary union and members	Dates	Single or multiple currency?	Single central bank?	Setter of monetary policy	Monetary arrangement and rules	Limits/rules on fiscal policy	Complementary arrangements	Reason for dissolution
Zollverein (twenty-six independent German States)	1837 to 1871	Multiple	No	State authorities	Silver standard	No	Customs union, common external tariff	Political unification
LMU (Belgium, France, Greece, Italy, Switzerland)[1]	1865 to 1927	Multiple	No	National authorities	Gold and silver standard	No	History of trade	Collapse of specie standard at WW I
SMU (Denmark, Norway, Sweden)[2]	1873 to mid-1920s	Multiple	No	National authorities	Gold standard	No	History of trade	Collapse of specie standard at WWI
Austro-Hungarian MU	1878 to 1922[3]	Single	Yes	Austro-Hungarian Bank	Silver standard until 1900, gold thereafter, seignorage sharing	No	Common market, common trade policy, common defense, common foreign policy	Collapse of specie standard at WW I
BLEU (Belgium, Luxembourg)	1922 to 1999	Multiple	Yes	Belgium	Belgian monetary policy	No	Membership in European Union	Joined EMU
EACB (Kenya, Swaziland, Tanzania, Uganda)[4]	1919 to 1977	Multiple	Yes until 1966	East African Currency Board until 1966; national authorities after	Currency board to sterling	No	Common market	Independent monetary policy undermined currency board

(continued)

Table 4.1. (*continued*)

Monetary union and members	Dates	Single or multiple currency?	Single central bank?	Setter of monetary policy	Monetary arrangement and rules	Limits/ rules on fiscal policy	Complementary arrangements	Reason for dissolution
CMA (Lesotho, Namibia, South Africa)[5]	1920s to present	Multiple	No	South Africa	Inflation targeting & currency board to rand, policy consultation, seignorage sharing	No	Customs union, common external tariff	Still in existence
ECCU (Anguilla, Antigua and Barbuda, Dominica, Grenada, Montserrat, St. Kitts and Nevis, St. Lucia, St. Vincent and the Grenadines)[6]	1950 to present	Single	Yes	East Caribbean Central Bank since 1983[7]	Currency board to US dollar, seignorage sharing, multilateral payments system	No	Common market, regulatory/ supervisory framework	Still in existence
CFA Zone in West Africa: WAEMU (Benin, Burkina Faso, Côte d'Ivoire, Guinea-Bissau, Mali, Niger, Senegal, Togo)[8]	1945 to present	Single	Yes	Central Bank of West African States since 1959[9]	Fixed peg to French franc, euro	Fiscal surveillance from 1990s	Customs union, common external tariff, ties to France, consolidated bank regulation & supervision	Still in existence

Table 4.1. (*continued*)

						Fiscal		
CFA Zone in Central Africa: CAEMC (Cameroon, Central African Republic, Chad, Congo, Equatorial Guinea, Gabon)[8]	1945 to present	Single	Yes	Bank of Central African States since 1959[9]	Fixed peg to French franc, euro	surveillance from 1990s	Customs union, common external tariff, ties to France, consolidated bank regulation & supervision	Still in existence
NOTE: EMU Prototype (Austria, Belgium, Finland, France, Germany, Greece, Ireland, Italy, Luxembourg, Netherlands, Portugal, Slovenia, Spain)	1999 to present	Single	Yes	European Central Bank	Price stability	Yes: Stability and Growth Pact	Common market (European Union)	Still in existence

[1] Greece was a de facto member from 1868 and joined formally in 1876.

[2] Norway joined in 1875.

[3] Dates provided by the Austrian National Bank (2005).

[4] Tanganyika joined in 1919; Zanzibar joined in 1936; the two countries merged to form Tanzania in 1964.

[5] Botswana participated until 1976; Namibia signed the formal agreement only in 1992.

[6] Trinidad and Tobago and British Guyana were founding members of the British Caribbean Currency Board in 1950 but withdrew in 1962 and 1965, respectively. Grenada joined in 1968. Anguilla and Montserrat are British territories, other members are independent states.

[7] Previously, the Eastern Caribbean Currency Board (1965–83) and British Caribbean Currency Board (1950–65).

[8] Membership has changed over time. Countries listed are current members.

[9] There was no centralized monetary authority until 1955 when each zone established a monetary institute in Paris.

89

Twentieth-Century Monetary Arrangements

World War I marked the end of monetary arrangements based on gold or specie. For the most part, the postwar monetary "unions" linked one or more smaller countries to a larger, dominant country and, in many cases, evolved from a colonial relationship.[23]

Belgium and its much smaller neighbor, Luxembourg, formed an economic union (BLEU) in 1921, and it was followed by monetary union in 1922. Each country printed its own currency and from 1935, the Belgian franc was legal tender in Luxembourg, being fully convertible at par into the Luxembourg franc.[24] The Luxembourg franc, however, was never granted legal tender status in Belgium. The Belgian central bank set monetary policy for the union; in fact, Luxembourg did not establish a central bank until 1998, in preparation for EMU, although it had a monetary institute from 1983.[25] The monetary union was dissolved in 1999 when both countries entered EMU.

Three British colonies, Kenya, Tanganyika, and Uganda, formed the East African Currency Board (EACB) in 1919 that tied their common currency, the East African shilling, to the pound sterling; Zanzibar joined the EACB in 1936.[26] Several years after political independence in the early 1960s, the countries[27] established national central banks and introduced national currencies; shortly thereafter, they formed the East African Community and Common Market and they agreed to exchange their national currencies at par and continue their convertibility into sterling. With the depreciation of sterling in the late 1960s and early 1970s, however, the link to sterling through the currency board was dismantled, and the central banks of the EACB countries began to pursue independent monetary policies. The monetary arrangement was formally dissolved in 1977 when

---

[23] Many of these involved currency boards. As indicated earlier, we review only those that involved several countries grouped together.

[24] The parity differed during World War II.

[25] Its primary role was the issuance of currency and the supervision of financial institutions.

[26] Honohan and Lane (2000) explain that the day-to-day operations of the British colonial currency boards were generally conducted in London.

[27] There were three countries at this point, as Tanganyika and Zanzibar had merged in 1964 to become Tanzania.

each country applied its existing exchange controls to the currencies of the other members.

So far, we have described monetary unions that are no longer in existence. Of these, most were dissolved for political reasons (see Table 4.1) following unification of the member states, absorption into a wider union, or war. From a study of six historical cases, Benjamin Cohen has concluded that political factors have been more important than economic factors in the break up of monetary unions.[28] But in a recent study of country pairs that shared a common currency over a fifty-year period, Volker Nitsch found both economic and political factors to be important in the dissolution of monetary unions: large differences in inflation among member countries, a low share of intra-union trade, and a change in political status are statistically important in predicting the break up of a monetary union.[29]

Turning to unions that still endure today, monetary linkages joining together several countries in southern Africa have existed in some form since the 1920s.[30] Initially, Botswana, Lesotho, Namibia, and Swaziland adopted the South African pound (later known as the rand) as their sole legal tender. This "dollarization" helped to promote trade among the countries and with their dominant partner, South Africa, but the arrangement did not provide the smaller countries with any influence over monetary policy or share of the seignorage revenue. In 1974, a formal agreement among Lesotho, South Africa, and Swaziland, with Namibia participating informally,[31] established what is now known as the Common Monetary Area (CMA).[32] Today, each CMA member has its own independent central bank. The dominant member, South Africa, sets monetary policy for the area through an inflation-targeting regime, whereas Lesotho, Namibia, and Swaziland maintain a currency board linked to the rand. Scheduled consultations among CMA central banks provide for input into monetary policy and coordination with regard to

---

[28] See Cohen (1993).
[29] Nitsch (2005) uses data on 245 country pairs that shared a common currency between 1948 and 1997.
[30] This discussion draws heavily on van Zyl (2003).
[31] It did not sign the formal agreement until 1992.
[32] Between 1974 and 1986, the CMA was known as the Rand Monetary Area.

the exchange rates of countries outside the region. The rand is legal tender in Lesotho and Namibia but not in Swaziland;[33] each country circulates a national currency that is pegged to the rand at par, is fully supported (100 percent) by foreign reserves and is legal tender only in the issuing country. The monetary agreement includes provisions for the sharing of seignorage revenue among the countries in which the rand circulates, and it is complemented by the South African Customs Union.

Many of the countries in the Caribbean have participated for more than fifty years in a monetary union governed by a currency board that issues a common currency.[34] In 1950, the British Caribbean Currency Board (BCCB) was set up for the British colonies in the eastern Caribbean as the sole issuer of the West Indian dollar, which was linked through a currency board arrangement to the pound sterling.[35] The arrangement required the BCCB to maintain 100 percent reserve backing of the domestic money stock and to guarantee convertibility. In 1965, the BCCB was replaced with the Eastern Caribbean Currency Authority (ECCA), and the currency was replaced with the Eastern Caribbean dollar pegged to the pound sterling at the same parity; the ECCA was required to maintain only 70 percent backing. In the mid-1970s, however, the required backing was cut to 60 percent, and the link to the pound sterling was shifted to the U.S. dollar.[36] Despite this reduction in required reserves, the *de facto* reserve cover has been in excess of 95 percent.[37] The substitution of the ECCA for the ECCB was aimed at creating "a central bank capable of playing a more active role in promoting the region's development."[38]

Membership in the Eastern Caribbean Currency Union (ECCU) has changed somewhat over time; current members include six independent states (Antigua and Barbuda, Dominica, Grenada, St. Kitts and Nevis, St. Lucia, and St. Vincent and Grenadines) and two British territories (Anguilla and Montserrat). The ECCA holds the stock of pooled foreign reserves, but each member government has unrestricted access to reserves

---

[33] Swaziland withdrew the rand from circulation in 1986.
[34] For a detailed history, see van Beek et al. (2000).
[35] The exchange rate between West Indian dollars and sterling was 4.8:1.
[36] The parity was set at 2.70 Eastern Caribbean dollars per U.S. dollar, and has remained at this level.
[37] See van Beek et al. (2000), pp. 6, 56.
[38] See van Beek et al. (2000), p. 4.

as necessary to back the currency in the domestic economy; seignorage revenue is distributed in proportion to the member's share of the currency. Other arrangements complement the monetary union, including a common market, a multilateral system for the clearing and settlement of interbank payments, and a regulatory and supervisory framework. Overall, the ECCU has fostered external currency stability for the very small and open economies of the eastern Caribbean.

In the countries of western and central Africa, two separate arrangements known collectively as the CFA Franc Zone have operated since 1945.[39] One arrangement, the West African Economic and Monetary Union (WAEMU), unites eight countries in western Africa (Benin, Burkina Faso, Côte d'Ivoire, Guinea Bissau, Mali, Niger, Senegal, and Togo); the other arrangement, the Central African Economic and Monetary Community (CAEMC), unites six countries in central Africa (Cameroon, Central African Republic, Chad, Congo, Gabon, and Equatorial Guinea).[40] The two unions operate separately but identically, each with its own central bank[41] and have a common currency known as the CFA franc; the two CFA francs are equivalent in value but are not legal tender outside the zone of issuance. Until 1999, the CFA franc was pegged to the French franc. It is now tied to the euro. [42]

---

[39] Between 1945 and 1958, the acronym "CFA" stood for "franc of the French colonies of Africa." Since 1958, it has meant "franc of the French Community of Africa." Masson and Pattillo (2005) provide a thorough history of the CFA zone, along with a discussion of its current operations.

[40] The names of the two unions and their memberships have changed somewhat over time. Five CAEMC members are former French colonies, while one (Equatorial Guinea) is a former Spanish colony; the Union of the Comoros, a republic in the Indian Ocean, is technically considered part of the zone but has its own currency and monetary authority. Seven WAEMU members are former French colonies, whereas one (Guinea Bissau) is a former Portuguese colony.

[41] The two central banks were established only in 1959. During the first decade of its operation, the CFA franc zones had no monetary authority; the right to issue currency notes was held by designated private banks. This system was changed in 1955, when each zone established a monetary institute that had issuance privileges. These institutes were lodged in Paris and were under the control of the French government. In 1959, the institutes were changed to central banks and were permitted to extend credit to member country governments, subject to certain limits.

[42] The initial parity in 1948 was one CFA franc to two French francs. On the introduction of a new French franc in 1960, the parity was reset at fifty CFA francs per French franc and maintained until the devaluation of the CFA franc in 1994 to 100:1. On the commencement of EMU, the CFA parity was translated into euros using the euro conversion rate for the French franc.

The operational mechanics of the CFA franc zone are quite different from those of systems that have their roots in British colonial currency boards. Unlike the former British colonies in East Africa, which severed ties to Britain, the countries in the CFA franc zone did not abandon their links to France after achieving political independence in the 1960s.[43] Each CFA central bank maintains an operations account with the French Treasury, which holds the pooled foreign reserves of the member countries. Furthermore, the convertibility of the CFA franc is effectively guaranteed by an overdraft facility that is tied to the operations account. The French Treasury has set conditions that govern the use of the operations account and the overdraft privilege: the account is intended to hold 65 percent of total reserves; emergency monetary policy measures must be taken if reserves drop below 20 percent of the CFA central bank's sight liabilities or the balance in the operations account turns negative; and market interest rates are charged on large deficits in the operations account.

The CFA region is integrally linked with France, not only through the operations account but also through policy surveillance, trade, foreign assistance, and military support. French representatives participate in WAEMU and CAEMC monetary policy meetings,[44] and set limits on central bank lending to member governments.[45] Intraregional trade is very low compared with the intraregional trade of other monetary unions.[46] Trade with France is substantial, however, at just under 40 percent of total trade, suggesting that exchange-rate stability *vis-à-vis* the franc (and now the euro) has contributed importantly to fostering ties with countries outside of Africa. French foreign assistance and military support to its former colonies in western and central Africa have been

---

[43] Honohon and Lane (2000) compare features of British and French colonial currency boards and claim that each reflects arrangements in the colonial power's own central bank (pp. 3–4); see also Masson and Pattillo (2005), pp. 15–17.

[44] France holds two (of sixteen) and three (of thirteen) seats on the central bank boards in the WAEMU and CAEMC, respectively.

[45] Since 1972–73, the stock of central bank lending to a member government in a given year has been limited to 20 percent of the prior year's fiscal revenues. Prior to that time, the limits were somewhat more restrictive. Both the WAEMU and CAEMC central banks have plans to phase out lending to member governments; see Masson and Pattillo (2005), p. 48.

[46] See Table 1.1. For a complete analysis of CFA trade patterns, see Boughton (1993), Honohan and Lane (2000), Masson and Pattillo (2005), and Yeats (1998).

sizable. Arguably, this web of ties to France has raised the cost of exit from the monetary arrangement and led to a more durable union.[47]

The CFA zone weathered a severe banking crisis in the 1980s, and it led to recession in many member countries and to the devaluation of the parity with the franc in 1994. The primary cause of the crisis was excessive lending by the CFA central banks to commercial and development banks (many owned or co-owned by the French); the loans were made on concessional terms and on-lent to governments of the CFA countries. Although these loans circumvented the restraints on central bank lending to governments put in place by the French authorities, French officials took no action.[48] In some cases, moreover, the French also increased their own foreign assistance. In the aftermath of the crisis, the CFA zone countries established two regional banking commissions to conduct banking supervision and regulation, and the French authorities linked the disbursement of additional aid to IMF conditionality. Each zone also instituted routine fiscal surveillance based upon specific convergence criteria,[49] and they lodged the responsibility for monitoring compliance with these criteria with a supranational institution. In 1999, the WAEMU countries agreed to a timetable within which member countries would be expected to meet the convergence criteria. This was done as part of the preparation process for a wider monetary union, ECOWAS, to which we now turn.

PROSPECTIVE MONETARY UNIONS

Since its founding in 1975, the Economic Community of West African States (ECOWAS) has had a broad agenda for regional integration,

---

[47] Stasavage and Guillaume (2002) examine monetary unions in twenty-nine former British and French colonies in Africa over the 1960–94 period and find empirical support for the hypothesis that countries with parallel or complementary arrangements are less likely to exit from a monetary union.

[48] See Honohan and Lane (2000), Masson and Pattillo (2005), and Stasavage (2000) for details and discussion of the crisis.

[49] Primary convergence criteria apply to the fiscal balance, stock of public debt, inflation, and payments arrears, whereas secondary criteria govern the public-sector wage bill, government revenue, public investment, and the current account. Numerical reference values are specified for each convergence criterion.

encompassing trade, common institutions, and monetary union. The members of ECOWAS include the eight countries in WAEMU plus four former British colonies (Gambia, Ghana, Nigeria, and Sierra Leone), a former French colony (Guinea), a former Portuguese colony in western Africa (Cape Verde), as well as Liberia, which was never a European colony. Unlike the WAEMU countries, the seven non-WAEMU countries in ECOWAS have not tied their monetary or exchange-rate policies together: each has its own currency, operates its own independent monetary policy, and has a floating exchange rate.[50]

A timetable for moving to monetary union was first outlined in 1987 in an ECOWAS Monetary Cooperation Programme (EMCP), which introduced convergence criteria and other measures aimed at strengthening regional integration.[51] The program sought to develop further the West African Clearing House, a payments mechanism for intraregional trade that dated back to the founding of ECOWAS, into a system of linked exchange rates tied to the clearinghouse unit of account (which was, in turn, linked to the SDR). Because of insufficient political commitment, however, little progress was made in achieving convergence, and the initial timetable, which called for monetary union by 1992, was postponed several times.

In 2000, the ECOWAS heads of state expressed new interest in moving forward with regional integration, and five non-WAEMU countries agreed to form a second monetary union in western Africa,[52] the West African Monetary Zone (WAMZ), and then to merge it with WAEMU to achieve a full ECOWAS union. A Convergence Council, composed of government ministers and central bank governors from ECOWAS member countries, was created to oversee this process. In 2001, the Council established the West African Monetary Institute (WAMI) to develop and prepare the technical aspects of the WAMZ among the non-WAEMU countries. In the first instance, the ECOWAS heads of state called for WAMZ in 2003, to be followed by a full ECOWAS union in 2004. Subsequently, the start of WAMZ was postponed until 2005. Yet WAMZ

---

[50] Cape Verde, however, pegs its domestic currency to the euro.

[51] Ojo (2003) provides additional detail on the EMCP.

[52] Six non-WAEMU countries signed the Accra Declaration on a Second Monetary Zone in April 2000, but, since then, Liberia has not been an active participant. Cape Verde was not a signatory to the agreement.

has still not been achieved, and it is not now clear when, or if, broad monetary integration will be realized in western Africa.

At the time that they agreed initially to move toward WAMZ, the six non-WAEMU countries developed a set of convergence criteria that are similar but not identical to those used by the WAEMU countries. The main criteria place limits on fiscal deficits and specify reference values for fiscal deficits as a share of GDP, for the central bank's financing of government expenditure, for inflation, and for gross official reserves. The ECOWAS central bank governors have agreed that, as with EMU, macroeconomic convergence should be achieved before monetary union and that exchange-rate stability is a necessary precondition. The latter is defined in terms of stability *vis-à-vis* the West African Unit of Account (WAUA), the numeraire of the West African Clearing House, and is to be achieved gradually as part of a phased integration process that involves pegging national currencies to the WAUA, then narrowing the fluctuation margins, and finally fixing parities irrevocably. As Paul Masson and Catherine Pattillo have pointed out, however, many details of the integration timetable have not yet been specified and important issues remain unresolved.[53] For example, the ECOWAS authorities have not indicated precisely how the convergence criteria will be applied, how WAMZ (once created) and WAEMU will merge to form the full ECOWAS union, what will happen to the institutions created for WAMZ once the full union is formed, or what role France will play in a broader union. [54]

Despite the interest of the western African governments in monetary integration, the theory of optimal currency areas suggests that the ECOWAS grouping is not ideally suited for a single currency. Trade integration is quite low (see Table 1.1 and Table 4.2). Furthermore, the European Union is a major trading partner of the WAEMU and WAMZ countries, which leads one to wonder whether the objective of monetary union is to promote integration within each of those two regions – an implausible objective – or to strengthen the region's already substantial trade ties to Europe. Furthermore, evidence presented by Masson and

---

[53] See Masson and Pattillo (2001, 2005).

[54] In addition, Masson and Pattillo have questioned the wisdom of creating new institutions (such as a supranational central bank) for WAMZ and then replacing these institutions when the wider ECOWAS union is formed.

Table 4.2. *ECOWAS patterns of trade, 2002*
(percent of trade with partner group)

	Exports	Imports
ECOWAS		
ECOWAS	11.0	10.1
European Union	35.1	40.4
Other	53.9	49.5
WAEMU		
WAEMU	12.7	8.9
WAMZ	7.6	9.7
European Union	45.1	42.8
Other	34.6	38.6
WAMZ		
WAMZ	3.6	4.6
WAEMU	4.2	3.4
European Union	28.0	42.2
Other	64.2	49.8

Source: Paul R. Masson and Catherine Pattillo (2005), *The Monetary Geography of Africa.* Washington, DC: The Brookings Institution.

Pattillo indicates that ECOWAS countries have experienced significantly different shocks to their terms of trade. In particular, the correlation of shocks among WAMZ countries is especially low, reflecting the performance of Nigeria, the largest country in the group and the only oil exporter.[55] In short, an ECOWAS monetary union would link countries that trade relatively little with one another and whose economies are very dissimilar.

This heterogeneity in western Africa stands in marked contrast to the homogeneity among the Gulf States that have proposed to establish a common market in 2010 and form a monetary union thereafter.[56] The six countries in the Gulf Cooperation Council (GCC), comprising Bahrain, Kuwait, Oman, Qatar, Saudi Arabia, and the United Arab Emirates, account for 42 percent of the world's oil reserves and 23 percent of global natural gas reserves. Thus, the GCC countries face a common

---

[55] Nigeria accounts for about 75 percent of the GDP of WAMZ countries.

[56] For additional detail, see Al-Bassam (2003), Al-Jasser and Al-Hamidy (2003), Al Falasi (2003), Fasano et al. (2003), and Sturm and Siegfried (2005).

source of shocks and heavy exposure to the dollar in which most of the world's oil trade is denominated. In addition, the GCC countries have similar political systems and share a common language and culture. Although trade among the GCC countries is quite low (about 5 percent for both exports and imports),[57] the impetus for monetary union arises from the desire to achieve exchange-rate stability and promote an integrated trade and financial-market platform that will spur investment in the region. Ultimately, the countries want to diversify their economies so as to be less dependent on oil and gas, and they see an integrated market (including a single currency) as the way to achieve this objective.

Since its founding in 1981, the GCC has focused primarily on policy coordination and regional economic integration. Over the past two decades, bilateral exchange rates have been stable, inflation has been low, and movements in domestic interest rates have been highly correlated. The Gulf countries have sound and well-supervised banking systems and have dismantled formal barriers to the cross-border movement of goods, capital, and labor.

Although a common currency has been a stated goal since 1982, the project did not gain momentum until 2000, when the GCC heads of state appointed a technical committee of central bank governors and finance ministers to outline a path to monetary union. This union would unite thirty-five million people with a combined GDP of nearly $470 billion.[58] By 2002, all six countries had adopted formal pegs to the dollar and have created a customs union with a common external tariff of 5 percent.

The GCC was slated to resolve many of the outstanding details of its monetary union during 2005, but accomplished nothing more than the design of a set of convergence criteria very similar to those used to judge European convergence.[59] Other important issues, such as the location of the future central bank and the name of the single currency, have not yet been decided, and, recent press reports have suggested that

---

[57] Sturm and Siegfried (2005) note that the similarity of factor endowments across GCC countries will ultimately limit the potential for trade integration.

[58] In 2004, the largest GCC country, Saudi Arabia, accounted for two-thirds of the population and more than half of the GDP.

[59] According to McSheehy (2005), GCC central bank governors agreed to convergence criteria for inflation, interest rates, government debt, and fiscal deficits.

there may be insufficient political commitment to move forward on these contentious issues. The ECB, which formally agreed in the spring of 2006 to assist the GCC in devising a blueprint for monetary union, may help to jump-start the process. The original timetable envisioned a four-year convergence process before full monetary union in 2010, but the timetable for the introduction of a common currency was postponed in mid-2007 following Oman's withdrawal from the monetary union project and Kuwait's abandonment of its exchange-rate peg to the dollar.

ECONOMIC PERFORMANCE UNDER ALTERNATIVE EXCHANGE-RATE REGIMES

We turn now to the economic performance of countries that have surrendered their domestic currencies by joining a monetary union or adopting another currency through dollarization. In Chapter 2, we asked what economic theory tells us about the potential benefits and costs of currency consolidation; here, we review the actual evidence by asking how countries' exchange-rate regimes influence inflation and output growth. A country that joins a monetary union rigidly fixes its exchange rate *vis-à-vis* the union's common currency (even if the union to which it belongs has a floating external exchange rate). The same is true for a country that adopts another country's currency through dollarization, because it employs a fixed exchange rate to replace its domestic currency with a foreign currency. According to the IMF, which publishes the exchange-rate regimes of all its member countries, currency consolidation, formally known as "exchange arrangements with no separate legal tender," is the most firmly fixed type of exchange rate on the spectrum of exchange-rate regimes that a country can adopt.[60] The literature that discusses the relationship between the exchange-rate regime and economic performance often uses a broad, three-way classification scheme in which countries' regimes are designated as pegged, intermediate, or floating. Within this three-way scheme, the pegged classification can include countries that have various sorts of hard pegs (such as currency board arrangements) in addition to those that have no separate legal tender.

[60] See IMF (2005a).

Much of the relevant literature on economic performance has been based on a country's official or *de jure* exchange-rate regime.[61] Recently, however, attention has turned to a different sort of exchange-rate classification system that takes into account the actual behavior of a country's exchange rate as well as other information, and thus distinguishes between the declared or *de jure* regime and the actual or *de facto* regime. The two will differ whenever a country might announce one exchange-rate regime but behave as if it were following another. This possibility has been widely noted. Guillermo Calvo and Carmen Reinhart observed that some countries with *de jure* floating exchange rates appeared to exhibit a "fear of floating" by actively using interest rates or foreign exchange reserves to stabilize their exchange rates.[62] Many of the emerging market countries that adopted floating rates during the 1990s in response to volatile capital flows and financial crises were in fact covertly limiting exchange-rate movements, suggesting the need to distinguish between what a country announces its exchange-rate regime to be and what it actually is. This distinction also can be applied to countries at the other end of the regime spectrum – those that formally fix or peg their exchange rates but in fact experience substantial movement as a result of frequent changes in their pegs.

There are several *de facto* classification systems that sort countries into exchange-rate regimes based upon their deeds rather than words. They differ in the information they employ when making their assessments and, not surprisingly, can arrive at different answers about the proper *de facto* classification of a given country. In the review that follows, we draw heavily on two different *de facto* classification systems, one developed by Atish Ghosh, Anne-Marie Gulde, and Holger Wolf and the other developed by Carmen Reinhart and Kenneth Rogoff.[63] The former uses the

---

[61] Countries are required to inform the IMF of their exchange rate regimes when they join the institution and whenever they make a change thereafter.

[62] See Calvo and Reinhart (2002). The authors identified the countries with a fear of floating by comparing the behavior of exchange rates, interest rates, and foreign exchange reserves in *de jure* managed floaters with three benchmark managed floaters (Australia, Japan, and the United States).

[63] See Ghosh, Gulde, and Wolf (2002) and Reinhart and Rogoff (2004). We do not discuss another frequently cited *de facto* scheme developed by Eduardo Levy-Yeyati and Federico Sturzenegger. They use a purely statistical procedure (cluster analysis) to group

actual exchange rates of 147 countries from 1970 through 1999 to eliminate instances when the stated regime is not consistent with exchange-rate
performance.[64] The "consensus" sample (the *de facto* classification) that
results is composed of countries whose stated regimes – pegged, intermediate, or floating – overlap with actual behavior. The Reinhart-Rogoff
system uses information from parallel or secondary foreign-exchange
markets, along with detailed country chronologies, and descriptive statistics on exchange rates and inflation to classify the regimes of 153 countries between 1940 and 1999.[65] The resulting "natural" scheme is composed of five *de facto* categories – pegged, limited flexibility, managed
floating, freely floating, and freely falling.[66] In sum, the Ghosh-Gulde-
Wolf method refines the *de jure* classification by eliminating hard floats
and soft pegs from the sample, whereas the Reinhart-Rogoff method
leads to a classification scheme that pays no attention to the *de jure*
one.

In general, *de jure* hard peg regimes are recategorized less frequently
than *de jure* intermediate or floating regimes. For example, according
to the "consensus" classification, the *de facto* pegged group includes 80
percent of the *de jure* pegs. This is much larger than for the *de facto*
intermediate and floating groups, which include only 31 and 42 percent,
respectively, of the corresponding, *de jure* observations.[67]

The IMF also has developed a *de facto* classification. Since 1999, the
Fund has used official documents, press reports, and observed behavior
in addition to a country's stated regime to classify the country's actual

---

exchange rates for 156 countries into four different categories over the 1974 to 2000
period. For a thorough discussion of their methodology and the resulting *de facto*
regimes, see Levy-Yeyati and Sturzenegger (2005).

[64] The authors compute an annual score for each country based on the mean and variance
of its nominal monthly exchange rate (weighted equally). The score is computed for
the country's bilateral exchange rate relative to each G-7 currency, the ECU, and the
SDR; the bilateral exchange rate with the smallest score (i.e., the lowest volatility) is
used to construct the *de facto* classification. For additional details, see Ghosh, Gulde,
and Wolf (2002), pp. 46–50.

[65] For a detailed discussion of the algorithm used to classify exchange-rate regimes, see
Reinhart and Rogoff (2004), pp. 14–18.

[66] The "freely falling" category is composed of countries whose twelve-month rate of
inflation exceeds 40 percent.

[67] See Ghosh, Gulde, and Wolf (2002), p. 51.

regime.[68] Currently, the IMF groups *de facto* regimes into one of eight categories,[69] and also indicates the monetary policy framework for countries with managed or independently floating exchange rates. But, unfortunately, the IMF's *de facto* classification begins only in 1990 and so provides too short a history for a proper assessment of economic performance.[70] For this reason, our discussion of performance relies on other *de facto* classification schemes.

Inflation Performance

Can a country that joins a monetary union or replaces its domestic currency through dollarization expect to improve its inflation performance? After all, a rigidly pegged exchange-rate regime imposes a form of monetary discipline and therefore could be expected to raise credibility, result in better policy, and lead to lower inflation.[71] Based on both simple and more sophisticated analyses of exchange-rate regimes across all countries, the answer appears to be a resounding "yes." When different categories of countries are examined separately, however, the answer depends importantly on the country's level of income and development.

Simple correlations between annual mean inflation and a broad, three-way categorization of exchange-rate regimes for 147 countries over a thirty-year period shows that inflation was much lower in countries that operated under pegged regimes than in those with intermediate or floating regimes (see Table 4.3). The superior inflation performance associated

---

[68] See IMF (1999) for the first discussion of the Fund's *de facto* methodology. The Fund no longer publishes the *de jure* regimes of its member countries.

[69] These categories are: exchange arrangements with no separate legal tender, currency board arrangements, other conventional fixed peg arrangements, pegged exchange rates within horizontal bands, crawling pegs, exchange rates within crawling pegs, managed floating with no predetermined path for the exchange rate, and independently floating.

[70] See Babula and Ötker-Robe (2002) for a discussion of the IMF's *de facto* classification since 1990.

[71] Ghosh, Gulde, and Wolf (2002) label lower money growth the "discipline" effect, and higher credibility the "confidence" effect. Dollarization, by completely removing monetary policy from the tool kit of the domestic government, has stronger discipline effects than a monetary union in which a supranational central bank retains responsibility for monetary policy.

Table 4.3. *Annual inflation in percent, 1970–1999*

	Mean inflation	Median inflation
De jure		
Pegged	13.3	8.0
Intermediate	22.0	9.6
Floating	24.3	9.0
De facto[1]		
Pegged	9.4	6.9
Intermediate	30.2	11.4
Floating	58.8	21.7

[1] "Consensus" classification.

Source: Atish R. Ghosh, Anne-Marie Gulde, and Holger C. Wolf (2002), *Exchange Rate Regimes: Choices and Consequences.* Cambridge, MA: MIT Press.

with pegging is apparent using both the *de jure* definition and the *de facto* "consensus" classification. There may be a bias here, however, because countries experiencing hyperinflation have much higher inflation rates and these countries are more likely to be classified as floaters, raising the mean inflation rate for the floaters. But the substitution of median for mean inflation rates removes that bias and still confirms the relative superiority of pegged rates in holding down inflation.[72]

Nevertheless, simple correlations can give misleading results, because there are no controls for other factors that influence inflation. For example, countries with pegged exchange rates may have lower money growth than countries with intermediate or floating regimes. Thus, it is important to remove the effects of lower money growth (as well as other factors affecting inflation) in order to assess accurately the separate effect of the

---

[72] The "natural" classification yields a somewhat different answer because it sorts countries into five categories and places high- and hyperinflation countries in the "freely falling" regime. Furthermore, the pegged category includes some regimes that would be put in the intermediate category in other studies. Thus, the "natural" classification indicates that the mean and median inflation rates of free floaters (but not those of managed floaters) are below those of the peggers. See Rogoff et al. (2004). The *de facto* scheme of Levy-Yeyati and Sturzenegger supports the relative superiority of pegged regimes, but finds that floating regimes outperform intermediate regimes with respect to inflation. See Levy-Yeyati and Sturzenegger (2001).

exchange-rate regime itself.[73] Even after controlling for a large number of other influences, including money growth, the evidence suggests that pegged exchange rates improve inflation performance by a substantial margin relative to floating rates and that this effect is highly signifi-cant statistically.[74] Thus, Kenneth Rogoff and his coauthors found that annual inflation was 5.2 percent higher with floating than with pegged exchange rates.[75] Furthermore, intermediate exchange-rate regimes per-form somewhere in between pegged and floating regimes in terms of inflation performance.

The clear superiority of pegged exchange rates with respect to inflation does not stand up in all cases when countries are sorted into different groups reflecting their levels of income and development.[76] Using the "natural" classification, pegged regimes in low-income developing coun-tries are associated with a 10 percent annual reduction in inflation relative to freely floating regimes. In emerging market countries, however, differ-ent exchange-rate regimes do not affect inflation in a statistically impor-tant way. Moreover, pegged rates in industrial countries are associated with 3 percent per year *higher* inflation relative to floating regimes. These different results may reflect the different challenges faced by the various country groups. Low-income developing countries have low exposure to volatile international capital flows and may thus benefit most from pegged regimes because pegs require commitment and thereby enhance credi-bility. In contrast, emerging market countries have open capital markets and can be buffeted by swings in capital flows; hence, pegged exchange

---

[73] Even so, it may not be possible to correct fully for endogeneity, the possibility that the exchange rate regime may have been chosen precisely because of its expected effects on inflation.

[74] Ghosh, Gulde, and Wolf (2002) and Rogoff et al. (2004) report results based upon the "consensus" and "natural" regimes, respectively. Each estimates equations in which the dependent variable, inflation, is a function of regime dummy variables, money growth, real GDP growth, trade openness, turnover of central bank governor, terms of trade, and the government's fiscal balance. Both studies also examine results from a two-step procedure in which money growth depends on the exchange-rate regime and inflation depends on conditional money growth and the other control variables. This two-step procedure also points to a substantial inflation advantage for pegged exchange rates relative to floating rates; see Ghosh, Gulde, and Wolf (2002), ch. 6 and Rogoff et al. (2004), ch. III.

[75] See Rogoff et al. (2004), p. 30.

[76] See Rogoff et al. (2004), p. 31.

rates in those countries may raise their exposure to financial crises. Finally, in mature economies with significant nominal rigidities, flexible exchange rates may play an important role in facilitating adjustment to shocks.[77]

Sebastian Edwards and Igal Magendzo have looked directly at the macroeconomic effects of currency consolidation by comparing infla-tion performance in thirty-two currency-union members and twenty dollarized countries between 1970 and 1998 with performance in a con-trol group of countries that have their own currencies.[78] Their approach has the advantage that it does not mix other hard pegs, such as cur-rency boards, with the currency-consolidation group. It has a disadvan-tage, however, because many of the economies covered by their study are extraordinarily small, raising questions about comparability with those in the control group. Using sophisticated statistical analysis, Edwards and Magendzo find that annual inflation is 12 to 14 percent lower in the currency-consolidation group than in the country group having their own currencies. Using a different statistical procedure they likewise find a differential, but it is about half as large.[79] All of their estimates are highly significant statistically and provide additional support for the proposi-tion that joining a monetary union or dollarizing can reduce inflation.

Growth Performance

Can countries that join a monetary union or adopt another country's currency expect to achieve higher growth as well as lower inflation? Here the answer is less clear. In theory, a rigid exchange-rate regime might

---

[77] Ghosh, Gulde, and Wolf (2002) find broadly similar results for countries grouped by income. Furthermore, they find that for countries with annual inflation rates of 10 percent or more, a pegged regime yields significantly better inflation performance than a floating regime. However, for countries with annual inflation rates lower than 10 percent, there is no identifiable difference between a peg and a float.

[78] See Edwards and Magendzo (2003). Their sample includes dependencies and territories that are not members of the IMF and are therefore excluded from the "consensus" and "natural" classifications. They exclude hyperinflation countries from their control group.

[79] The authors use a treatment-effects model to obtain the first result and a matching estimator model to obtain the second.

Table 4.4. *Annual real GDP growth per capita in percent, 1970–1999*

	De jure	*De facto*[1]
Pegged	1.2	1.3
Intermediate	2.4	2.6
Floating	1.2	−0.9

[1] "Consensus" classification.

Source: Atish R. Ghosh, Anne-Marie Gulde, and Holger C. Wolf (2002), *Exchange Rate Regimes: Choices and Consequences.* Cambridge, MA: MIT *Press.*

raise market confidence, reduce domestic interest rates and uncertainty, and lead to higher growth. Yet it may instead have adverse implications for growth, because an irrevocably fixed exchange rate cannot adjust in response to shocks. Unfortunately, the available empirical evidence does not help us to sort out this issue. It fails to provide consistent answers.

Simple correlations for 147 countries over a thirty-year period, using both *de jure* and "consensus" classifications of exchange-rate regimes, show that intermediate regimes have been associated with higher annual growth in per capita real GDP than pegged or floating exchange rates (see Table 4.4). However, the floating-rate category includes countries with very high inflation; once these countries are removed, the growth rates of countries with floating regimes are higher than shown in Table 4.4 – on the order of $1\frac{3}{4}$ percent per year according to Rogoff and his coauthors.[80]

The message from these simple correlations does not survive completely in more sophisticated statistical testing. When using the "consensus" classification and controlling for a broad set of other factors that influence growth, Ghosh, Gulde, and Wolf find again that pegged and intermediate regimes result in higher growth in per capita real GDP than do floating exchange rates.[81] But when they employ econometric methods

[80] This finding is based on analysis using the "natural" regime classification. The freely falling regime composed of countries with very high inflation is associated with a decline in per capita real growth of 1.3 percent per year; see Rogoff et al. (2004), pp. 32–33.

[81] They estimate equations in which the dependent variable, growth in per capita real GDP, is a function of regime dummy variables, the share of investment in GDP, trade openness, terms of trade growth, average years of schooling, the share of taxes in GDP,

that control for country-specific effects and correct for reverse causality, they find that the estimated effects are lower both in magnitude and statistical significance. Thus, it is not clear that pegged or intermediate regimes have implications for growth different from those of floating exchange rates. Rogoff and his coauthors concur, having run similar growth regressions using the "natural" classification scheme and controlling for a host of important factors.[82]

Separating countries according to income and development changes the results. Rogoff and his coauthors find a statistically significant relationship between growth and exchange-rate regimes for industrial countries but not for emerging markets or developing countries. Industrial countries with floating regimes grow faster by $2\frac{3}{4}$ percentage points per year than do countries with pegged regimes.[83]

A study by three Bank of Canada economists obtains definitive results for growth by adopting a different approach. It takes account of the monetary policy framework in addition to the *de facto* exchange-rate regime.[84] Although countries operating under pegged exchange-rate regimes have a clear nominal anchor (the exchange rate), some countries operating under intermediate or floating regimes do not. A country with a floating exchange rate and an inflation-targeting framework for monetary policy can be considered to have a clear nominal anchor, whereas one with a floating rate but no such monetary policy framework may have no such anchor. Once the monetary policy framework is taken into account,

---

the government's fiscal balance, initial income relative to U.S. income, population growth, and population size. They also examine results from a two-step procedure that first predicts the investment share and/or trade openness as a function of regime dummies and other controls. The two-step results also point to a significant growth advantage for pegged and intermediate regimes.

[82] They use explanatory variables identical to those used by Ghosh, Gulde, and Wolf (2002).

[83] See Rogoff et al. (2004), pp. 32–33. To complicate matters, however, Levy-Yeyati and Sturzenegger (2003) come to a conflicting conclusion. Using their own *de facto* classification of regimes, they find that pegged and intermediate exchange rates reduce growth in per capita real GDP by about $\frac{3}{4}$ to 1 percent per year relative to floating rates. But when they separate countries into industrial and nonindustrial groups, they find that this result does *not* hold for the industrial countries, but is large and statistically significant for the nonindustrial countries.

[84] Bailliu, Lafrance, and Perrault (2003) examine the growth performance of sixty countries from 1973 to 1998.

exchange-rate regimes with an anchor are associated with higher growth in real GDP per capita relative to regimes with no anchor.[85] Furthermore, pegged exchange rates raise real per capita growth by $1\frac{1}{4}$ percent per year, whereas intermediate and floating regimes with a nominal anchor raise it by only $\frac{3}{4}$ of 1 percent per year.

Another approach is to abandon regime classifications altogether, focusing only on countries that do not have independent currencies and assessing their growth relative to countries with their own national currencies. In a study discussed earlier, Edwards and Magendzo found that countries that have surrendered their national currencies have higher per capita real growth – on the order of 0.75 to 1.2 percent per year – relative to countries having their own currencies.[86] But the authors find that the ECCU countries in the sample account entirely for these results; other monetary-union countries and dollarized economies perform no differently in terms of growth relative to countries with national currencies.

Overall, it is hard to know what to make of the proliferation of conflicting estimates, not only because of the differences in results but also because of the differences in methodology. The major studies that examine the implications of exchange-rate regimes rely importantly on different *de facto* classifications and this, more than anything else, may account for the differences in results.[87] Perhaps, in the end, the best that can be said is that there is no convincing evidence that pegged exchange rates have adverse growth effects.

Finally, a pegged exchange rate should, at least in theory, raise the volatility of real growth in an economy with nominal rigidities, because fixing the exchange rate forecloses a mode of adjustment. But here, too,

---

[85] The authors use a hybrid exchange-rate classification scheme that combines the *de jure* regime with actual behavior: *de jure* pegged exchange rates are classified as *de facto* pegged regimes, while intermediate and floating rates are classified according to the actual volatility of the nominal rate.

[86] See Edwards and Magendzo (2003). Their results contrast with those of Frankel and Rose (2002), who find that membership in a currency union has no independent effect on per capita real growth. Frankel and Rose, however, include countries that operate currency boards, whereas Edwards and Magendzo do not.

[87] Frankel (2003) makes this point. Ghosh, Gulde, and Wolf (2002), Levy-Yeyati and Sturzenegger (2003), and Rogoff et al. (2004) all use very similar sets of countries, time periods, statistical approaches, and sets of control variables. The main difference across studies is the *de facto* regime classification.

the empirical evidence is mixed. Although empirical work using a *de jure* classification provides support for the theoretical argument, the "consensus" classification suggests that floating rates raise the volatility of real growth, and the "natural" classification yields no effects of the exchange-rate regime on volatility. [88]

ECONOMIC PERFORMANCE AND EMU

Our discussion of economic performance has thus far been a general one, but we would not want to neglect an obvious candidate for analysis: the euro area. There has indeed been a great deal of discussion about the effects of Europe's monetary union on the economic performance of its members.[89] As mentioned in Chapter 3, average annual inflation across euro area countries was slightly above 2 percent in most years after 1999. And for many countries (including Greece, Italy, Spain, and Portugal), the monetary discipline of EMU has brought with it a decline in domestic inflation rates from the high rates that prevailed in the early to mid-1990s, a result broadly consistent with the empirical studies of the effects of hard peg exchange-rate regimes discussed in the previous section. But, after robust growth in the first two years of EMU, a substantial slowdown in France, Germany, and Italy led some to ask whether a "one size fits all" monetary policy has had deleterious implications for growth.[90]

Much of the discussion about the effects of EMU, however, has focused not on the *levels* of inflation and growth but rather on their *dispersion* (as measured by the unweighted standard deviation of annual inflation or

---

[88] See Ghosh, Gulde, and Wolf (2002) for the results using the *de jure* and "consensus" classifications, and Rogoff et al. (2004) for the results using the "natural" classification. When countries are separated into groups, Rogoff et al. (pp. 33–34) find that the volatility of real growth increases with exchange-rate flexibility for industrial and emerging market countries. Levy-Yeyati and Sturzenegger (2003) find higher volatility in countries with pegged regimes, but this effect holds only for nonindustrial countries when the sample is subdivided. Edwards and Magendzo (2003) find higher growth volatility for the countries without an independent currency.

[89] Recall that a monetary union is classified as a hard peg exchange rate regime for each of its members.

[90] Unlike our earlier discussion of growth performance under different exchange rate regimes, we refer here to growth in real GDP not per capita growth. See Lane (2006) for detail on growth asymmetries among EMU member countries.

growth rates). Differences in the growth rates of EMU member countries has received relatively little attention because their standard deviation has fluctuated around 2 percent since the 1970s with little or no change since 1999.[91] Inflation, however, is another matter. During the 1990s, there was a dramatic decline in inflation differentials across countries in the euro area. Since 1999, the dispersion of inflation rates has been broadly stable at about one percentage point.[92]

How does the inflation dispersion of EMU members compare with that of another large monetary union, the United States? The European Central Bank and its officials have emphasized the comparability of euro-area inflation differentials with those within the United States.[93] Based on Census data for fourteen Standard Metropolitan Statistical Areas (SMSA), inflation dispersion in the United States has been broadly stable at about one percentage point over a long period. However, Ignazio Angeloni and Michael Ehrmann have asked whether these fourteen SMSAs provide the appropriate benchmark against which to compare euro-area inflation differentials; that is because these U.S. cities are generally smaller than European countries and their inflation rates are therefore more volatile.[94] Another benchmark, based on the four U.S. Census regions (for which the standard deviation of annual inflation rates averages about 0.5 percentage point), suggests that euro-area inflation dispersion may still be above levels associated with monetary union.

But even if inflation differentials in the euro area are not quite comparable to those in the United States, there is an even greater problem. The differentials between European countries' inflation rates are highly persistent. Unlike the United States, where regions exhibit both positive

---

[91] See European Commission (2004a) and González-Páramo (2005), who argue that current growth differentials owe primarily to trend or structural factors, as business cycles since 1999 have been highly synchronized.

[92] On these facts, all the studies agree. See, for example, Angeloni and Ehrmann (2003), European Central Bank (2005b), Issing (2005), González-Páramo (2005), and Lane (2006). The dispersion dropped below one percentage point in the late 1990s, and rose above it in the first years of EMU before stabilizing. For a detailed discussion of the pattern of inflation differentials, see European Commission (2004a). Furthermore, as might be expected, inflation differentials across euro-area countries have been higher for services than for traded goods; see Lane (2006), Table 1.

[93] See European Central Bank (2005b), Issing (2005), and González-Páramo (2005).

[94] See Angeloni and Ehrmann (2004), p. 9.

and negative differences relative to average inflation, EMU countries have exhibited inflation rates that are consistently higher or lower than the euro-area average.[95] This persistence in inflation dispersion results in protracted differences in real interest rates and competitiveness across countries, with attendant consequences for growth and its composition.[96] For example, countries in the periphery (Greece, Ireland, Italy, Portugal, and Spain) experienced the largest decline in *ex post* real short-term interest rates as a result of monetary union, due to a larger drop in nominal interest rates as well as higher inflation than in the core countries. These lower real rates have provided stimulus to domestic demand that has been reinforced, *ceteris paribus*, insofar as domestic demand has spurred additional domestic inflation.[97]

The persistence of inflation differentials has had dramatic consequences for member countries' competitiveness. Greece, Ireland, Italy, the Netherlands, Portugal, and Spain have all experienced an appreciation of their real exchange rates by more than 5 percent since joining EMU (see Chart 4.1), whereas France and Germany have experienced substantial real depreciations. Such changes in competitiveness, by depressing net exports in countries with higher inflation rates and raising them in countries with lower inflation,[98] offset to some extent the effects of different real interest rates on domestic demand. But there is no doubt that persistent inflation differentials across countries in a monetary union will, over time, produce significant changes in competitiveness and this may be a source of serious tension within the union.

---

[95] See Angeloni and Ehrmann (2004) and Lane (2006).

[96] González-Páramo (2005) reports that seven of the twelve countries in EMU have experienced annual inflation rates either consistently above or below the euro-area average since 1999.

[97] Lane (2006), Table 3, reports data on *ex post* real short-term interest rates. Ahearne and Pisani-Ferry (2006) discuss effects on the composition of growth. There is some debate about whether to it is better to measure real interest rates *ex ante* or *ex post* using expected or actual inflation. This is an important consideration when assessing the dispersion, but not the level, of interest rates before and after 1999. See Issing (2005) and European Central Bank (2005b).

[98] Inflation is not the entire story, however, because the euro's external value has also changed since 1999. Moreover, Ireland is an exception to the general case because its net exports have increased despite real appreciation. The rise in inflation reflects increased productivity (the so-called Balassa Samuelson effect). For a discussion of these issues, see Honohan and Lane (2003) and Lane (2006).

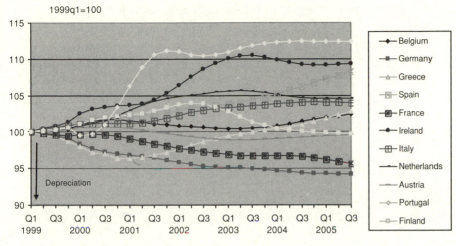

Chart 4.1. Real Exchange Rates
Source: Alan Ahearne and Jean Pisani-Ferry (2006), "The Euro: Only for the Agile," Policy Brief 1, Brussels: Bruegel. Reprinted with the permission of Bruegel and of the authors.

Differentials in inflation rates across countries and their persistence must be distinguished from the issue of convergence in price *levels*, a subject that also has received attention and on which we will touch briefly. One of the conjectured benefits of EMU was that it would lead to greater transparency of prices across member countries and spur the convergence of price levels. The convergence process may produce different inflation rates, however, and without a separate examination of price levels, we cannot know whether the observed differences in inflation rates reflect convergence or divergence.

Charles Engel and John Rogers studied the actual prices of 139 traded and nontraded products across eighteen European cities from 1990 to 2003 and found that a substantial amount of price convergence occurred in the 1990s prior to EMU but could find no evidence of additional convergence after 1999.[99] The authors conclude that the integration process was more important for the convergence of price levels than monetary union itself. However, another study that used data on the prices of two

---

[99] See Engel and Rogers (2004). Goldberg and Verboven (2004) studied the European car market and arrived at a similar conclusion.

hundred consumer goods in fifteen EU countries from 1995 to 2002 arrived at a different conclusion. Nigel Allington, Paul Kattuman, and Florian Waldmann have found that prices have converged more since 1999 in countries that adopted the euro than in EU countries outside the monetary union.[100] Whether the arrival of the euro has brought with it additional price convergence is something we are not likely to know with any certainty until more time has passed.

[100] See Allington, Kattuman, and Waldmann (2005).

5

Monetary Union in the Americas?

INTRODUCTION

We now turn our discussion to the Americas and examine the prospects for monetary integration in the northern and southern hemispheres. Canada and Mexico have floating exchange rates, which are often described as the best regime for a country in bed with an elephant – the huge U.S. economy. It is important to know, however, just how much economic insulation Canada and Mexico have actually enjoyed, and whether NAFTA has changed the situation – the claim made by some Canadians who advocate monetary union with the United States or adoption of the U.S. dollar. For Mexico, a key issue is whether growing competition from China strengthens or weakens the case for tighter monetary integration with the U.S. dollar.

This chapter also looks at whether MERCOSUR should take steps toward an *internal* monetary union – one that would not include the United States. The recent addition of Venezuela to MERCOSUR, along with leftist anti-American sentiment in several other countries, may revive the quest for a single currency. The composition of MERCOSUR's trade, however, will influence the economic benefits, costs, and possible strains arising from a monetary union. To the extent that financial dollarization has already occurred, moreover, use of the U.S. dollar may impede prospects for an internal monetary union. We thus compare the benefits and costs of internal monetary union with those that would result from unilateral dollarization.

Finally, the chapter will turn to a discussion of dollarization and the countries which appear likely to adopt this sort of exchange-rate regime. We explain why *de facto* dollarization or euroization in medium and large emerging-market countries seems unlikely in the future to evolve toward the *de jure* replacement of national currencies with the dollar or euro. In smaller countries, however, *de facto* dollarization or euroization may well presage *de jure* dollarization or euroization, and the chapter provides a discussion of the two groups of countries where this may be appropriate. First, following El Salvador, other countries in Central America with large trade ties to the United States and small, undeveloped domestic financial markets may turn to dollarization. Second, several countries in Eastern Europe would seem to be equally well suited to adopt the euro. However, suitability is in this case less relevant than their desire to join EMU, because European officials have ruled out using the euro as legal tender for any country that aspires to become a full-fledged member of the monetary union.

NORTH AMERICAN MONETARY UNION

A North American monetary union (NAMU) involving Canada, Mexico, and the United States would differ from EMU in several key respects: size, number of member countries, symmetry, openness, level of development across the member economies, and institutional infrastructure. First, a NAMU would be substantially larger than the current euro area, with 40 percent more people and 47 percent more economic output (based on data for 2005, see Table 5.1.). Second, NAMU would have only three member countries compared with the current thirteen of the euro area and potentially more than twenty-five members. We would expect that this smaller membership might be associated with less complex negotiations and a smaller institutional apparatus compared with Europe.[1] Third, a NAMU would be dominated by a single country, the United States, which contains 69 percent of North America's population

---

[1] This assumes that Canada and Mexico are willing to form a monetary union with the United States on terms largely dictated by the latter, as we discuss later on.

Table 5.1. *Indicators of size, NAMU countries and EMU*

	Population (millions)	Nominal GDP (trillions of U.S. dollars)	Openness[1] (percent)	GNI per capita (U.S. dollars)
NAMU:	431.9	14.4	14	33,341
United States	296.4	12.4	20	41,890
Canada	32.3	1.1	60	33,375
Mexico	103.1	0.8	57	10,751
Euro Area:	313.9	10.0	31	29,162

[1] Merchandise trade as a percent of nominal GDP.

Source: World Development Indicators (2007) *Direction of Trade Statistics* (2006), and European Central Bank (2006), *Monthly Bulletin* (December). Data are for 2005, except for openness for NAMU countries, which is for 2004. Gross National Income (GNI) per capita is computed by converting domestic currency values to U.S. dollars using purchasing power parity exchange rates and dividing by population.

and produces 87 percent of its output. By contrast, Germany, the single largest country in EMU, accounts for 27 percent of total population and 29 percent of euro-area GDP. Thus, NAMU would be a far more asymmetric union than EMU.

In addition, NAMU would differ markedly from EMU in terms of openness. Canada and Mexico are very open economies (total exports and imports are 61 and 58 percent of GDP, respectively) and the United States is each country's largest trading partner. Given that the United States is a relatively closed economy, the external trade of a NAMU would be much smaller – only 14 percent of GDP – than the external trade of EMU (31 percent of GDP). This suggests that fixing the internal exchange rates in a North American monetary union would provide larger benefits to Canada and Mexico than to the United States.[2]

Furthermore, although Canada falls somewhere between France and Italy in terms of income per capita, Mexico has a lower standard of living than any of the thirteen countries in the euro area. Although the

[2] As we will argue later, it is necessary to evaluate the pattern of shocks to the member countries and the required adjustment to them before concluding that fixing the nominal exchange rate is the best policy. Buiter (1999, p. 295) argues that neither openness nor the concentration of trade with the United States has "any obvious bearing" on the desirability of a North American currency.

wealthiest EMU member country (Germany) had an income per capita more than two times that of the poorest member country (Portugal) at the start of monetary union, U.S. income per capita is six times that of Mexico. With a per capita income between that of Estonia and the Slovak Republic, Mexico should be viewed in the same light as some of the prospective EMU members that joined the EU in 2004. Thus, the process of convergence, which has received substantial attention with respect to the EU accession countries, also would be important in a debate over NAMU. For example, Mexico would naturally grow more rapidly and experience a higher inflation rate than Canada or the United States as part of its convergence process. Exactly how NAMU monetary policy makers would choose to respond to these differences is not clear.[3]

Finally, North America lacks Europe's institutional infrastructure. The North American Free Trade Agreement (NAFTA) signed in 1993 created only a free trade area, not a customs union or common market. NAMU would require, at a minimum, agreement to create a common central bank and would perhaps necessitate the creation of other consultative bodies or supranational structures. In the absence of other institutions, the creation of a supranational central bank would raise questions about legitimacy and accountability. Willem Buiter has argued that without a North American counterpart to the European Parliament (or some other body to which the NAMU central bank could be accountable), the transfer of national sovereignty that would occur under NAMU would not be perceived as legitimate.[4]

We also must note that there is little or no political will for regional monetary integration in any of the three North American nations at the present time. There was a debate in Canada that began in 1998 following Argentina's flirtation with dollarization (we will come back to Argentina and dollarization later in the chapter), and North American monetary integration was discussed on several occasions in the Canadian

---

[3] Higher-equilibrium inflation results from higher productivity growth in the converging economy and is a manifestation of the Balassa-Samuelson effect. See Kenen and Meade (2004) for a discussion of these issues.

[4] Buiter (1999) also notes that monetary unions that are not preceded by political unification are generally not very durable. Pastor (2001) discusses the lack of North American institutions and lays out an agenda for deepening the regional infrastructure.

parliament.[5] Mexico entertained the idea as well.[6] But even if the sentiment in Canada and Mexico were to favor NAMU strongly, we think it highly unlikely that the United States would become a vigorous proponent of regional monetary integration.[7] The reason is due primarily to the asymmetry we noted above. Given the size and dominance of the United States and the international status of the U.S. dollar, America would likely gain little economically from a monetary union with its northern and southern neighbors. And, in the continuing aftermath of NAFTA, a NAMU would face political hurdles as well.[8] In fact, Benjamin Cohen has written that the United States could suffer some loss of political power if it were required to obtain approval from Ottawa and Mexico City in order to wield its monetary influence.[9]

Edwin Truman claims that, were North American monetary integration to occur, the terms would "almost certainly" be dictated by the United States and based on existing U.S. institutions.[10] We agree. Thus, in what

---

[5] See the articles published in *International Management* (2003) in a thematic issue on "Business and Policy Views on the Monetary Integration of North America." Carr et al. (1999) provides a transcript of one hearing before the Canadian Senate's Committee on Banking, Trade, and Commerce. Cohen (2003a) cites a 2001 survey of public opinion in which 55 percent of Canadians favored some form of monetary integration with the United States. Helleiner (2006, ch. 8) notes that the support in Quebec, particularly among those favoring political sovereignty, was stronger than in other provinces of Canada.

[6] In 1999, for example, the Mexican Bankers Association announced its support for a North American common currency; see Courchene and Harris (2003). The enthusiasm in Mexico was voiced mainly by business in the border region, while public officials indicated their support for continuing with a floating exchange rate.

[7] The lack of U.S. support for regional monetary integration has been widely noted. See Chriszt (2000) and Cohen (2003a, 2006). Robson and Laidler (2002) cite poll results in which 84 percent of U.S. respondents opposed the idea of a common currency in North America. Courchene and Harris (1999) and Grubel (2003) argue that as EMU grows larger and the euro threatens to displace the dollar as the premier international currency, the United States will feel pressure to enlarge the dollar area. We do not see this as likely in the near term.

[8] As Salvatore (2007) points out, a NAMU would require the amendment of Article I, Section 8 of the U.S. Constitution, which assigns to the U.S. Congress the power to coin money and regulate its value.

[9] See Cohen (2006).

[10] See Truman (2003b), p. 1. Laidler (2002), p. 1, expresses a similar view and concludes that "the degree of U.S. hegemony over Canadian [and Mexican] affairs that is implicit in any monetary arrangement to which the U.S. might be willing to be party presents a serious political deterrent" to monetary integration.

follows, we discuss the form that the United States would be most likely to support were it to decide that regional monetary union was in its interest: the enlargement of the Federal Reserve System to include Canada and Mexico. We then compare this regime with current monetary arrangements. Finally, we complete our discussion with some remarks about the economic case for NAMU and whether North America comes close to being an optimum currency area.

A North American Federal Reserve

The Federal Reserve System[11] could be readily expanded to incorporate Canada and Mexico, and this seems to us to be a more likely outcome than the creation of an entirely new institution of the sort advocated by Canadian economist Herbert Grubel.[12] Canada, with about $7\frac{1}{2}$ percent of North American output, lies somewhere between the Dallas and Richmond Federal Reserve districts in economic size. Mexico accounts for another $5\frac{1}{2}$ percent of regional GDP, putting it on a par with the Cleveland Federal Reserve district.[13] Hence, the NAMU Fed could be constructed by adding Canada and Mexico as additional Federal Reserve districts or, as Edwin Truman has suggested, by redrawing the lines of the existing twelve districts.[14] While the former would be more straightforward, it would be subject to the criticism that some district Presidents on a NAMU Federal Open Market Committee (FOMC) were basing their views and votes on economic developments in their own countries, rather than upon average inflation and output in NAMU as a whole.[15] Thus, a system in which Federal Reserve districts were drawn across national and state borders would make more sense.[16] The districts could align economic interests: the U.S. and Canadian Pacific Northwest, the U.S. and Mexican border regions, and so on. In Truman's scheme, six of the

---

[11] Box 3.2 summarizes key features of the Federal Reserve System.

[12] Grubel (1999, 2003) advocates the creation of a new institution, the North American Central Bank, which would issue a new currency, the amero.

[13] These estimates are approximate. Meade and Sheets (2005b) provides data on the size of each Federal Reserve district.

[14] Truman (2006). We do not address the complexities of the requisite treaty and associated legislation necessary to achieve this result. See also Helleiner (2006) for a discussion of an enlarged Federal Reserve System.

[15] This sort of criticism has been voiced with regard to the ECB's Governing Council.

[16] The Federal Reserve districts drawn in 1914 do not observe state boundaries.

twelve districts would combine regions of the United States with parts of Mexico or Canada.[17]

If we assume that the United States would demand continuity with current voting arrangements on the FOMC, then twelve of the nineteen NAMU policy makers would cast a vote at any given meeting. Seven Board members appointed from the three countries would each cast one vote, as would the President of the New York district bank, and four other votes would rotate annually across the other eleven district banks in a prescribed fashion. None of this is set in stone, however. It is possible to conceive of many different ways to structure voting in the NAMU Fed, although it is hard to imagine that the Canadian and Mexican representatives would cast a large number of votes, given the lesser economic importance of their countries in a combined monetary area. Thus, the policy domain of a NAMU Fed would be dominated by the United States, and it is likely that a U.S.-oriented monetary policy would result.

An interesting question is whether a NAMU Fed would maintain the mixture of public and private interests that characterizes the current Federal Reserve System. For instance, would the district Bank Presidents continue to be nominated by each district Bank's board of nine directors (six of whom are selected by private banks in the district),[18] or would NAMU require a more democratic process for making those appointments? Obviously, NAMU would need to establish an appointments process as well as designate reporting requirements of the NAMU Fed to Canadian, Mexican, and U.S. legislatures or to some new supranational body.

A NAMU would presumably include a rule for the sharing of seigniorage revenue. A reasonable formula would allocate seigniorage based on the sizes of the NAMU members – perhaps according to shares in income.[19] Under such a formula, Canada and Mexico would gain seigniorage income relative to the status quo.[20] Because of substantial

---

[17] See Truman (2006).

[18] The appointment of the district Bank Presidents is subject to the approval of the Federal Reserve Board. See *Purposes and Functions* (2005), p. 10, for a complete description of the appointments process.

[19] In light of the relatively large population of Mexico, we deem it unlikely that seigniorage allocation would be based on a combination of income and population as it is in EMU.

[20] Buiter (1999), Cohen (2006), and Truman (2003b) make this point.

holdings of U.S. dollars outside of the United States, the fraction of U.S. dollars in total NAMU currency outstanding (the sum of U.S. dollars, Canadian dollars, and Mexican pesos) is larger than the U.S. share in regional GDP.[21] In addition, under the assumption that the NAMU currency would remain as attractive to hold as the U.S. dollar, the amount of currency outstanding could be expected to rise more rapidly than the stock of Canadian dollars or Mexican pesos would have grown under monetary sovereignty.

Would there be an entirely new currency – the amero, as Herbert Grubel has advocated[22] – or would a NAMU issue the U.S. dollar under a more inclusive name – the NAMU dollar perhaps? We find it difficult to imagine circumstances under which the United States would agree to give up its dollar. To do so would impose tremendous switch-over costs on international investors and multinational businesses, risking damage to the dollar's reputation worldwide. Thus, the United States would presumably demand that both its central bank and its currency be retained in a regional monetary union.

The effective functioning of the North American monetary area would require the integration of banking, financial, and payment systems. Furthermore, there would have to be some harmonization or coordination of bank supervision, as well as designation of the NAMU Fed as the lender of last resort. Here, too, the United States would presumably insist that its approach be extended throughout the region.[23]

The Status Quo: Inflation Targeting

As we have already argued, monetary policy in a NAMU would likely be very similar to Federal Reserve policy, because of the size of the United States in the region's policy domain. To weigh the potential gains and

---

[21] Judson and Porter (1996) estimate that as much as two-thirds of U.S. currency in circulation is held abroad. According to Truman (2003b), U.S. dollars, Canadian dollars, and Mexican pesos as a fraction of total currency outstanding in North America were 93 percent, 4 percent, and 3 percent, respectively, as of mid-2000.

[22] See Grubel (2003).

[23] Robson and Laidler (2002) provide a comparison of current bank supervision and regulation in the United States and Canada, and the steps that would be necessary to harmonize their systems.

losses from a NAMU, we need to examine the current policy regimes in Canada and Mexico, as they would change more dramatically than the U.S. regime. Both countries' central banks combine inflation targeting with a floating exchange rate. Canada, which adopted inflation targeting in 1991, has had consistently good inflation performance; annual increases in inflation have ranged between 1 and 3 percent since 1992. Mexico adopted inflation targeting in 1995 in order to reduce its very high inflation rate, which exceeded 35 percent in that year.[24] Inflation has declined rapidly and steadily, however, falling to 4 percent in 2005.

When the exchange rate floats, of course, it cannot anchor the price level. Therefore, many countries with floating exchange rates use inflation targeting as their guide to making monetary policy. They do not try to keep the inflation rate constant at each point in time. Rather, they seek to contain it within a range consistent with price stability over the medium term.[25] To do that, of course, they have to forecast future inflation, using econometric models of their own, forecasts made by others, and, when available, forecasts implied by the difference between market interest rates on ordinary bonds and market interest rates on inflation-indexed bonds. Inflation forecasts are required, because monetary policy cannot affect inflation today; it can only affect future inflation. By publishing their forecasts, moreover, central banks can convey information, not only about future inflation but, more important, about the future paths of their monetary policies. A number of industrial countries other than Canada have adopted this regime, including New Zealand (the first to do so), Australia, Switzerland, and the United Kingdom.[26] In

---

[24] Mexico introduced an inflation target in 1995 but supplemented it in the early years with a monetary aggregate target, which was eliminated in 2001. See Truman (2003a).

[25] The Bank of Canada has a target range for inflation of 1 to 3 percent, and it aims to keep annual consumer price inflation at 2 percent over the medium term. The Bank of Mexico aims for annual consumer price inflation of 3 percent.

[26] Although price stability is the primary objective of the ECB, it is not classified as an inflation-targeting central bank, largely because it has an asymmetric policy target – keeping inflation below but close to 2 percent – rather than seeking to keep inflation within a preannounced range. Furthermore, as was noted in Chapter 3, it uses a second target, the growth rate of a broad monetary aggregate, in the formulation of its monetary policy.

addition to Mexico, moreover, central banks in twelve emerging-market countries, including three East Asian countries,[27] have adopted inflation targeting.

Critics of this regime often claim that inflation targeting forces a central bank to ignore other important dimensions of economic performance, such as real output or the exchange rate. That is not entirely true. Lars Svensson has noted that even the strictest inflation-targeting central banks move inflation back to target only gradually because they want to minimize the variability of output as much as possible while meeting their inflation target.[28] And, in some situations, a monetary policy aimed at an inflation target also stabilizes the exchange rate. Consider three cases in which an economy starts at full employment:[29]

(1) A spontaneous fall in aggregate domestic demand will depress output and imports, and the fall in imports will cause the domestic currency to appreciate under a floating exchange rate. With output below its potential level and an appreciation of the domestic currency, inflation can be expected to fall. If, then, the central bank believes that the fall in domestic demand is not merely temporary, it will reduce short-term interest rates by enough to take the economy back to full employment. The interest-rate cut will induce a net capital outflow, which will tend to reverse the appreciation of the domestic currency. In this case, then, an inflation-targeting monetary policy will serve to stabilize output, inflation and the exchange rate.

(2) A spontaneous change in investors' preference that raises the demand for domestic assets will attract a net capital inflow and thus cause the domestic currency to appreciate. The appreciation will worsen the trade balance by raising imports and reducing exports and will therefore reduce domestic output, as in the previous case. Furthermore, it will lead to lower expected inflation, both directly through the appreciation and by way of its impact on domestic output.

---

[27] These three are Korea, the Philippines, and Thailand. See IMF (2005b, ch. IV), which provides a review of experience with inflation targeting and of the relevant literature. It also compares two groups of emerging-market countries, thirteen inflation-targeting countries, and twenty-nine other emerging-market countries, and its findings are quite striking. Although both groups of countries reduced their inflation rates during the period under study, the inflation-targeting countries reduced them further, and they did so without suffering more output volatility. See also Ito (2004) on inflation targeting by Asian central banks and Truman (2003a).

[28] Svensson (1997) originated the term "flexible inflation targeting" to describe central banks that take a gradualist approach.

[29] In what follows, we implicitly assume a model of exchange-rate determination based upon the trade balance and uncovered interest parity.

If the central bank expects the capital inflow to continue, it may again reduce short-term interest rates. By doing that, the central bank will reduce the capital inflow, the appreciation of the domestic currency, and the deterioration of the trade balance. Once again, the monetary-policy response will tend to stabilize output, inflation, and the exchange rate.

(3) A spontaneous fall in foreign demand will cause a reduction in exports, a deterioration of the trade balance, and a depreciation of the domestic currency. The fall in domestic output resulting from the reduction in exports will work to reduce expected inflation, but the depreciation of the domestic currency will have the opposite effect. The central bank's response will therefore depend on its judgment about the relative sizes of the two effects. If it expects inflation to fall, it will reduce interest rates; that will induce additional depreciation and higher expected inflation, and it will also stimulate output. If it expects inflation to rise, it will raise interest rates; that will limit or reverse the depreciation and stabilize inflation, but it will cause a larger output loss.[30]

This is not to say that the combination of inflation targeting and a floating exchange rate can work to stabilize inflation and the exchange rate in every macroeconomic situation. Consider an adverse supply shock, such as a sharp decline in the availability of an important input. This will raise production costs directly, and depress output and imports. The declines in output and income will reduce imports and thus lead to exchange-rate appreciation. The increase in the output gap and the appreciation will create downward pressure on prices but not by enough to outweigh the higher prices resulting from the supply shock itself. If the central bank thinks that the supply shock will be temporary, it may make no change in monetary policy. If it is uncertain about the duration of the shock or expects it to last for some time, it will respond by raising interest rates. It might nevertheless weigh the loss of output against the increase in inflation, and the extent to which it raises interest rates will depend importantly on the weight it assigns to stabilizing output under its inflation-targeting regime. Whatever the size of the interest rate increase, however, the tightening in monetary policy will further depress output and imports. In this case and others like it, then, an inflation-targeting monetary policy will stabilize inflation but at the cost of greater variability in output and the exchange rate.

[30] Ogawa, Ito, and Sasaki (2004) come to a similar conclusion.

Costs and Benefits of a North American Currency Area

The question facing Canada and Mexico, then, is whether they would be better served by their current regimes – inflation targeting and a flexible exchange rate – or by a monetary union with the United States.[31] As both countries trade substantially with the United States and the bulk, if not all, of that trade is paid for in U.S. dollars,[32] a single North American currency would eliminate currency conversion costs and exchange-rate risk. According to Bank of Canada estimates, the elimination of currency conversion would generate annual savings of $3 billion.[33] Moreover, competition from China is challenging Mexico's global export market share. Although the share of U.S. imports from Mexico has risen from just under 7 percent when NAFTA was signed in 1993 to $10\frac{1}{2}$ percent in 2004, the share of U.S. imports from China has grown from $5\frac{1}{4}$ to nearly 14 percent over the same period. The IMF estimates that Mexico and China compete directly in products that amount to 75 percent of the total value each country's exports to the United States.[34] If the elimination of currency conversion costs and exchange-rate risk gave Mexican producers some room to reduce their export prices, they might make some small gains relative to their Chinese counterparts.[35]

---

[31] Cuevas and Werner (2003) point to Mexico's success in achieving monetary credibility and reducing inflation under a floating exchange-rate regime. Their analysis thus suggests that Mexico might suffer by joining NAMU and giving up an independent monetary policy. To be sure, the NAMU central bank would focus on price stability but we have not concerned ourselves with the form of the central bank's mandate – whether it would be an inflation target, or something broader like that of the Federal Reserve. It is sufficient to note that the Fed has been successful in delivering low and stable inflation and thus behaves in many ways like a central bank with an inflation target even though its formal mandate is different.

[32] In 2004, Canada and Mexico shipped 85 and 88 percent, respectively, of their total exports to the United States; imports from the United States were 59 and 55 percent, respectively, of their total imports.

[33] According to Murray (2003), a $3 billion reduction of transactions costs in Canadian foreign exchange markets per year, when discounted at a real interest rate of 4 percent, would have a present value equal to one-tenth of Canada's GDP.

[34] The IMF estimates that direct competition affects about one-half of all products produced by Mexico and China for export to the United States. See IMF (2005b).

[35] It goes without saying that an appreciation of China's renminbi relative to the dollar would help Mexico's exporters as well. We discuss China's exchange-rate policy in Chapter 6.

Table 5.2. *Composition of output*[1]

	Agriculture	Industry	Services
Canada	2.3	33.7	64.0
Mexico	4.2	28.0	67.8
United States	1.2	24.2	74.6

[1] Share of value-added in GDP.

Source: World Development Indicators (2006).

In addition, monetary union with its northern neighbors could be expected to yield credibility gains for Mexico, despite its good performance since the adoption of inflation targeting. A narrowing of the differential between yields on Mexican and U.S. dollar-denominated government securities – about one hundred fifty basis points in 2005 – could generate a substantial reduction in Mexico's borrowing costs.[36] But, as Portugal's experience in EMU has shown, lower interest rates can be a mixed blessing. Although borrowing costs are lower because monetary policy is more credible, the lower interest rates boost demand and can lead to an overheated economy.

A proper assessment of the appropriateness of a single North American currency, however, can be made only after evaluating the extent to which the countries appear to form an optimum currency area. At first glance, the composition of output, shown in Table 5.2, appears relatively similar, although the United States produces more services and relies less on agriculture and industry than do Canada and Mexico. However, this broad decomposition of output masks a fundamental difference between the United States and its northern and southern neighbors, having to do with the share of primary commodities in production and trade. For example, the production of primary commodities in Canada is three times as large (as a share of the economy) as it is in the United States; the former is a net exporter of commodities, whereas the latter is a net importer.[37] In the

---

[36] Interest rates on Canadian government securities are comparable to yields on U.S. Treasuries, so Canada could not expect to benefit much, if any, from credibility gains.

[37] Murray, Schembri, and St-Amant (2003) report that commodity exports were 12 percent of Canada's GDP in 1997, compared with only 1 percent in the United States. See also Robson and Laidler (2002). Bank of Canada Governor David Dodge has ruled

future, moreover, Canada may depend to an even greater extent on commodity production if it continues to unearth the vast oil reserves buried in Alberta's tar sands. Mexico too depends heavily on commodities; the production of oil and related products accounts for about one-third of government revenues and more than 10 percent of exports.

More than a decade ago, Tamim Bayoumi and Barry Eichengreen compared European countries with U.S. regions; their results were summarized in Table 2.1. Soon thereafter, moreover, the same two authors extended their previous work on Europe by asking how closely the countries of North America resembled an optimum currency area.[38]

They began, as before, by using econometric methods to extract and quantify two types of shocks – demand shocks and supply shocks – affecting Mexico and regions of Canada and the United States. Next, they asked how closely the shocks affecting one area were correlated with the shocks affecting other areas in North America (a higher correlation between shocks provides a stronger case for forming a monetary union). They focused primarily on the results for supply shocks, arguing that those shocks were likely to reflect exogenous disturbances to commodity prices whereas demand shocks were likely to reflect both exogenous disturbances and responses to monetary and other macroeconomic policies.[39] In other words, an assessment of supply shocks is critical to determining North America's suitability for a common currency.

Table 5.3 reproduces their main findings. The variability of supply shocks ranges from highest in Mexico to lowest in the U.S. South East region. Not surprisingly, the greatest variability is found in Mexico and in the other two regions that are large producers of raw materials, Western Canada and the U.S. North West. The correlation of supply shocks across North America suggests that disturbances affecting Canada and Mexico are largely asymmetric when compared with disturbances affecting most

---

out a monetary union with the United States on the basis of differences in economic structure. He noted, however, that: "From a strictly economic perspective, it is always possible that, at some future time, the structures of our two economies could converge to a point that the benefits of a common currency could outweigh the macroeconomic costs of abandoning our flexible exchange rate." See Dodge (2001).

[38] See Bayoumi and Eichengreen (1994a, 1994b).

[39] The key point is that a monetary union would eliminate demand shocks arising from different monetary policies.

Table 5.3. *Supply shocks to Mexico and to Canadian and U.S. regions (Blanchard-Quah shock extraction)*

Country or region	Standard deviation	Correlations									
		E. Can.	W. Can.	New Eng.	Mid-East	G. Lakes	Plains	S. East	S. West	Calif.	N. West
Eastern Canada	0.019	1.00									
Western Canada	0.037	0.30	1.00								
New England	0.014	0.11	0.01	1.00							
Mid-East	0.012	0.15	−0.26	0.88	1.00						
Great Lakes	0.013	0.06	−0.07	0.77	0.81	1.00					
Plains	0.016	0.37	−0.10	0.34	0.30	0.46	1.00				
South East	0.011	−0.03	−0.52	0.44	0.67	0.66	0.49	1.00			
South West	0.019	−0.05	0.54	0.11	−0.14	−0.08	−0.52	−0.56	1.00		
California	0.013	0.23	0.14	0.68	0.61	0.67	0.47	0.43	0.07	1.00	
North West	0.025	0.05	0.52	0.29	0.03	0.27	0.14	−0.29	0.55	0.59	1.00
Mexico	0.053	0.14	0.57	−0.09	−0.35	−0.43	−0.50	−0.64	0.77	−0.17	0.33

Source: Adapted from Tamin Bayoumi and Barry Eichengreen (1994a), "Monetary and Exchange Rate Arrangements for NAFTA," *Journal of Development Economics*, 43, pp. 125–165, Tables 10 and 11.

of the United States. Supply shocks to Western Canada are highly correlated with those to Mexico, the U.S. Northwest, and the U.S. Southwest
but not with those to Eastern Canada.[40] Supply shocks to Mexico are
highly correlated only with those to Western Canada and the U.S. Southwest, and are in fact negatively correlated with six of the eight U.S. regions,
including California.[41] When Bayoumi and Eichengreen compared these
results to those for EU countries, they found that supply disturbances
within the "core" European countries were much more highly correlated
than those within North America.[42]

In another study, three Bank of Canada economists updated the work
of Bayoumi and Eichengreen to include more recent data and used a
technique that allowed them to separate demand shocks due to monetary
policy from those due to other sources.[43] Their findings were quite similar
to those of Bayoumi and Eichengreen. The average correlation of supply
and nonmonetary demand shocks was substantially higher for regions
of the United States with each another than it was for U.S. regions with
either Canada or Mexico.[44]

---

[40] These results are broadly consistent with Mundell's original suggestion that two optimum currency areas could be formed by joining eastern Canada and the United States
on the one hand, and western Canada and the United States on the other; see Mundell
(1961).

[41] The correlations of demand shocks, not shown in the table, do not make a stronger
case for North American integration; the only high correlation is internal to Canada,
between its Eastern and Western regions; see Bayoumi and Eichengreen (1994a), p. 155.

[42] The "core" countries were Belgium, Denmark, France, Germany, and the Netherlands;
see Bayoumi and Eichengreen (1994a), pp. 157–60.

[43] See Murray, Schembri, and St-Amant (2003). The estimation period for the demand
and supply shocks was 1976 to 1999.

[44] The average correlation of demand and supply shocks between U.S. regions was 0.68
and 0.48, respectively. In contrast, the average correlation of demand and supply shocks
between Canada and U.S. regions was 0.22 and 0.23, respectively, and between Mexico
and U.S. regions was −0.13 and −0.03, respectively. See Murray, Schembri, and St-
Amant (2003), p. 213. Beine and Coulombe (2003) examine the synchronization of
business cycles between the United States and the regions of Canada. They find that the
business cycles of Quebec and Ontario, which are Canada's manufacturing centers and
account for about two-thirds of the country's output, are highly asynchronous with the
business cycles in other Canadian regions. Moreover, the Quebec and Ontario business
cycles are well synchronized with the U.S. business cycle and have become more so
over time. They conclude that Canada does not itself form an optimum currency area.
This point has some practical significance, in light of Quebec's past flirtations with
autonomy.

Much of the Canadian debate about NAMU has focused precisely on this issue. The defenders of Canada's floating exchange rate claim that shocks to commodity prices have generally moved the terms of trade in Canada and the United States in opposite directions. Moreover, Canada's nominal exchange rate relative to the U.S. dollar has moved to cushion swings in commodity prices, appreciating when commodity prices rise and depreciating when they fall.[45] Because of this, they maintain, Canada has successfully operated with a floating exchange rate for most of the period since 1950.[46]

Proponents of a NAMU have countered that a secular depreciation of Canada's nominal exchange rate has caused a fall in the standard of living relative to the United States. Falling commodity prices followed by depreciation of the Canadian dollar have propped up commodity production, providing no incentive for this sector to shrink over time. Moreover, "lazy" Canadian manufacturers have relied on exchange-rate depreciation to boost their competitiveness and have not undertaken necessary productivity improvements.[47] Underlying these claims is the rather strong assumption that fixing Canada's nominal exchange rate to the U.S. dollar in a monetary union would bring about constancy of the bilateral real exchange rate. Interestingly, the appreciation of the Canadian dollar relative to the U.S. dollar since 2003 has quieted the calls for monetary union.

In addition, NAMU advocates have argued that the use of the U.S. dollar as a unit of account, medium of exchange, and store of value in

---

[45] See Lafrance and Schembri (2000), Laidler (1999, 2002), Murray (2003), and Thiessen (1999). Murray (2003) reports on a "Bank of Canada" equation, developed by Bank of Canada economists Robert Amano and Simon van Norden, that relates changes in the U.S.-Canada real exchange rate to the terms of trade of energy, the terms of trade of other commodities, and the differential in short-term interest rates. This equation tracks movements in the U.S.-Canada real exchange rate very well over a long time period. See Amano and van Norden (1995), and Issa, Lafrance, and Murray (2006) for a recent update.

[46] Between May 1962 and May 1970, Canada had a pegged exchange rate of the sort prescribed by the Bretton Woods System.

[47] See Courchene and Harris (1999, 2003) and Grubel (1999, 2003). The "lazy" manufacturer point is attributed to McCallum (1998) who first noted a correlation between the depreciation of the Canadian dollar and the decline in manufacturing productivity relative to the United States.

Canada has been on the rise and that this increased dollarization should be followed by a formal monetary union.[48] However, there is scant evidence of rising dollarization in the Canadian economy.[49]

Finally, we want to touch briefly on two issues raised initially in Chapter 2 because they are important for determining whether North America is or could become an optimum currency area. First, recall that Mundell emphasized labor mobility as a means of facilitating the adjustment to asymmetric shocks. It is nearly impossible to imagine circumstances under which the United States would permit unrestricted or even relatively free movement of Mexican workers across the U.S. border. Second, recall that fiscal transfers can play an important role in facilitating adjustment. Although both Canada and the United States have well-functioning domestic systems for fiscal transfers, a transnational North American system would not be politically viable and would also pose difficult challenges because of the wide difference in the three countries' per capita incomes.[50]

MONETARY INTEGRATION AND MERCOSUR

In contrast to North America, which has a successful free trade area but little political will for further integration, South America's largest regional trade area – the Common Market of the South or MERCOSUR – has been slow to liberalize but may be gaining some political momentum. The seeds of MERCOSUR were sown in the 1980s when Argentina and Brazil negotiated two bilateral agreements.[51] The Treaty of Asunción that created MERCOSUR in 1991 added two small countries, Paraguay and Uruguay, to the group. Nevertheless, MERCOSUR's objectives, the

---

[48] See Courchene and Harris (1999).

[49] See Murray (2003), who makes an important distinction between the increasing use of the U.S. dollar by Canadian firms that operate in U.S. markets and firms that operate in Canadian markets. He cautions against confusing the expected effects of globalization and diversification with dollarization. See also Laidler and Poschmann (2000) and Murray and Powell (2003).

[50] Pastor (2001) has suggested that North America establish an institution similar to the European Investment Bank (or expand the remit of the North American Development Bank) in order to facilitate Mexico's economic development.

[51] The Cooperation and Integration Act, signed in 1986, removed trade barriers in some sectors. This agreement was followed by the Integration, Cooperation, and Development Treaty of 1988, which established the principle of free trade and called for the gradual coordination of monetary, fiscal, and exchange-rate policies.

timetable for achieving those objectives, and the obstacles to realizing them have always been determined by the group's two largest members, Argentina and Brazil.

At the start of MERCOSUR, the member countries reduced bilateral tariffs substantially and agreed to a timetable for their full elimination, with the goal of creating a common market and establishing a common external tariff by 1995. At the Ouro-Preto Summit in 1994, however, the four countries agreed to retain internal tariffs on some products until 2001,[52] and allowed exceptions to the common external tariff until 2006. In addition, they established a network of regional institutions designed to oversee and facilitate the integration process.[53] Later, in 2000, the MERCOSUR members agreed to harmonize national statistics and set some common macroeconomic goals (inspired by the convergence criteria in the Maastricht Treaty); these were to be monitored by a new regional institution, the Macroeconomic Monitoring Group.

While the initial years of MERCOSUR were quite successful, a diminishing commitment to trade liberalization combined with two important events – the massive depreciation of Brazil's currency in 1999 and Argentina's financial crisis in 2001 – resulted in some major setbacks. Thus, despite early progress, trade within MERCOSUR remains burdened by trade barriers. Some products are afforded special treatment; some are exempt from the common market altogether; there are exceptions to the common external tariff; and there are in addition frequent trade tensions and disputes. Critics have described MERCOSUR as chaotic and dysfunctional, and have noted a widening gap between the group's stated agenda and its actual implementation.[54]

---

[52] The number of exempt products was large: 223 for Argentina, 29 for Brazil, 272 for Paraguay, and 1018 for Uruguay. Moreover, sugar and steel were left entirely outside of the agreement. See Levy-Yeyati and Sturzenegger (2000).

[53] These institutions are: the Common Market Council and Common Market Group that reports to it, the MERCOSUR Trade Commission, the Joint Parliamentary Commission, the Socio-Economic Consulting Forum, and the MERCOSUR Administrative Secretariat.

[54] Da Motta Veiga (2004) is particularly critical. He notes that domestic laws have not been amended to incorporate MERCOSUR's agreements, member countries have been resistant to disciplines, and compliance with rules has been modest. MERCOSUR is not rule-based like NAFTA and the EU, and it suffers from a "growing deficit in the implementation of agreed measures" (p. 5). In addition, MERCOSUR's institutions are overlapping and lacking in real authority. See also Singh et al. (2005).

In addition to its four founding members, MERCOSUR has had six associate members: Bolivia, Chile, Colombia, Ecuador, Peru, and Venezuela.[55] In mid-2006, however, Venezuela became a full member, following an unusually rapid negotiation and its abrupt withdrawal from the Andean Community prompted by objections to the bilateral trade agreements that two other Andean Community members, Colombia and Peru, had signed with the United States.[56] At ceremonies marking Venezuela's formal entry into MERCOSUR, the country's leftist president, Hugo Chávez, loaded his remarks with anti-American rhetoric. Given the political climate in South America – with populist anti-American leaders in Venezuela and Bolivia, a pragmatic leftist in Brazil, and MERCO-phile leaders in both Argentina and Uruguay – the regional trade area may be gaining solidarity.[57] Nevertheless, MERCOSUR is still years away from becoming a true customs union. According to the terms of accession, Argentina and Brazil will open their markets to Venezuela in 2010, while Paraguay and Uruguay will follow three years later. In return, Venezuela will grant free access to the exports of its MERCOSUR partners in 2012. It is not surprising, then, that Paraguay's leader, Nicanor Duarte Futos, remarked at Venezuela's signing ceremony that MERCOSUR "must develop more open commerce and not just make statements about regional integration that don't always coincide with what is practiced."[58]

Could MERCOSUR be heading toward an eventual monetary union? With the addition of Venezuela, such a monetary union would encompass about 260 million people and a combined GDP of more than $1 trillion (75 percent of South American output).[59] Although the emphasis here should be on the word "eventual," it is important to recognize that

---

[55] Bolivia and Chile became associate members in 1996, and Colombia, Ecuador, Peru, and Venezuela were added in 2003.

[56] The Andean Community, founded in 1969, now comprises Bolivia, Colombia, Ecuador, and Peru.

[57] Early in 2006, before Evo Morales nationalized Bolivia's oil and natural gas industry in which Brazil held a vital stake, Lula da Silva had invited Bolivia to become a full member of MERCOSUR.

[58] See Associated Press (2006).

[59] Brazil produces 67 percent of MERCOSUR's output, Argentina and Venezuela together produce about 30 percent, while Paraguay and Uruguay together account for less than $2\frac{1}{2}$ percent.

monetary integration was mentioned repeatedly in the late 1990s as one of MERCOSUR's longer-term goals.[60] More recently, since Néstor Kirchner's election in Argentina, there has been talk again about an eventual monetary union, whereas Celso Amorim, Brazil's foreign minister, has indicated that a single currency is among MERCOSUR's "objectives."

Does an Internal MERCOSUR Currency Make Sense?

There was a tremendous expansion of trade in the early years of MERCOSUR that reflected the effects of the regional arrangement itself as well as broader trade liberalization throughout Latin America.[61] From the mid-1980s, fifteen countries in Central and South America signed the multilateral General Agreement on Tariffs and Trade (GATT), and these countries negotiated more than 30 bilateral or regional initiatives during the 1990s.[62] From 1985 to 1997, tariff rates in Argentina, Brazil, Paraguay, and Uruguay fell from an average of more than 35 percent to 12 percent on trade with outside countries and 4 percent on trade with MERCOSUR partners.[63] As a result, the four MERCOSUR countries experienced rapid overall export and import growth, and the share of intraregional trade in total trade more than doubled, rising to nearly 20 percent.

But this analysis misses a major point. Despite the expansion of trade, MERCOSUR countries – particularly Argentina and Brazil – remain relatively closed economies.[64] The IMF has thus noted that a distinctive

---

[60] After Argentine President Carlos Menem first proposed it in 1997, a single regional currency was mentioned repeatedly by Argentine and Brazilian officials. The communiqué of the Ushuaia Summit in 1998 referred to "considering other aspects [initiatives] that could in the future facilitate the establishment of a single currency in the Southern Common Market." See Eichengreen (1998) and Giambiagi (1999).

[61] Thus, Levy-Yeyati and Sturzenegger (2000) note that MERCOSUR itself did not "bring about trade reorientation but . . . instead simply accompanied the opening process that the economies of the region experienced during this period." Belke and Gros (2002) draw a similar conclusion.

[62] See Singh et al. (2005) for additional detail.

[63] See Estevadeordal, Goto, and Saez (2000). The decline in tariffs in Argentina and Brazil dates from the first bilateral agreement in 1986, whereas the drop in tariffs in Paraguay and Uruguay dates from the Treaty of Asunción in 1991.

[64] In 2005, openness (total exports plus imports as a share of nominal GDP) was 25 percent in Brazil, 37 percent in Argentina, 41 percent in Uruguay, and 54 percent in Paraguay.

feature of Latin America, compared with other developing regions, has been the low degree of trade openness combined with highly liberalized financial markets.[65] Accordingly, the reduced transactions costs conferred by a single MERCOSUR currency are not likely to confer large efficiency gains. Furthermore, high financial openness renders the countries of South America particularly vulnerable to large and volatile external capital flows. There is no obvious anchor country within MERCOSUR, no counterpart to Germany in EMU, from which an internal monetary union could draw credibility. Thus, it is difficult to see how a regional monetary union would add substantially to credibility and thereby diminish the volatility of external capital flows.[66]

Finally, there is nothing to suggest that the MERCOSUR countries constitute an optimum currency area. For evidence we turn again to the work of Bayoumi and Eichengreen,[67] who used the methods described above to extract and quantify demand and supply shocks affecting the MERCOSUR countries. As before, we look at the extent to which the supply shocks affecting one such country are correlated with the supply shocks affecting the other MERCOSUR countries. The estimates in Table 5.4 suggest that these shocks are highly asymmetric; the MERCOSUR region appears to be an even less promising candidate for a common currency than North America.[68] And because domestic labor markets in the

---

[65] See Singh et al. (2005). The authors compute a measure of financial openness defined as the sum of external assets and liabilities deriving from foreign direct investment plus portfolio investment, divided by GDP.

[66] Levy-Yeyati and Sturzenegger (2000) point out that a major benefit of the single European currency does not exist for MERCOSUR. In Europe, the main source of speculative attack was the possibility of changes in parities among European currencies, and EMU eliminated that. In MERCOSUR, by contrast, the main source of speculative attack arises from expectations of changes in parities *vis-à-vis* external currencies.

[67] See Bayoumi and Eichengreen (1994b).

[68] Levy-Yeyati and Sturzenegger (2000) discuss other studies that arrive at similar conclusions. Supply shocks estimated from a later sample period than that used by Bayoumi and Eichengreen indicate some increase in the correlation of shocks between Argentina and Brazil, but the evidence is too weak to suggest that the MERCOSUR region forms an optimum currency area. Williamson (2003) takes a different approach. He evaluates the MERCOSUR countries according to five criteria: size, openness, trade diversification, similarity of shocks, and liability dollarization. He concludes that MERCOSUR is a reasonable candidate for monetary union, and that it would gain more from a single currency than from dollarization.

Table 5.4. *Supply shocks to MERCOSUR countries (Blanchard-Quah shock extraction)*

Country	Standard deviation	Correlations				
		Argentina	Brazil	Paraguay	Uruguay	Venezuela
Argentina	0.033	1.00				
Brazil	0.084	0.34	1.00			
Paraguay	0.094	0.06	0.22	1.00		
Uruguay	0.049	−0.48	−0.06	−0.08	1.00	
Venezuela	0.062	0.27	0.13	0.12	0.05	1.00

Source: Adapted from Tamin Bayoumi and Barry Eichengreen (1994b), "One Money or Many? Analyzing the Prospects for Monetary Unification in Various Parts of the World," *Princeton Studies in International Finance 78*. Princeton, NJ: Princeton University International Finance Section, Tables 5 and 6.

MERCOSUR countries are relatively rigid, we should not expect intraregional migration to facilitate adjustment to such highly asymmetric shocks.[69]

Would Dollarization Be Better?

When the monetary integration of the MERCOSUR countries was actively discussed in the late 1990s, dollarization was often mentioned as a possible alternative to a single regional currency. At the time, Argentina was flirting with the idea of replacing its then-successful currency-board regime with dollarization, and Congressional hearings at least hinted at the prospect for a monetary cooperation agreement with the United States. (Box 5.1 describes Argentina's proposal and the U.S. response to it.) Replacement of the national currencies of the MERCOSUR countries with the U.S. dollar would permit a tie to the world's most prominent currency and to the Fed's credible monetary policy. If all went well, then, dollarization would solve the credibility problem inherent in an autonomous regional currency. (These credibility gains were discussed at some length in Chapter 2.) At the very least, regional dollarization would

[69] For a discussion of regional labor market rigidities, see Arroyo (2002) and Levy-Yeyati and Sturzenegger (2000).

Box 5.1. **Argentina, Dollarization, and the International Monetary Stability Act**

Early in 1999, Argentine officials began discussing openly the possibility of replacing their domestic currency, the peso, with the U.S. dollar. The peso had been tied to the dollar under a currency board regime at a parity of one-to-one since 1991 as part of Argentina's Convertibility Plan. Although the currency board had generally been regarded as quite successful, financial crises in a number of emerging-market countries, along with the substantial devaluation of the Brazilian *real,* had heightened volatility in financial markets and led Argentine officials to fear that speculators could attack the currency board. Hence, the Argentine government was looking to demonstrate its commitment to the dollar peg, and dollarization seemed a logical next step.

Dollarization was regarded as the ultimate fix. Because it was presumed to be irreversible, it could enhance credibility and lock in lower interest rates. Furthermore, because there was already a high degree of *de facto* dollarization in Argentina, adopting the dollar officially did not seem to be a particularly radical move. The dollar was already used alongside the peso as a medium of exchange in everyday transactions, and the banking sector had a very high share of dollar-denominated deposits (nearly 60 percent of total deposits).

There are two problems with dollarization, however, that arise when a country undertakes the policy unilaterally. The first problem is that the country loses seigniorage income. For a country with a sovereign currency, seigniorage is the revenue that accrues to the government because it does not have to pay interest on its outstanding currency stock. Furthermore, as the public's holdings of currency rise over time, so does seigniorage. When a country dollarizes, the government exchanges its dollar reserves for U.S. currency notes. By trading in its reserves, the government forgoes its annual interest earnings on those reserves as well as any earnings that would arise from an increase in currency holdings over time. Dollarization in Argentina would have involved a loss of seigniorage on the $15 billion currency stock as well as the loss on the approximately $1 billion annual increase in currency outstanding. Andrew Berg and Eduardo Borensztein estimated the initial seigniorage costs to Argentina to be about $700 million per year (0.2 percent of GDP); over a ten-year period, as the holdings of currency rose, that cost would double.[1]

The second problem with dollarization is that a country loses its domestic lender of last resort. When a domestic central bank serves as a lender of last resort, it stands ready to provide liquidity as necessary to an illiquid banking system. But with dollarization, the domestic central bank cannot print money at will. Therefore, something else must happen. If the domestic central bank has excess dollar reserves (those that were not used when replacing the domestic currency stock), they can be used to prop up the banking system; alternatively, foreign banks operating in the country can agree to provide the central bank with lines of credit for use in emergencies. As banking crises can arise suddenly and the resources required to quell them can be extensive, the loss of the lender of last resort in a dollarizing country is a major concern.[2]

When Argentina's then central bank governor Pedro Pou announced that the country was considering dollarization in January 1999, he indicated that Argentina was in discussions with U.S. authorities about the possibility of a treaty. The U.S. Congress held hearings on several occasions to investigate the issues involved in dollarization[3] and Senator Connie Mack introduced the International Monetary Stability Act. This legislation set out conditions under which the U.S. Secretary of the Treasury would certify a dollarizing country and thereby qualify it to receive a payment in lieu of seigniorage.[4] In Senate testimony, Lawrence Summers (Deputy Secretary of the Treasury) and Alan Greenspan (Chairman of the Federal Reserve) expressed concern that treaty-based dollarization might be perceived as obligating U.S. authorities to consider the dollarizing country when setting U.S. policies and goals. Although Senator Mack's legislation explicitly stated that the Federal Reserve would have no obligation to consider economic conditions in dollarized countries or to act as a lender of last resort, there nevertheless remained a political concern that such legislation would be misinterpreted. The International Monetary Stability Act did not progress beyond the committee level.

---

[1] See Berg and Borensztein (2003).

[2] For a thorough discussion of this issue, see Berg and Borensztein (2003) and Gulde et al. (2004).

[3] The Senate Committee on Banking, Housing, and Urban Affairs held hearings in April and July of 1999 and February of 2000. See U.S. Senate (1999a, 1999b, 2000).

[4] Several schemes for the allocation of seigniorage income were discussed, but we do not review them here. See Berg and Borensztein (2003), Bogetić (2000), Michael Gavin's statement in U.S. Senate (1999b), and Schuler and Stein (2000). The latter provides an extensive discussion of the proposed legislation and its provisions.

eliminate the possibility of exchange-rate changes *vis-à-vis* the dollar and thereby narrow the risk premium attaching to domestic interest rates.[70]

MERCOSUR dollarization would also prevent recurrence of the problem that arose in 1999 when Brazil devalued the *real* by nearly 40 percent. With Argentina's peso fixed at one-to-one against the U.S. dollar, the sharp drop in the Brazilian *real* provided a boost to Brazil's competitiveness which Argentina could ill afford. Tying the MERCOSUR countries to the dollar would be problem-free, however, only if the bulk of the region's trade were conducted with the United States or denominated in dollars, and that is not the case. Although more than 20 percent of MERCOSUR's external trade is with the countries of North America, another 20 percent or more is with countries in the European Union. As the dollar's value rose against the euro in 1999 and 2000, Argentina suffered a further loss of competitiveness, this one against its European trading partners. Writing in 1998 before the *real*'s fall, the dollar's rise, and Argentina's subsequent problems, Barry Eichengreen noted:

Pegging each of the MERCOSUR currencies to a common external numeraire like the U.S. dollar is an extremely indirect way of solving the problem of intra-MERCOSUR exchange-rate variability. It forecloses not just intra-MERCOSUR exchange-rate changes as an instrument of adjustment but also, in effect, changes in the exchange rate vis-à-vis the rest of the world. This is such a Byzantine solution to MERCOSUR's exchange-rate problem that we can safely ignore it.[71]

Dollarization may seem the logical choice, however, for an economy that has already experienced a high degree of *de facto* dollarization, and this was true of Argentina in the late 1990s under its currency-board regime. Since Argentina's crisis, however, the degree of *de facto* dollarization has fallen substantially (see Table 5.5). The share of foreign-currency denominated deposits and loans in Argentina's banking system is now just slightly higher than in Brazil; in general, financial dollarization is low for the large MERCOSUR countries.

---

[70] Berg and Borensztein (2003) analyze the risk premium in developing-country interest rates, and the extent to which that risk premium can be expected to decline with dollarization. Although devaluation risk is eliminated with dollarization, sovereign (default) risk is not; yet, the possibility of exchange-rate changes may raise the sovereign risk premium and the question is, if so, by how much. They provide a model for evaluating these possibilities and some estimates for Argentina.

[71] See Eichengreen (1998), p. 24.

Table 5.5. *The extent of financial dollarization*

| | Foreign currency denominated | | | |
| | Deposits (percent of total deposits) | | Loans (percent of total loans) | |
	2001	2004	2001	2004
Argentina	71.5	10.7	80.0	14.1
Brazil	6.1	6.5	18.0	12.0
Paraguay	66.6	47.0	52.8	51.7
Uruguay	83.0	83.0	66.0	70.0
Venezuela	0.2	0.1	0.7	0.6

Source: Robert Rennback and Masahiro Nozaki (2006), "Financial Dollarization in Latin America," Working Paper 06-7. Washington, DC: International Monetary Fund.

THE FUTURE OF DOLLARIZATION

Less than a decade ago, a number of prominent economists advocated dollarization for a broad set of emerging-market countries as the best way to restore credibility and address the volatile swings in external capital flows.[72] At the time, emerging-market countries were abandoning their intermediate exchange-rate regimes and were faced with choosing between regimes at polar ends of the exchange-rate spectrum: freely floating their currencies or rigidly fixing them through dollarization.[73] Although many emerging-market countries did replace their pegged regimes with floating exchange rates,[74] there was no such rush to dollarize; only two countries, Ecuador and El Salvador, have unilaterally dollarized since 1999 and other countries are not lining up to do so.

Why, then, were so many economists enthusiastic about dollarization? It was not because many emerging-market countries were deemed to

---

[72] In this section, we use the term "dollarization" to denote the replacement of the domestic currency with a foreign legal tender whether it is the U.S. dollar, the euro, or some other currency. See, for example, Barro (1999), Calvo (1999), Hinds (2004, 2006), Schuler and Stein (2000), and Steil and Litan (2005), all of whom advocate dollarization. Edwards (2003) takes a more skeptical view.

[73] See Fischer (2001).

[74] According to the IMF, 77 developing countries maintained *de facto* managed or independently floating exchange rates as of end-2004, while only nine countries (all developing) used a foreign currency as legal tender.

meet the conditions for forming an optimum currency area with an issuer of an important international currency. Rather, proponents emphasized two primary reasons for choosing dollarization. First, as we discussed in Chapter 2, dollarization provides a way to import the credibility of the currency issuer.[75] If the domestic central bank has made a mess of monetary policy, importing credibility through dollarization can reduce interest costs significantly. Second, there was growing recognition in the late 1990s that financial dollarization was extensive[76] and posed grave potential problems. Proponents of dollarization emphasized financial conditions in the public and private sectors; they examined balance sheets, the volume of assets and liabilities denominated in foreign currency, and the size of the mismatch between those assets and liabilities.

An older literature on currency substitution had long recognized that when inflation is high, a country's residents will hold a foreign currency for transactions purposes and hold foreign-currency bank deposits where that is permissible. What was not recognized in the discussion of currency substitution was the phenomenon that gained widespread attention beginning with Mexico's tequila crisis in 1994. An emerging-market government or private firm seeking to borrow had a strong incentive to *borrow* in foreign currency in order to reduce its interest costs and attract a large number of lenders. This is known as "liability dollarization" because it shows up only on the liability side of the balance sheet, not on the asset side, where foreign-currency deposits are recorded. A mismatch between foreign-currency assets and liabilities can be particularly problematic. If the liabilities are larger than the assets – which was the case in the emerging-market crises of the 1990s – a devaluation of a pegged exchange rate will increase the mismatch even further. This is a serious problem for a government, as in the case of Mexico, but an even larger problem for the private sector, which has no recourse to policy action or to official assistance. Devaluation in the presence of sizable foreign-currency liabilities can mean bankruptcy for firms and

---

[75] See Berg and Borensztein (2003).

[76] Baliño, Bennett, and Borensztein (1999) classified eighteen countries as highly dollarized (defined as a ratio of foreign currency deposits to broad money in excess of 30 percent) and another thirty-four countries as moderately dollarized.

banks, and this is exactly what happened to them in the crisis-stricken countries.[77] Advocates of dollarization recognized that full unilateral dollarization would rectify the problem of liability dollarization by eliminating the mismatch between assets and liabilities denominated in foreign currency.

So why haven't more emerging-market countries dollarized? Because optimum currency area theory matters and most emerging-market countries – the ones plagued by volatile capital flows and frequent crises – do not form optimum currency areas with the United States or the euro zone.[78] What we observe today is some degree of partial dollarization in many developing countries combined with floating exchange rates.

Does this *de facto* dollarization decline over time if policies are better managed? Barry Eichengreen and Ricardo Hausmann asked this question several years ago.[79] As *de facto* dollarization was commonly deemed to reflect a country's history of high inflation and repeated depreciation, they concluded that many developing countries would not be able to reduce their foreign-currency exposure after adopting a floating exchange rate. Yet recent empirical findings suggest exactly the opposite.[80] Using data from the balance sheets of private nonfinancial firms in Latin American countries, three studies have found compelling evidence of a drop in foreign-currency borrowing and a decline in the currency mismatch several years after the adoption of a floating exchange-rate regime.[81]

---

[77] See Goldstein and Turner (2004) for a detailed analysis of the currency mismatch problem.

[78] Williamson (2003, p. 172), unlike other authors, includes liability dollarization among his five "criteria drawn from the optimum currency area (OCA) literature."

[79] See Eichengreen and Hausmann (1999). It is worth noting that the degree of *de facto* dollarization is often quite high in countries or regions in the midst or immediate aftermath of conflict. In Bosnia-Herzegovina and Kosovo, the euro was legalized as an official parallel currency, and the dollar was used that way in East Timor. This type of dollarization does not reflect a lack of trust in macroeconomic policies so much as it reflects the absence of political stability.

[80] See Kamil (2006), who uses data for more than two thousand firms in seven Latin American countries from 1992 to 2005. Cowan, Hansen, and Herrera (2005) and Martinez and Werner (2002) study firms in Chile and Mexico, respectively.

[81] Another study by Reinhart, Rogoff, and Savastano (2003) found little evidence that successful disinflation in seventeen countries was accompanied by a decline in dollarization. They measured dollarization using a mix of data on public- and private-sector exposure to foreign currencies on the asset and liability sides of the balance sheet.

Most of the world's fully dollarized countries are extraordinarily small (see Table 5.6). With the exception of Ecuador (which replaced its domestic currency with the U.S. dollar in 2000 amid a financial crisis), dollarized countries are very open, trade primarily with a single larger partner, and have small and relatively undeveloped domestic financial markets. In our view, these characteristics, combined with some degree of *de facto* dollarization, describe the leading candidates for *de jure* dollarization.[82]

So where are these countries and how likely are they to dollarize? There are two regions, Central America and Eastern Europe, where some if not all of the countries display the characteristics listed earlier. Two such countries in Central America have already dollarized: El Salvador adopted the dollar unilaterally in 2001 in order to reduce domestic interest rates, encourage foreign lending, and further its ongoing integration process;[83] Panama has used the dollar since 1904.[84] And the dollar is recognized legally as a parallel currency in Guatemala. These and the other Central American countries have similar characteristics. They are very small, highly open, and trade heavily with the United States.[85] Furthermore, financial dollarization is quite high in the region. According to IMF estimates for 2003, 40 percent of total financial assets were

[82] Others have emphasized the importance of these characteristics, particularly size. See, for example, Edwards (2003), Salvatore (2003), and Williamson (2003).

[83] Hinds (2004) makes two points worth noting here. First, before dollarization, El Salvador's economy was stable and inflation was low; thus, dollarization was not pursued in response to a crisis, as in the case of Ecuador. Second, El Salvador had a relatively low rate of *de facto* dollarization prior to 2001; foreign-currency deposits in the banking system never exceeded 8 percent of total deposits during the 1990s, even though dollar remittances from emigrants were extraordinarily large.

[84] Edwards (2003) provides a critical analysis of Panama's experience with dollarization. He points to Panama's high fiscal deficits, its severe banking crisis in 1988–89, and its heavy reliance on official assistance (seventeen IMF programs between 1973 and 2000) as evidence that dollarization does not automatically solve all macroeconomic problems.

[85] Average GDP in Central America is comparable to that of Luxembourg. Exports and imports of goods and services as a share of GDP averaged 92 percent in Costa Rica, 95 percent in the Dominican Republic, 47 percent in Guatemala, 84 percent in Honduras, and 74 percent in Nicaragua over the 1999–2003 period. Furthermore, exports to the United States as a share of total exports were very large over the same period: 62 percent for Costa Rica, 86 percent for the Dominican Republic, 63 percent for Guatemala, 69 percent for Honduras, and 38 percent for Nicaragua. See Kim and Papi (2005).

Table 5.6. *Countries using another sovereign currency as legal tender*[1]

Country	Population[2]	Political status	Currency used	Since
Andorra	71,000	Independent	Euro (Frenc franc and Spanish peseta since 1278)	2002
Cyprus, Northern	218,000	De facto independent	Turkish lira	1974
East Timor	1.1 million	Independent with U.N. troops	U.S. dollar	2000
Ecuador	13.5 million	Independent	U.S. dollar	2000
El Salvador	6.8 million	Independent	U.S. dollar	2001
Kiribati	105,500	Independent	Australian dollar	1943
Liberia	3 million	Independent	U.S. dollar	1847– 1982
Liechtenstein	34,000	Independent	Swiss franc	1921
Marshall Islands	60,500	Independent	U.S. dollar	1944
Micronesia	108,000	Independent	U.S. dollar	1944
Monaco	32,500	Independent	Euro (French franc since 1865)	2002
Montenegro	630,500	Independent	Euro (German mark since 1999)	2002
Nauru	13,500	Independent	Australian dollar	1914
Niue	2,000	Independent, in free association with New Zealand	New Zealand dollar	1901
Palau	20,500	Independent	U.S. dollar	1944
Panama	3.2 million	Independent	1 balboa = 1 US $; uses dollar notes	1904
San Marino	29,500	Independent	Euro (Italian lira since 1897)	2002
Tuvalu	12,000	Independent	Australian dollar	1892
Vatican City	1,000	Independent	Euro (Italian lira since 1929)	2002

[1] Omits dollarized economies that are not independent: commonwealths (Northern Mariana Islands, Puerto Rico), self-governing regions (Cook Islands), territories (American Samoa, British Virgin Islands, Channel Islands, Cocos (Keeling) Islands, Greenland, Guam, Norfolk Island, Pitcairn Island, Saint Helena, Tokelau, Turks and Caicos Islands, U.S. Virgin Islands), and regions under U.N. administration (Kosovo).

[2] In thousands unless otherwise noted.

Sources: Adapted from Željko Bogetić (2000), "Official Dollarization: Current Experiences and Issues, *Cato Journal, 20:2*, pp. 179–213, Tables 1 and 2, and Eduardo Levy-Yeyati and Federico Sturzenegger (2002), "Dollarization: A Primer," in E. Levy-Yeyati and F. Sturzenegger, eds., *Dollarization.* Cambridge, MA: MIT Press, pp. 1–52, Table 1.1. Updated using *CIA Factbook* (2006), *EIU Country Reports*, and http://www.worldatlas.com.

denominated in dollars.[86] Finally, a free trade agreement signed with the United States in 2005 should provide a further boost to trade and integration.[87] A recent study of the region applying the theory of optimum currency areas suggests that the countries of Central America are less suited for a common currency than were the EMU countries in the 1970s.[88] In our view, however, the Central American region is quite ripe for further *de jure* dollarization, although that may take several more years.

Finally, there is another region, Eastern Europe, where some of the smaller countries appear to be prime candidates for the unilateral adoption of a foreign currency, in their case, the euro. We will not explore this possibility, however, because, as we have noted, the European Commission and ECB have ruled out use of the euro as legal tender in any way other than membership in EMU, and this precludes euroization for any country that aspires to membership in that monetary union.[89]

---

[86] The figure rises to 55 percent when El Salvador and Panama are included. See Morales and Schipke (2005), who report that dollarization for transaction purposes is somewhat lower, "but in some countries certain contracts (such as mortgages, rents, and suppliers' contracts) are predominantly in U.S. dollars" (p. 101).

[87] The Central America-Dominican Republic-United States Free Trade Agreement (CAFTA-DR) has seven signatories: Costa Rica, the Dominican Republic, El Salvador, Guatemala, Honduras, Nicaragua, and the United States, and has been ratified by all but Costa Rica.

[88] See Kim and Papi (2005), who construct an optimum currency index by estimating the relationship between bilateral exchange-rate variability with the anchor country (the United States in the case of Central America) and several other variables. They conclude that, although Central America's suitability for dollarization has increased, it still remains low relative to that of the EMU countries. Interestingly, some Central American countries had index levels comparable to those of Greece, Ireland, Portugal, and Spain in the 1980s and 1990s.

[89] For a discussion of the issues involved, see Kenen and Meade (2004).

6

Monetary Integration in East Asia?

INTRODUCTION

Some of the country groups examined in previous chapters are more homogeneous than East Asia. That is certainly true of the EU. East Asia, indeed, is hugely heterogeneous, economically and politically. Peace prevails within the ten-country ASEAN group,[1] and ASEAN itself has helped to resolve dangerous disputes between some of its members. Yet some of its members have experienced political turmoil, whereas Myanmar, Cambodia, Laos, and Vietnam fall far short of being democracies, and others, such as Indonesia, the Philippines, and Thailand, are struggling to contain ethnic tensions. Beyond ASEAN itself, moreover, tensions abound. There is the chronic threat of conflict in the Taiwan Straits, and there is still the smoldering legacy of past Japanese aggression against China and Korea – a legacy inflamed periodically by unresolved territorial claims. To the south, Australia and New Zealand have not decided wholeheartedly whether they belong to East Asia or to a larger Pacific community symbolized by the Asia Pacific Economic Cooperation (APEC) forum – a body so loosely organized that the last word of its name is not even capitalized.

And then there is Japan, the only Asian member of the G-7. It has the largest East Asian economy, accounting for more than half of East Asia's GDP, even on the broadest definition of the region. Its economic

---

[1] ASEAN was founded in 1967 and had five members initially (Indonesia, Malaysia, the Philippines, Singapore, and Thailand); it now has five more members (Brunei-Darussalam, Myanmar, Cambodia, Laos, and Vietnam).

preeminence, however, is threatened by its own demographic dynamics; its population will shrink sharply in the next few decades. And its preeminence is also threatened by China's rapid growth – the growth of trade even more than the growth of output.

Consider, finally, the differences among East Asian polities. Myanmar and China, although totally different, are both autocratic – the one run by generals, the other by the self-perpetuating leadership of the Communist Party. Yet some of the region's other countries are democracies, where elections are contested freely and fairly, including, of course, Japan and South Korea, and others are now moving in the same direction.

These and other differences among the East Asian countries – differences in economic size as well as differences in domestic governance – are apt to limit the extent of monetary integration. It is hard to believe that the Chinese leadership will move soon to grant operational independence to the People's Bank of China, let alone delegate the making of monetary policy to an Asian version of the ECB. And there are no Asian institutions similar in form or function to those of the EU – those needed to produce the legislation required to integrate financial markets and set common standards for the supervision of financial institutions. It would be very difficult, moreover, to devise an acceptable distribution of seats on the governing body of an Asian counterpart to the ECB. The forthcoming enlargement of EMU has posed problems for the future governance of the ECB, and the solution devised by the ECB has itself been criticized.[2] It would be far harder for the East Asian countries to set up a governing board that gave appropriate voice and vote to the largest countries – China, Japan, Korea, and Indonesia – while likewise recognizing the key role of Singapore as a financial center.

There may, in the end, be an Asian monetary union, but it is unlikely to span the whole region. China and Japan are likely to keep their own national currencies, whereas the ASEAN countries or a subset of its members could form a monetary union of their own. Yet there are some other ways in which East Asian countries might undertake monetary cooperation, and this chapter will examine them closely, along with the longer-term prospects for a monetary union encompassing some or all of the East Asian countries.

---

[2] See, e.g., Meade (2003).

Why Asia Is Different and Why That Matters

Although East Asia is heterogeneous in many respects, intraregional trade has grown rapidly, especially trade between China and Japan, on the one hand, and the middle-income ASEAN countries, on the other. Trade started to grow rapidly in the early 1990s, when Japanese firms began to promote an intraregional division of labor within their own companies by setting up affiliates in low-cost countries to supply them with parts and components and to export to third markets, such as the United States. Here is how Peter Katzenstein describes the result:

Japan's growing economic enmeshment in northeast and Southeast Asia helped create an integrated Asian regional economy. It also reinforced a triangular trade structure in which Japanese exports and investments resulted in a rapid expansion of exports to Western markets, primarily the United States. Backed by a surge in foreign investment, trade, and the largest aid disbursements in the region, the Japanese government also sought to influence business and government abroad by exporting, with minor modifications and more or less successfully, its prized system of administrative guidance.[3]

But China also has contributed strongly to East Asian integration. There was, first, the unifying influence of the Chinese diaspora and its family-owned firms, which have played a major role in the growth and integration of the Southeast Asian countries. There was, next, the remarkably rapid growth and transformation of China's own economy, a process that may soon make China the world's largest exporter.[4]

Even in its trade dimension, however, East Asian integration is different from European integration, and the difference is stressed strongly in the growing literature contrasting the two regions.[5] European integration was fostered strongly by the region's governments and accompanied by the creation of strong supranational institutions. By contrast, Asian integration has been in large measure a market-led process. There is, indeed, an "institutional deficit" in East Asia. Although there are many regional entities that aim at promoting economic, financial, and

---

[3] Katzenstein (2005), p. 63.
[4] See OECD (2005).
[5] See, e.g., Hamilton-Hart (2000) and Katzenstein (2005); also Padoa-Schioppa (2004b) and Wyplosz (2001, 2004), who focus on differences especially relevant to monetary integration.

monetary cooperation, they do not have the prominence or powers of the EU institutions.

There are, of course, many trade agreements within Asia, such as the ASEAN Free Trade Agreement, which aims at dismantling barriers to intra-ASEAN trade, and the number of agreements is growing rapidly as China and Japan become involved. In 2002, for instance, China entered into a framework agreement with ASEAN, which includes an "early harvest" of reductions in trade barriers. In 2003, moreover, Japan entered into an agreement with ASEAN looking to the creation of a free trade area, and Japan is also forging a network of bilateral agreements with individual ASEAN countries.[6] All of these free trade agreements, however, including the ASEAN agreement itself, contain exemptions and exclusions, and they also require the use of "rules of origin," because each participating country retains its own national tariffs on imports from the outside world. Furthermore, the trade policies of the ASEAN countries are not monitored by a body comparable to the European Commission, which monitors the policies of the EU countries.

Most Asian economists and officials writing on monetary cooperation are fully aware of the institutional deficit in Asia. Nevertheless, they rarely stress its implications for the feasibility of a full-fledged monetary union. They focus on the various economic benefits of having a single currency, but they rarely tell their readers that you can't have a single currency without having a single central bank to issue and then manage it.[7]

The Antecedents of Monetary Cooperation

Monetary cooperation in East Asia began paradoxically, with a unilateral decision by Japan. At the start of the 1990s, the Japanese government

---

[6] For an overview of trade liberalization in Asia, see, e.g., Lincoln (2004); also the inventory of free-trade agreements in Sakakibara and Yamakawa (2003).

[7] Although Ito and Park (2004) are well aware of the institutional deficit, they make no mention whatsoever of the need for a single central bank, whereas Kuroda (2004) concludes his description of the path to monetary union by saying that a move to a single currency would force the national central banks to give up making independent monetary policies and subject them to a "single central authority" but does not say anything more about it.

decided to promote the international use the yen,[8] a task soon taken up by others, notably Chi Hung Kwan, who proposed the formation of a yen bloc in Asia.[9]

The advent of monetary union in Europe at the start of 1999 also attracted attention in Asia, not only from academics, many of whose writings are cited here, but in the Asian business community as well.[10] In 1998, moreover, the ASEAN governments agreed to study the feasibility of a common currency system,[11] and the Asia-Europe Meeting of finance ministers organized a very ambitious study, the Kobe Research Project, on the feasibility and merits of an Asian monetary union.[12]

It is widely agreed, however, that the Asian financial crisis was the main driver of monetary cooperation. That crisis began in the summer of 1997, when Thailand suffered a massive capital outflow, exhausted its foreign-currency reserves, and had to abandon the baht's peg to the dollar, allowing the baht to depreciate hugely. The crisis spread rapidly to other ASEAN countries, most notably Indonesia, and was then deflected northward to Hong Kong and Korea when Taiwan devalued its currency in a preemptive move to ward off the effects of the crisis.[13]

---

[8] On subsequent Japanese efforts to promote the international use of the yen, see Castellano (2000) and de Brouwer (2002). On the actual role of the yen in East Asian currency trading see Ho, Ma, and McCauley (2005), who show that several Asian currencies, including the Korean won, the Taiwan dollar, and some of the ASEAN currencies show much sensitivity to movements in the yen.

[9] See Kwan (2001), p. xiv, where he explains that his proposal was inspired by the shift in Japanese policy, although he is content to propose that other Asian countries, such as Korea and Taiwan, adopt basket pegs heavily weighted with yen. He gives two reasons for that proposal: achieving greater exchange-rate stability within East Asia and constraining the policy autonomy of the United States. In the longer run, he argues, the yen could become the common currency of East Asia, with the Bank of Japan setting monetary policy for the whole region (pp. 167–70). Other Japanese economists have likewise proposed basket pegs heavily weighted with yen – more heavily than those proposed by most other advocates of basket pegs. Yet Barro (2004), who finds strong empirical evidence of well-defined dollar and euro areas, finds no such evidence of a yen area.

[10] A 2002 poll of corporate executives found that 43 percent of the respondents favored eventual monetary union; Lincoln (2004), p. 325.

[11] See Bird and Rajan (2002), p. 27.

[12] See the overview by the Regional Economic Monitoring Unit (REMU) of the Asian Development Bank (ADB 2002a).

[13] For an account of the crisis, see, e.g., Kenen (2001), pp. 26–43, and the sources cited there.

Asian governments drew numerous lessons from the nature and virulence of the crisis and from the ways in which the international community responded to it. There was dissatisfaction with the size and speed of the response by the International Monetary Fund and with the failure of the United States to offer financial support comparable to the support it had offered Mexico in 1995, when that country suffered a grave crisis of its own. The United States declined to participate in multilateral financing for Thailand, an effort organized by Japan, and when it agreed thereafter to furnish financing for Korea, it restricted the use of its money to serve as a "second line of defense" rather than making it available up front to replenish Korea's dwindling reserves.[14]

Asian dissatisfaction with the IMF focused largely on the number and nature of the policy conditions attached to IMF financing during the Asian crisis, and some Asian critics of the IMF believe that it was acting at the behest of the United States, which they accused of seeking to supplant an indigenous Asian model of economic development with an Anglo-American model.[15] Yet Asians are not alone in criticizing the nature and large number of the policy conditions imposed by the IMF, especially those that called for structural reforms that were of dubious relevance to the resolution of the Asian crisis. The Fund's own Independent Evaluation Office did that too. The reforms required in the Indonesian case were, it said, aimed at restoring confidence by committing

---

[14] The failure of the United States to provide funding for Thailand is often ascribed to the so-called D'Amato Amendment – legislation adopted after the Mexican crisis limiting the freedom of the U.S. Treasury to use the Exchange Stabilization Fund (ESF) as it had in the Mexican case. Yet Robert Rubin, the Treasury Secretary at the time, while citing the D'Amato Amendment and concerns about a possible tightening of Congressional restrictions on the future use of the ESF, gives other reasons for deciding against U.S. financing for Thailand; see Rubin and Weisberg (2003), pp. 218–20. On Asian criticism of the U.S. role in the Korean crisis, see Nemoto (2003); on the common assertion that the United States has provided or endorsed ample financing for countries of special importance to Washington but not for the Asian countries, see, e.g., Chang and Rajan (2001). It should be noted, however, that the United States took a leading role in the successful effort to induce foreign banks to roll over their maturing claims on Korean banks.

[15] Chang and Rajan (2001) suggest that this view influenced Japanese policy, including Tokyo's decision to furnish large-scale financing to Thailand and other Asian countries caught up in the crisis (the so-called New Miyazawa Initiative). It also explains Japan's decision, discussed later, to propose the creation of an Asian Monetary Fund.

the government of President Suharto to a "radical change in its way of doing business," but they fell short of that objective. And the list of reforms required in the Korean case "was broader than seemed necessary, covering not only financial sector reforms but also trade liberalization, corporate governance, and labor market reform."[16]

Having taken the lead in mobilizing financial support for Thailand, the Japanese government went further. In September 1997, even before the IMF had called for far-reaching structural reforms in Indonesia and Korea, Tokyo proposed the creation of an Asian Monetary Fund (AMF). The proposal, however, was strongly opposed by the United States and the IMF, failed to win Chinese support, and died very quickly.[17]

The Chiang Mai Initiative

Two years, later, however, China adopted a "proactive stance" toward regional monetary cooperation.[18] It began to involve itself in efforts to develop regional debt and capital markets, and it suggested what was to become the first annual meeting of the finance ministers of the ASEAN+3 countries.[19] The meeting took place in 2000, at Chiang Mai in Thailand, where the finance ministers agreed to exchange data on capital flows, a step toward the development of an early warning system as a safeguard against future crises, and Japan proposed the development of the bilateral credit arrangements now known as the Chiang Mai Initiative (CMI). Hugh Patrick describes the meeting as the "start of meaningful East Asian regional cooperation."[20]

---

[16] IEO (2003), p. 42.

[17] Amyx (2005) suggests that China was reluctant to antagonize the United States while China was seeking accession to the World Trade Organization; she also suggests that the Japanese blundered diplomatically by using the Hong Kong Monetary Authority to elicit Chinese support; only later did they seek support directly from the People's Bank of China. Eichengreen (2001b, 2002) and Keijzer (2001) suggest that China also feared Japanese dominance of an AMF – as did the United States, which also feared that competition between the AMF and IMF would degrade the quality of conditionality.

[18] Amyx (2005), p. 2.

[19] They had met in Manila in 1999 at the invitation of the ASEAN countries, where they declared that monetary and financial cooperation had become "priority areas of shared interest and concern" and thus agreed to a Chinese suggestion that they hold regular meetings thereafter; see Nemoto (2003).

[20] Patrick (2005), p. 18.

Earlier, in 1977, the ASEAN countries had agreed to create a network of short-term bilateral swap agreements under which each ASEAN country could obtain U.S. dollars in exchange for its own national currency. A swap could last for no more than three months but could be renewed for three more months.[21] As the amounts involved were small, however, the swaps were rarely activated and were not used at all during the Asian crisis.

At Chiang Mai, China, Japan, and Korea agreed in principle to negotiate bilateral swap agreements with each ASEAN country, as well as bilateral agreements between themselves. Most of the agreements put in place thereafter were patterned after the earlier ASEAN swap agreements; a country seeking financial support uses its national currency to buy U.S. dollars. The agreement between China and Japan, by contrast, allows China to purchase yen with renminbi and Japan to purchase renminbi with yen.[22]

These agreements involve much larger amounts of money than the earlier ASEAN agreements; some of those signed by Japan allow bilateral dollar purchases as large as $3 billion. But they contain two provisions that may limit the amount of financing actually available. First, a potential provider of financing can opt out at its discretion. Second, a country cannot draw more than 10 percent of the total amount potentially available unless it has reached or is close to reaching an IMF agreement. This provision served to allay the concerns produced by the earlier Japanese proposal for an Asian Monetary Fund – that it could impair the ability of the IMF to influence the national policies of the Asian countries.[23] Furthermore,

---

[21] For details, see Henning (2002), pp. 14–15. Shortly after the Chiang Mai agreement, the ASEAN swaps were enlarged, raising the overall size of the ASEAN swap network to $1 billion. Furthermore, the duration of a drawing was raised from three to six months, as was the duration of the renewal period.

[22] The agreements involving Korea also permit two-way swaps; Korea can buy dollars from others, and they can buy dollars from Korea; see Henning (2002), p. 18.

[23] Henning (2004, p. 3) attaches particular importance to this provision. It shows, he says, that the CMI was not merely a manifestation of Asian objections to IMF policies during the Asian crisis; it was instead a response to the view then prevalent in the U.S. Congress that the IMF should not provide large-scale financing in the event of future crises.

it allowed the participants to adhere to a basic ASEAN tenet – noninterference in the internal affairs of other ASEAN countries.[24]

Although no country has yet sought to draw on the bilateral swap agreements, the participating governments have already decided to make several changes in the existing regime. At the Istanbul meeting of the Asian Development Bank (ADB) in 2005, they agreed on four objectives: (1) integrating economic surveillance into the CMI with the aim of developing effective regional surveillance capabilities complementary to those of the IMF; (2) clarifying the activation process and devising a collective decision-making mechanism as a first step toward multilateralization; (3) increasing the sizes of the bilateral swap agreements; and (4) raising from 10 to 20 percent the amount that a country can draw without having an IMF program.[25]

Others have gone further than the finance ministers, proposing the conversion of the CMI into a genuine reserve pool or a full-fledged AMF, although the advocates of the latter are fully aware of the problems that an AMF would face in conducting intrusive surveillance, let alone imposing policy conditions analogous to those imposed by the IMF.[26]

There have been other efforts to foster cooperation in Asia, and some have already borne fruit. The Executives' Meeting of East Asia and Pacific Central Banks (EMEAP) has sponsored the creation of two bond funds. The first, created in 2003, was a $1 billion fund to be used for buying dollar-denominated bonds issued by Asian governments. The second,

---

[24] Nemoto (2003, p. 23) emphasizes this particular feature; it was not meant mainly to avoid conflict with the IMF but rather to protect potential creditors from the need to design and impose onerous policy conditions of their own.

[25] *Joint Ministerial Statement of the 8th ASEAN+3 Finance Ministers' Meeting* (May 4 2005).

[26] On the case for reserve pooling, see Rajan and Siregar (2004). On the case for a full-fledged AMF, see, e.g., Bergsten and Park (2002), who suggest that an AMF could provide financial support for a common currency (by which they really seem to mean a common currency *basket* of the sort discussed later in this chapter). See also Bird and Rajan (2002), Montiel (2004, p. 24), and especially de Brouwer (2004a); he discusses the idea at length and appears to endorse it as a way to compensate partially for the underrepresentation of Asia in the IMF. In 1999, moreover, before the advent of the CMI, the ADB also had urged the creation of an AMF, because it could serve as a complement to the IMF in providing funds to crisis-stricken countries and could develop an early warning system to ward off future crises; see Chang and Rajan (2001), p. 12.

created in 2004, established a set of bond funds to invest and trade in local-currency bonds (a Pan-Asian Bond Index Fund and eight single-country index funds). Both initiatives were meant in part as learning exercises, aimed at detecting and removing obstacles to the integration of Asia's bond markets.[27]

Although the two bond funds may make only a modest contribution, in and of themselves, they are part of a more ambitious effort to strengthen financial markets and financial systems in the East Asian countries, and Barry Eichengreen argues strongly that this task is more urgent and apt to be more fruitful than any effort to promote monetary integration.[28] He is surely right about the need for reform and development of the financial sector, and he may be equally right to question the likelihood and benefits of monetary integration. Yet others have been less skeptical and have therefore devoted much attention to monetary integration and to the various forms it might take.

Squaring an Obdurate Circle

Before assessing the benefits and costs of monetary integration, we need first to confront a difficult problem: squaring the reluctance of Asian governments to criticize each other – the principle of nonintervention – with the need for intensive surveillance of national policies when countries

---

[27] On the creation of the bond funds and the lessons learned, see Ma and Remolona (2005). For a skeptical assessment, see Eichengreen and Luengnaruemitchai (2004), who find that Asian bond markets are not abnormally small, given the sizes of the Asian economies and some of their other characteristics; see also Eichengreen and Park (2005), who ascribe the faster integration of European bond markets to the earlier abolition of capital controls. On the possible merits of using an Asian Currency Unit (ACU), analogous to the ECU, to promote bond-market integration; see Plummer and Click (2005) and Eichengreen (2006). The ADB has since undertaken to construct an ACU, but not for the purpose of integrating Asian bond markets, nor for the more ambitious purpose of fostering monetary integration. It is meant to be used as a benchmark for monitoring movements in Asian exchange rates as part of the surveillance process conducted by the ADB's Office of Regional Economic Integration (the successor to REMU). The task of constructing an ACU, however, has proved harder than expected, because of disagreements about the currency composition of the ACU and the weights to be assigned to the constituent currencies; *Financial Times*, March 27, 2006.

[28] See Eichengreen (2001b, 2002), where he proposes the creation of an Asian Financial Institute to foster and oversee financial-sector reform in Asia.

adopt a single currency or undertake looser forms of cooperation in monetary matters.[29]

The need for some sort of surveillance was recognized speedily during the Asian crisis, and it focused at first on the need to devise an early warning system to forestall future crises and, failing that, to limit the sort of cross-country contagion that occurred in the wake of the Thai crisis.

The earliest effort began in 1997, during the crisis itself, when APEC sponsored the creation of the Manila Framework Group (MFG). Its membership, however, was too broad to foster candid dialogue among East Asian governments; it included only the larger East Asian countries but also Australia, Canada, New Zealand, the United States, and the main multilateral institutions. In fact, some Asians viewed the MFG as a foreign body – an agent of the IMF and U.S. government that they would use to foster reform in Asia, when what Asia truly needed was a forum in which the Asian countries could grapple with intraregional issues.[30]

In 1998, the ASEAN governments responded to this need by organizing their own surveillance process with technical assistance from the ADB.[31] The process begins with the preparation of a confidential staff report, which is then reviewed and finalized by a meeting of senior officials from the finance ministries and central banks of the ASEAN countries. It is then discussed at a finance ministers' meeting meant to be a forum for peer review, and it finds its final expression in an agreed ministerial statement. In 2000, moreover, China, Japan, and Korea began to participate in a similar process now known as the ASEAN+3 Economic Policy Review and Dialogue Process.

The ASEAN and ASEAN+3 processes differ substantially from the sort of surveillance conducted by the IMF. Like all such processes, they begin

---

[29] The principle of nonintervention in other countries' affairs is not unique to ASEAN. It permeates relations among all Asian countries. See Girardin (2004), who suggests that the principle is grounded in "Asian values." Citing Kahler (2000), he argues that Asians are less concerned with demonstrating right and wrong than with avoiding conflict, and he concludes that Asian surveillance cannot be effective unless it is based on national ownership of the resulting recommendations. Manzano (2000) makes the same point.

[30] See de Brouwer (2004b), p. 46.

[31] The description that follows draws heavily on Girardin (2004) and on Wang and Woo (2004).

with staff work. In the case of the IMF, however, a staff mission is sent annually to each member country. Furthermore, the Fund encourages the publication of the voluminous report prepared by the staff mission, and a large number of IMF members now consent to publication of the staff report on their own economy.[32] At the end of the process, moreover, the IMF issues a Public Information Notice summarizing the views of the Fund's Executive Board about the findings and recommendations in the staff report. There is no attempt, however, to obtain agreement between the staff and the government concerned regarding those recommendations, whereas the ASEAN+3 process ends with the publication of an agreed communiqué.

Here is a recent critique of the ASEAN+3 process:[33] First, it needs to specify precisely the sorts of information each and every government is required to provide, rather than giving the governments wide discretion; absent such standardization, it is hard to draw comparisons between countries' situations. Second, the ASEAN process cannot provide an early warning of potential risks, because the discussion at the ASEAN+3 meetings tends to focus mainly on recent developments and only on the information each country chooses to provide. The substance of the policy recommendations and their subsequent implementation remain to be developed.

Clearly, more must be done for regional surveillance to have any appreciable impact on the policy-making processes of the East Asian governments. The present approach, even if based on standardized data and aimed explicitly at drawing attention to potential problems, would still be inadequate. A draft prepared by staff in the expectation that it will be vetted by deputy ministers and then passed on to ministers, seems doomed to yield an anodyne document, and a reading of the ministers' recent statements strongly supports that supposition. No such document

---

[32] At an early stage in East Asian surveillance, these IMF staff reports were used extensively as the most readily available source of information on recent economic developments in the Asian countries, because they were available to the Asian governments, even those that were not published; see ADB (2002b).

[33] This is a summary of the critique offered by Wang and Woo (2004), p. 444. That critique, taken together with the comments made in the next paragraph, call into question Amyx's assertion that the ASEAN+3 has "an institutionalized program of policy dialogue and information exchange that surpasses in frequency and depth that found in any other forum" (Amyx, 2005, p. 2).

can be expected to name and shame, not even to generate a polite discussion about incipient risks.

It is probably unrealistic to envision the early adoption of a more confrontational approach, in which the finance ministers would offer candid criticism of their colleagues' policies. There is, however, another *modus operandi*, akin to the one adopted by the OECD. There, each government confronts the analysis and recommendations of the staff and has to respond to them. There is thus "peer pressure" whenever a member's own forecasts or policies are criticized by the staff and other governments echo the staff's view. Yet governments are not obliged to quarrel with each other, although they can still quarrel with a government's objections to the staff's recommendations.[34] And though the final version of the staff's analysis takes note of the government's objections, there is no attempt to negotiate a communiqué papering over disagreements. A comparable process is employed by the Council of Ministers of the European Union, where the analyses and recommendations of the European Commission provide the focus for debate.

If and when some of the Asian countries cooperate more closely in matters involving exchange-rate management and the associated national policies, let alone a full-fledged monetary union, they must adopt a more intrusive process. They must come to distinguish between constructive criticism, aimed at improving the functioning of their exchange-rate arrangements, and breaching the Asian tradition of nonintervention in their neighbors' internal affairs. An exchange rate is, by definition, a shared variable. It is not the property of a single government. And the same can be said about the exchange rates that link Asian currencies to outsiders' currencies. The renminbi-dollar rate is not Chinese property; it is "owned" jointly by Beijing and Washington.

Some Asian economists go even further. It is essential, they say, that the policy recommendations agreed by the Asian governments should be made public, so that market pressure will reinforce peer pressure. Furthermore, governments failing to implement the recommendations to which they have themselves agreed should be barred from access to short-term financing of the sort available *via* the CMI.[35]

---

[34] We owe this analogy to Grenville (2004); see also Wang (2002, 2004).
[35] Wang and Woo (2004), p. 453.

The Evolution of Exchange-Rate Arrangements in Asia

Let's recall the range of exchange-rate arrangements prevailing in East Asia before the Asian crisis of the late 1990s. At one extreme, Japan had a floating exchange rate, although it engaged in substantial intervention to influence the path and rate of change of the yen-dollar rate. At the other extreme, China had a rigidly fixed exchange rate *vis-à-vis* the U.S. dollar, whereas Hong Kong and Brunei had even stricter currency-board regimes, based on the U.S. dollar and Singapore dollar, respectively. As for the other ASEAN countries and Korea, most of them described themselves officially as having flexible exchange rates, although numerous studies have shown that most of them pegged their currencies more or less firmly to the U.S. dollar, partaking of what Ronald McKinnon described as the Asian dollar standard.[36] (Singapore's regime was and remains exceptional, and it is described later in this chapter.)

During and after the Asian crisis, however, most of the ASEAN countries began to do what they had claimed to do before – letting their exchange rates fluctuate more freely. Malaysia was the clear exception, as it switched to a strict dollar peg backed by the imposition of new capital controls. In July 2005, however, Malaysia loosened its tie to the U.S. dollar on the same day that China revalued the renminbi by 2.1 percent *vis-à-vis* the dollar and announced that its exchange-rate policy would henceforth be guided by the behavior of a multicurrency basket.[37]

The move to more flexible exchange rates in Asia was roundly condemned by McKinnon, who continues to call for resurrection of the Asian dollar standard. The widespread use of the dollar for pricing tradable goods, he argues, allows a country that pegs to the dollar to "import" price stability. He now concedes, however, that the Asian dollar standard cannot survive unless Tokyo and Washington agree to stabilize the

---

[36] See McKinnon (1998). On the very large weights they attached to the dollar when managing their currencies, see McKinnon (2000a, 2000b), (2004), and (2005); also Frankel and Wei (1994) and Kawai and Akiyama (2000).

[37] One month later, the Governor of the People's Bank of China said that the basket would include the dollar, euro, yen, Korean won, and several other currencies, including those of Australia, Britain, Canada, Malaysia, Russia, Singapore, and Thailand, all of which figure importantly in China's foreign trade; but he did not disclose the weights attaching to each currency; *Asia Times*, August 12, 2005.

yen-dollar rate. That rate, he says, was the "loose cannon" that under-mined the dollar standard and was in part responsible for the Asian crisis. As Tokyo and Washington are hardly likely to take his advice, his case for the Asian dollar standard is gravely weakened, along with the case for any other single-currency peg.[38] What, then, are the options available to the East Asian countries? Consider first two single-country options, then two multicountry options.

Two Single-Country Options

There is still a strong aversion to exchange-rate flexibility in East Asia, but not for the reason most often adduced, that uncertainty depresses trade. There is by now some evidence supporting that assertion but, as noted in Chapter 2, the adverse effects on trade appear to be quite small.[39] The aversion derives instead from Asia's long-standing reliance on export promotion as a way to foster economic development. It is, in effect, an aversion to real appreciation, not to exchange-rate flexibility *per se*. That aversion, moreover, was reinforced by the Asian crisis, when some Asian countries lost out to others in their major export markets, not only Asian markets but other markets, too, when their competitors' currencies depreciated sharply. A depreciation of the Thai baht or Indonesian rupiah was, in effect, an appreciation of the Malaysian ringgit and Korean won, even if there was no change in their U.S. dollar values.

---

[38] We do not mean to imply that currency boards are inappropriate for Hong Kong or Brunei, although it is worth considering other options. There has been some discussion of a "Greater China" monetary union involving the Chinese mainland, Hong Kong, Macau and, politics permitting, Taiwan as well. It cannot be formed, however, until the reminbi has become fully convertible; see, e.g., Cheung and Yuen (2005) and Genberg et al. (2005), p. 58. Brunei could replace its strict link to the Singapore dollar by linking itself to a single ASEAN currency, if and when that currency is introduced; alternatively, it could become a full member of a future ASEAN monetary union, one of the options discussed later in this chapter.

[39] See Frankel and Wei (1994) and the papers cited by Kawai and Takagi (2005), and Rajan (2002); see also the suggestion by Eichengreen (2001b, p. 12) that exchange-rate fluctuations may discourage foreign direct investment by vertically integrated firms. It must be noted, however, that the same uncertainty about future exchange rates that inhibits trade and direct investment also helps to inhibit unhedged foreign-currency borrowing by a country's banks and firms, and that sort of borrowing was one of the proximate causes of the Thai crisis and of the grave damage suffered by Indonesian firms when the crisis spread and the rupiah depreciated significantly.

Some say that East Asia has outgrown the need for export-oriented growth. Barry Eichengreen concedes that it played a major role in Asian development strategies during the second half of the twentieth century, but he argues that it will not be essential to their development strategies in the current century.[40] Elsewhere, moreover, he draws attention to the efforts of some Asian countries to stimulate consumption, although he concedes that "the traditional model may have some way to run," especially in China and other lower-income countries.[41] Even in China, however, there is awareness of the need to stimulate consumption, rather than rely for growth on exports and investment. Yet other economists in Asia and elsewhere, including Takatoshi Ito and John Williamson,[42] still favor exchange-rate regimes aimed at achieving stable exchange rates, although there are very few advocates of strict single-currency pegs.[43]

A FLOATING EXCHANGE RATE COMBINED
WITH INFLATION TARGETING

Those who believe that Asia has outgrown the need to manage exchange rates intensively recommend that Asian countries move to floating exchange rates. They do not say that governments should forgo *any* intervention in foreign-exchange markets to limit the size or speed of exchange-rate movements. Barry Eichengreen makes that very clear: "Leaning against the wind in foreign exchange-markets is integral to the operation of inflation targeting in open economies,"[44] and it does not

---

[40] Eichengreen (2001b), p. 5.

[41] Eichengreen (2002), p. 30.

[42] See Ito (2002) and Williamson (1999, 2001); also Dornbusch and Park (1999), Ito and Park (2004), and Kuroda (2004); some of these authors go further, proposing the adoption of a common basket to reinforce intraregional exchange-rate stability. That option is examined later in this chapter.

[43] McKinnon, cited earlier, and Robert Mundell are the leading advocates, although Mundell approaches the issue obliquely. He begins by proposing that Asian countries peg their national currencies to a common currency unit defined by a basket containing the dollar, euro, and yen, but he then adduces reasons for dropping the euro and yen, which leaves him with a dollar peg; see Mundell (2002, 2003). On the several merits of the dollar peg in the pre-crisis era, see Kawai (2004), who argues that it lost its luster when the yen depreciated in the mid-1990s.

[44] Eichengreen (2002), p. 33.

imply benign neglect of the exchange rate. It merely means that monetary policy should cease to be driven by a rigid reaction function linking
exchange rates and interest rates or by some target value for a country's
currency.[45]

In the previous chapter, we set out the case for combining a flexible
exchange rate with inflation targeting, and there is no need to repeat
what we said there, but two points deserve emphasis. First, inflation targeting is a forward-looking strategy; it involves the use of interest-rate
changes to hold the future inflation rate within a band deemed to be
consistent with price stability over the medium term. For this reason,
of course, a central bank adopting this strategy must make forecasts of
future inflation. By publishing those forecasts, moreover, a central bank
can convey information about the outlook for inflation and, more important, the future path of its monetary policy. Second, as we emphasized
in Chapter 5, flexible inflation targeting does not compel a central bank
to ignore other important dimensions of economic performance, such
as real output or the exchange rate. There are, we noted, certain cases,
notably supply shocks, in which conflicts will arise. In such cases, the
central bank may adopt a less aggressive monetary policy, involving a
more gradual return to price stability, but it cannot always resolve completely the intrinsic conflict between the pursuit of price stability and the
stabilization of output and the exchange rate.

A SINGLE-COUNTRY BASKET PEG

At the opposite extreme, a country can tie the value of its currency explicitly to a basket of foreign currencies, typically those of its main trading
partners, and then intervene in the foreign-exchange market to keep the
actual basket value within the boundaries of a band surrounding the
targeted path of the basket value. It does not have to intervene in each
and every currency entering its basket. If, for example, it pegs to a basket
comprising the dollar, euro, and yen, and the yen appreciates *vis-à-vis*
the domestic currency, it can stabilize the value of its currency basket by
selling dollars instead of yen.

[45] Eichengreen (2002), p. 35; see also Goldstein (2002) and Eichengreen (2004).

Three reasons are usually adduced for adopting a fairly wide band around the target value of a currency basket: (i) the need to limit the size and frequency of intervention; (ii) the need to create a modest amount of exchange-rate uncertainty in order to deter speculation by market participants and a buildup of currency mismatches on the books of domestic banks and firms; and (iii) the freedom to devalue or revalue the target value of the basket without forcing market exchange rates to jump between nonoverlapping bands – a result that would unduly enhance the profitability of speculation.[46]

How should a country choose the currencies and weights for its own currency basket? Clearly, it should include the currencies of its main trading partners and weight them according to their importance in its foreign trade. Yet simple trade weights cannot be optimal; they cannot allow for the ways in which trade flows respond to price changes and, therefore, exchange-rate changes. And when you compare theoretical papers on the choice of optimal trade weights, you find that the authors' results depend on their definitions of optimality; some aim to stabilize the trade balance, whereas others aim to minimize the variance of domestic output.[47]

---

[46] One advocate of this regime, John Williamson, while favoring wide bands, would let a country using a currency basket allow the market value of the basket to breach the limit of its band when it confronts strong speculative pressures. In fact, he describes the boundaries of the band as "reference values" rather than fixed limits. He also suggests that a country using this regime allow the target value of its currency basket to rise or fall gradually so as to offset a gradual change in its country's competitive position. That's why this regime is often called the BBC regime – for basket, band, and crawl in the target value. For his full-fledged treatment of the BBC regime, see Williamson (2000); on his case for using it in East Asia, see Williamson (1999), in which he argues that the BBC regime can be combined successfully with inflation targeting. In Williamson (2000), incidentally, he explains that his use of the term "common" in the title of his previous paper was not meant to suggest that the Asian countries should adopt identical basket pegs of the sort discussed in the next section of this paper. He meant merely to suggest that each Asian country adopt its own basket, then use it in a fashion appropriate to its particular needs.

[47] There is a large literature on this subject; see, e.g., Ito, Ogawa, and Sasaki (1998), Ogawa and Ito (2002), and Yoshino, Kaji, and Suzuki (2002). It is often suggested that trade weights be adjusted to take account of another complication – the extent to which a country's trade is not invoiced in the currency of its trading partners but rather in the currency of some third country, such as the U.S. dollar; see, e.g., Eichengreen (2001b),

Advocates of currency baskets see them as a way to achieve exchange-rate stability without incurring the rigidity and risks of defending a single-currency peg – including the risk that the single currency chosen for that purpose fluctuates in terms of third countries' currencies, conferring less stability than it seems to promise. Some countries, however, use currency baskets for a different purpose. In July 2005, China announced that it would use a currency basket to influence its future exchange-rate decisions. And Singapore uses a currency basket as a policy instrument to maintain price stability. The Monetary Authority of Singapore has an inflation target but does not rely on interest-rate changes to achieve its target. There are two reasons. First, its financial markets are tightly integrated with international markets, and it has very little control over short-term interest rates. Second, its goods markets are likewise integrated with international markets. In fact, its exports exceed its gross national product. For that same reason, moreover, changes in the value of the Singapore dollar affect domestic prices strongly, and Singapore can influence domestic prices to maintain price stability by intervening in the foreign-exchange market rather than the money market.[48]

Singapore does not disclose the composition of its currency basket, although it does publish a time-series chart, showing the path of the basket value. China, by contrast, has listed publicly some of the currencies that enter importantly into its currency basket, but it has not yet published the weights of those currencies, nor any time-series chart on the basket value of the renminbi. It also has confounded observers by deciding to retain

p. 19. This point has validity insofar as trade is based on long-term contracts setting the prices of traded goods in terms of a third currency. Absent such contracts, however, the relevant exchange rates are those of the country's trading partners, not those of the currency in which trade is invoiced. Suppose that a Korean firm exports electric motors to Japan but prices them in dollars. Suppose further that the dollar appreciates by 10 percent *vis-à-vis* the won and yen. The Korean exporter can afford to lower its dollar price by 10 percent, as it will then still receive the same number of won for its dollar earnings. If it does that, moreover, the Japanese importer can buy the same number of electric motors for the same number of yen. When, as here, each party measures its profitability in its own national currency, it is the yen-won exchange rate that matters, and it has not changed in this example.

[48] On Singapore's experience, see Khor, Robinson, and Lee (2004); see also Cavoli and Rajan (2007), who provide an econometric analysis of Singapore's regime.

a rather narrow daily trading band for the renminbi-dollar rate, which would seem to deprive the currency basket of any operational influence over China's exchange-rate policy.[49]

Critics of basket pegs sometimes say that they lack credibility because they are not sufficiently transparent.[50] Credibility is important, not only for the viability of a basket peg but also for the conduct of monetary policy. Transparency *per se*, however, is far less important than consistency – a point illustrated by the regimes described in the previous paragraph. Although the Monetary Authority of Singapore declines to disclose the composition of its currency basket, it enjoys credibility because it behaves consistently.[51] The People's Bank of China falls far short on that score, because its exchange-rate regime appears to contain an internal inconsistency and because it is not the final arbiter of exchange-rate policy – nor, for that matter, of monetary policy.

Two Multicountry Options

There are two quite different ways for a group of countries to manage exchange rates collectively: adopting a common currency basket to limit exchange-rate fluctuations, or forming a full-fledged monetary union and thus adopting a single currency and single monetary policy. The first can be regarded as a permanent arrangement or as a way-station on the road to monetary union.[52] The second requires the creation of a single

---

[49] The initial description of China's exchange-rate reform appeared to say that the position of the renminbi-dollar band would be adjusted daily in light of the previous day's behavior of the renminbi-dollar rate. That procedure, however, would not guarantee close consistency between the evolution of the renminbi-dollar rate and of the multicurrency basket unless the target value of the basket was likewise adjusted daily. No firm judgment on these matters can be made, however, without knowing the weights used in the basket, as well as the target value of the basket and the width of the band around it.

[50] See, for example, the critique in Bayoumi, Eichengreen, and Mauro (2000).

[51] Rajan (2002, p. 158) makes the same point, likewise citing Singapore, and de Brouwer (2002) takes it further; an excess of transparency, he argues, may expose a basket peg to speculative pressures.

[52] It should be noted, however, that the Europeans set up the European Monetary System (EMS) in 1979, a full decade before they took the first steps toward full-fledged monetary union. They saw it as a way to fashion a "zone of monetary stability" within Europe, not as a precursor to monetary union.

central bank, the institutions needed for its governance, safeguards for its independence, and ways to render it accountable for its decisions and performance. It also requires the integration of its members' money markets and their banking systems, although it does not necessarily require the lifting of all capital controls. A monetary union can be created without the unification of prudential supervision, but it does require strict adherence to common standards by those responsible for prudential supervision.[53] Finally, it requires a well-defined way to manage the common external exchange rate of the monetary union.

We have discussed the principal problems involved in designing a currency basket for a single country; we look next at the problems involved in designing a common currency basket and then turn to the harder task of setting up and managing a monetary union.

DESIGNING A COMMON BASKET PEG

When a single country decides to adopt a currency basket, it has merely to decide which foreign currencies it wants to put into the basket and what weights to give them. For reasons already mentioned, no simple set of trade weights will give optimal results; optimality itself is a multidimensional notion, and no one really knows enough about the relevant parameters to modify the trade weights in a satisfactory way.

The task is doubly difficult, however, when a group of countries have agreed in principle to adopt a common basket. Even if they choose to use trade weights, they are apt to disagree about the sizes of those weights, because their trade patterns are quite likely to differ. Consider the East Asian countries. Korea trades far more heavily with Japan than do most ASEAN countries. Within ASEAN itself, moreover, Indonesia and Thailand trade more heavily with Japan than with the United States, whereas Singapore trades more heavily with the United States.[54]

---

[53] Recall that the ECB plays no significant role in bank supervision, but the national agencies responsible for supervision in each EU country must adhere to the common standards embodied in EU legislation. See the discussion in Chapter 3, however, which suggests that the decentralization of supervision may deprive the ECB of prompt access to the information required to cope with a major banking crisis.

[54] For more on these asymmetries, see de Brouwer (2002).

Most important, the governments must make a fundamental choice between two types of basket: an *external* basket containing only the currencies of outsiders, such as the dollar and euro, and an *internal* basket containing the currencies of the participating countries.[55] The need for the choice does not arise when a single country decides to adopt a currency basket. All of the currencies in that basket are, by definition, external currencies. It arises acutely, however, when a group of countries decides to adopt a common basket, and it has extensive implications.

If countries agree to adopt a common external basket and thus undertake to stabilize their national currencies within a band surrounding the target value of that basket, each participating country will then limit fluctuations in its domestic-currency value of the external basket. But they will also achieve another objective. When each of them limits fluctuations in its domestic-currency value of the external basket, they will also limit fluctuations in the relative values of their own national currencies. In other words, adherence to an external basket will confer a degree of exchange-rate stability between the participants' national currencies and the set of currencies entering the basket, but it will also confer a degree of stability on the cross-rates between their own national currencies. If, for example, Thailand and Malaysia adopt a common external basket containing the dollar, euro, and yen, they will limit fluctuations in the exchange rates connecting the baht and ringgit to those three currencies. In the process, however, they will also limit fluctuations in the cross rate between the baht and ringgit and will thereby preclude large fluctuations

---

[55] Many economists writing on this subject fail to draw this distinction clearly, and it is often hard to know which type of basket they have in mind. Montiel (2004) provides a good discussion of the differences between them, although he fails to make a point emphasized below: an external basket limits the variability of the participants' currencies relative to the currencies in the basket, but it also limits the variability of the participants' bilateral exchange rates. Note that the three-currency external basket discussed in the text is based on the implicit but plausible supposition that Japan will not want to peg the yen to an external basket. Note further that the three-currency external basket might soon become a four-currency basket, because the renminbi might be included even before becoming a fully convertible currency. (Note also that an arrangement mentioned in Chapter 5, collective dollarization by the MERCOSUR countries, may be viewed as special case of common external basket pegging, but with only one currency, the dollar, in the external basket.)

in intra-ASEAN exchange rates like those that were so damaging during the Asian crisis.

To honor their obligations under this regime, each participating country must hold or be able to borrow enough dollars, euros, or yen keep its currency sufficiently close to the target values defined by the common external basket.[56] That might, of course, be done by greatly increasing the size of the bilateral swap lines set up by the CMI, but it might also require the multilateralization of those swap lines, curtailing the right of potential creditors to opt out of their obligations, and loosening the link between the CMI and IMF. Alternatively, countries such as China and Japan might agree to use or lend some of their very large dollar reserves to set up a new facility that would make short-term dollar loans when other Asian countries need them to keep their countries' currencies close to the target values set by the external basket.

By adopting instead an internal basket, the participating countries will achieve one of the two objectives served by an external basket – stabilizing within limits the values of their countries' currencies *vis-à-vis* the other currencies in the internal basket. But they will not achieve the other objective – stabilizing the values of their currencies in terms the dollar, euro, and yen (unless, of course, the yen is included in the internal basket). Instead, their currencies will float jointly against those three key currencies.

There will, of course, be need for intervention to stabilize the participants' currencies *vis-à-vis* an internal basket, and there are two ways to finance it: using dollars, euros, and yen, as in the case of an external basket, or using the national currencies of the other participating countries.[57]

Both sorts of intervention were used by European countries in the EMS. Countries wanting to keep their currencies well within the bilateral limits

---

[56] Recall, however, that the basket value of a country's currency can be stabilized by intervening in just one of the component currencies; there is no need for intervention in every currency. (Intervention in a single currency, however, can affect the basket values of others tied to the same basket and may therefore require that they also intervene.)

[57] Note in this connection a point made by Padoa-Schioppa (2004b); intervention in the participants' own currencies requires a liquid foreign-exchange market for each currency pair involved.

(so-called intramarginal intervention) often intervened in dollars. When one exchange rate reached the limit of its band, however, the rules of the EMS required that both of the countries directly involved – the strong-currency country and the weak-currency country – intervene together. Alternatively, the strong-currency country, usually Germany, had to make open-ended short-term loans to the weak-currency country. There were two reasons for this practice. Intervening in dollars was not a very efficient way to influence directly the exchange rate between the German mark and French franc. Furthermore, France might not have enough dollar reserves to do the whole job by itself. When Germany lent marks to France, however, it necessarily raised the German money supply, and the Bundesbank was fearful of the impact on its monetary policy. Therefore, it reserved the right to limit its lending, and when it invoked that right in 1992, Italy had to devalue the lira, and that is what triggered the crisis that drove both Italy and Britain out of the EMS.

Note finally another important difference between the two types of baskets. When a group of countries adopt a common external basket, they import to some degree the monetary policies of the United States, the euro zone, and Japan – the countries whose currencies are most likely to comprise the external basket. When, instead, a group of countries adopts a common internal basket, the countries have no obvious anchor for their monetary policies. They can, of course, adhere to inflation targeting, but some of them may fail to pursue it faithfully or in a manner fully consistent with their partners' practices. In the EMS, of course, the monetary policy of the Bundesbank constrained and thereby anchored the monetary policies of the other member countries. There is no Asian counterpart, however, to the Bundesbank.[58]

The two distinguishing features of an internal basket – its inability to stabilize its member countries' currencies *vis-à-vis* the dollar, euro,

---

[58] Genberg et al. (2005, p. 59) stress this point but fail to note that it applies with particular force to an internal basket; see also Bayoumi and Mauro (1999), pp. 12–13. Hefeker and Nabor (2005) suggest that China could play that role in Asia, but they confuse two phenomena. China may soon be dominant in Asia and by a larger margin than Germany was in Europe. Yet the People's Bank of China is far from being the dominant central bank in Asia in the way that the Bundesbank was the dominant central bank in the EMS.

and yen, and the absence of an anchor for monetary policy – combine strongly to suggest that a common external basket would be superior to a common internal basket if some of the mid-sized Asian countries decided to adopt a common basket.[59]

DESIGNING A MONETARY UNION

Should some or all of the East Asian countries plan instead to form a monetary union? The theory of optimum currency areas, discussed in Chapter 2, cannot answer that question decisively. Nevertheless, empirical work inspired by that theory can shed some light on two key questions: Does a particular country group come sufficiently close to being an optimum currency area? Does a particular subset of countries within East Asia look to be a better group for a monetary union than some other subset?

In Chapters 2 and 5, we presented research results obtained by Tamin Bayoumi and Barry Eichengreen aimed at ascertaining whether various country groups come close to being optimum currency areas. They quantified demand and supply shocks for each member of a particular country group and then computed correlations between the shocks affecting each of the country pairs in that country group. The higher the correlations for a particular country pair, the lower potential cost of forming a monetary union between that country pair. The authors also asked how rapidly

---

[59] In Chapter 7, however, we note that a common external basket could severely limit the flexibility of the East Asian currencies *vis-à-vis* the dollar, and they would thereby limit the contribution of exchange-rate changes to the reduction of global imbalances. The increased rigidity of the monetary system would not be severe if the ASEAN countries by themselves adopted a common external basket, but if they were joined by China, Japan, and Korea, the monetary system might become much more rigid These and related matters are examined in two recent papers. Williamson (2005) assumes that nine Asian countries adopt a common external basket comprising the dollar, euro, and yen, and he finds that this regime tends to stabilize substantially the nominal effective exchange rates for eight of the nine countries (the exception being Singapore). Ogawa and Shimizu (2006) assume that all of the ASEAN+3 adopt a common internal basket (in effect, a trade-weighted ACU of the sort discussed earlier in this chapter), and they find that it imparts more stability to the nominal effective exchange rate in five of the seven country cases covered by both papers (the exceptions being China and Malaysia). Unfortunately, neither paper shows how the two regimes – the external basket used by Williamson and the ACU basket used by Ogawa and Shimizu – affect the behavior of the dollar and euro *vis-à-vis* the currencies of East Asia.

Table 6.1. *Cross-country correlations of demand shocks in EU and East Asian countries (Blanchard-Quah shock extraction)*

EU Countries

	Ger	Fra	Net	Bel	Den	Aus	Ita	UK	Spa	Por	Ire	Swe	Fin
Germany	1.00												
France	0.30	1.00											
Netherlands	0.21	0.34	1.00										
Belgium	0.36	**0.53**	**0.52**	1.00									
Denmark	0.35	0.32	0.20	0.30	1.00								
Austria	0.32	**0.50**	0.29	**0.56**	0.30	1.00							
Italy	0.22	**0.62**	0.24	**0.49**	0.06	**0.44**	1.00						
UK	0.09	0.20	−0.05	−0.03	0.00	−0.08	0.05	1.00					
Spain	−0.10	**0.53**	0.11	0.26	0.25	0.30	**0.43**	0.23	1.00				
Portugal	0.24	**0.47**	0.05	**0.45**	0.30	**0.60**	**0.63**	0.24	0.32	1.00			
Ireland	0.06	0.09	0.39	0.00	0.34	−0.12	−0.08	0.25	0.02	−0.01	1.00		
Sweden	0.10	0.18	0.29	0.36	0.18	0.02	0.25	0.18	−0.01	0.08	0.30	1.00	
Finland	0.10	**0.47**	0.32	**0.60**	0.36	**0.53**	**0.65**	0.16	**0.40**	**0.54**	0.17	0.33	1.00

East Asian Countries

	Jap	Tai	Kor	Tha	HK	Sin	Mal	Ind	Phi
Japan	1.00								
Taiwan	−0.01	1.00							
Korea	0.19	0.33	1.00						
Thailand	−0.04	**0.54**	0.32	1.00					
Hong Kong	0.23	0.22	0.05	**0.43**	1.00				
Singapore	−0.09	**0.44**	0.27	**0.70**	0.37	1.00			
Malaysia	0.12	**0.41**	**0.43**	**0.58**	**0.54**	**0.67**	1.00		
Indonesia	0.16	0.17	0.17	0.36	**0.62**	**0.64**	**0.58**	1.00	
Philippines	0.29	0.09	0.16	0.15	−0.19	−0.05	−0.11	0.04	1.00

Source: Tamim Bayoumi and Barry Eichengreen (1994b), "One Money or Many? Analyzing the Prospects For Monetary Unification in Various Parts of the World," *Princeton Studies in International Finance* 78, Princeton, NJ; Princeton University, International Finance Section Table 6.
All correlations equal to or higher than 0.40 are shown in bold type, as they approach or exceed levels commonly accepted as being statistically significant.

each country individually adjusted to each type of shock. Their results for Europe and East Asia are reproduced in Table 6.1, which deals with demand shocks.[60] (Their results for supply shocks are summarized in Table 6.2, in which they are compared with those obtained by another study.)

There are fewer large positive correlations in the East Asian section of Table 6.1 than in the EU section, but that is because there are fewer countries in the East Asian section. When, as in Table 6.2, the number of large positive correlations is expressed as a percentage of the country pairs appearing in Table 6.1, they exceed the corresponding percentage in the EU section of the table (33.3 percent of the East Asian cases, compared with 24.4 percent of the EU cases). The same result obtains, moreover, with respect to supply shocks. Bayoumi and Eichengreen also showed that the East Asian countries adjusted more rapidly to both sorts of shocks than did the EU countries.[61] Accordingly, they concluded that East Asia came as close as the EU to being an optimum currency area.[62]

Several other studies have reached similar conclusions,[63] and the most recent study reinforces them. Conducted by Masahiro Kawai and Taizo Motonishi, the study used two methods for extracting shocks and it included China, unlike most other studies.[64] The results are summarized

---

[60] Table 6.1 omits two European countries (Norway and Switzerland) that were included in their study, as they are not EU countries, and it omits two EU countries (Greece and Luxembourg) that were not included in their study. In addition, the table omits Australia and New Zealand, which were included in their study, and it omits China, which was not included in their study for want of reliable time-series data when the study was conducted.

[61] On the more rapid adjustment of the Asian countries, see Ngiam and Yuen (2001), who suggest that it may reflect the role played by high cross-border labor mobility.

[62] They also noted, however, that two subsets of Asian countries came even closer to being optimum currency areas: a Northeast Asian bloc comprising Japan, Korea, and Taiwan, and a Southeast Asian bloc comprising Hong Kong, Indonesia, Malaysia, Singapore and, possibly, Thailand.

[63] See Bayoumi and Mauro (1999), who used the same techniques but more recent data, and Eichengreen and Bayoumi (1999) who used a wholly different method but were still able to conclude that East Asia is nearly as good a candidate as the EU for an internationally harmonized monetary policy. See also Kawai and Tagaki (2005) and Lee, Park, and Shin (2004). Contrast their results, however, with those of Brandão de Brito (2004), who worked with a subset of Asian countries, used another way of extracting shocks, and found that the number of strong positive cross-country correlations was much higher in his Asian subset.

[64] Kawai and Motonishi (2005).

Table 6.2. *Summary of cross-country correlations in EU and East Asian countries*

Source, country group, and methodology	Summary statistics	
	Number of outcomes	Percentage of country pairs
Bayoumi-Eichengreen:		
Using Blanchard-Quah Shock Extraction:		
EU Countries (78 country pairs):		
Large correlations of demand shocks	19	24.4
Large correlations of supply shocks	17	21.8
East Asian Countries (36 country pairs):		
Large correlations of demand shocks	12	33.3
Large correlations of supply shocks	10	27.8
Kawai-Motonishi		
Using Blanchard-Quah Shock Extraction:		
East Asian Countries (55 country pairs):		
Large correlations of demand shocks	8	14.5
Large correlations of supply shocks	25	45.5
Using Clarida-Gali Shock Extraction:		
East Asian Countries (55 country pairs):		
Large correlations of nominal shocks	9	16.4
Large correlations of output shocks	23	41.8

Sources: Based on data in Table 6.1 and in Masahiro Kawai and Taizo Motonishi (2005), "Macroeconomic Interdependence in East Asia: Empirical Evidence and Issues," in *Asian Economic Cooperation and Integration: Progress, Prospects, and Challenges.* Manila: Asian Development Bank, pp. 213–268.

in Table 6.2, where they can be compared with those obtained much earlier by Bayoumi and Eichengreen.[65] There is not much difference between the results produced by the two methods used for extracting shocks – the Blanchard-Quah technique[66] and the Clarida-Gali technique.[67] When Kawai and Motonishi used the Blanchard-Quah technique, they obtained

[65] The summary in Table 6.2 omits eight countries that were included in the Kawai-Motonishi study (the United States, Australia, New Zealand, India, Vietnam, Cambodia, Laos, and Myanmar) as well as a fifteen-country EU composite. It does include two countries, Brunei and China, which were not included in the Bayoumi-Eichengreen study.

[66] See Blanchard and Quah (1989).

[67] See Clarida and Gali (1994).

twenty-five large positive correlations between countries' supply shocks; when they used the Clarida-Gali technique, they obtained twenty-three large positive correlations between countries' output shocks. There is a bigger difference, however, between the results of the Bayoumi-Eichengreen study and the results of the Kawai-Motonishi study. When both studies used the Blanchard-Quah technique, the Kawai-Motonishi study found fewer large positive correlations between countries' demand shocks but more numerous correlations between countries' supply shocks,[68] and a similar difference arose when the Clarida-Gali technique was used instead. The most striking result of the Kawai-Motonishi study, however, pertains to China. There were only two large positive correlations between the shocks affecting China and those affecting other countries (and those two involved Vietnam and Cambodia rather than the principal East Asian countries).

There are other compelling reasons for wondering whether China should belong to an Asian monetary union, assuming for the moment that some of its neighbors want to move in that direction. China is growing and changing faster than its Asian neighbors, and there may therefore be need for a significant depreciation of the real exchange rates of most other Asian countries *vis-à-vis* the renminbi.[69] Such changes can, of course, be made within a monetary union by endogenous changes in labor costs and product prices, but that can be a slow and painful process.[70] It may be far easier to make them by changing the nominal exchange rate between the renminbi and other Asian currencies.

Even today, moreover, the Chinese currency is one of the world's principal currencies. It is not a key currency in the conventional sense, and it cannot become one until it is fully convertible. Yet the renminbi-dollar exchange rate may be more important for the proper functioning of the

---

[68] The much larger number of positive supply shocks may reflect the difference in time periods involved. The Bayoumi-Eichengreen study was concluded before the Asian crisis of the late 1990s; the Kawai-Motonishi study includes the crisis period. This difference, however, does not fully explain why the Kawai-Motonishi study found fewer strong positive correlations between countries' demand shocks.

[69] See, however, Tan and Khor (2005), especially pp. 16–20, where they argue that China's cost competitiveness may be eroded by rising real incomes, allowing its trade partners to retain their competitiveness in a wide range of products.

[70] See the discussion of European experience in Chapter 5.

international monetary system than the dollar-euro rate or dollar-yen rate. There is, in other words, a need to replace the present G-7 with a new G-4, to oversee the macroeconomic management of the world economy. It would comprise China, the Euro Area, Japan, and the United States.[71]

Finally, there is the matter of size, a point already raised in Chapter 5 with regard to NAFTA. The difference in size between China and any ASEAN country is far larger than the difference in size between Germany and the next largest country in the euro area, and the difference will get bigger in the years ahead. It would therefore be difficult to reach agreement on the composition of the policy-making body of an Asian central bank. Furthermore, the data on which that body would base its policy decisions would be dominated by the Chinese data, with the result that economic developments in China would dominate the making of monetary policy by an Asian central bank. In fact, economic conditions in China would determine the policy stance of an Asian central bank to a much greater degree than economic conditions in Germany determine the policy stance of the ECB.[72] Similar problems would arise if Japan joined an Asian monetary union and China did not, although the internal asymmetries might be somewhat less pronounced.

For other reasons, however, an Asian monetary union could not readily include Japan without including China and could not readily include China without including Japan. Few other countries in East Asia would want to tie themselves tightly to one of those countries at the potential expense of its relations with the other. It may therefore be far better to contemplate a smaller monetary union comprising the six original ASEAN countries and, perhaps, Korea, but one that would be open to other ASEAN countries and to Taiwan as well.[73] Such a union also might

[71] See Kenen et al. (2004), ch. 4. The newly introduced arrangements for multilateral surveillance by the IMF may prove to be a viable and more flexible alternative, but it is too early to know whether that process will lead to closer cooperation among the key countries involved.

[72] The same problem was raised in Chapters 2 and 5, in which we noted that a monetary union between a very large country and a much smaller country would not be very different from the small country's viewpoint than the unilateral adoption of the large country's currency. We encountered the same problem in Chapter 5, when discussing the possibility of a monetary union between Canada, Mexico, and the United States.

[73] Genberg (2006) entertains a similar scenario. See, however, Eichengreen (2005), who believes that a monetary union that did not include China would have very little appeal

include Australia and New Zealand, should they care to join, although they may choose to form their own monetary union.[74]

There are, of course, large differences among the ASEAN countries. Income per capita in Singapore was $24,220 in 2004, compared to $4,650 in Malaysia and $2,540 in Thailand, and it was only half as high in Indonesia and the Philippines as it was in Thailand.[75] And it was much lower in Cambodia, Laos, and Vietnam, but they are far from ready for a monetary union, because their monetary and financial systems are far less developed. Bilateral trade between the ten ASEAN countries accounts for only a quarter of those countries' total trade, a fraction smaller than the one for the euro area, but still substantial; see Table 1.1. Singapore, moreover, might have grave reservations about replacing its unique monetary policy, which relies heavily on exchange-rate management, with a single ASEAN monetary policy.

How long might it take to form this sort of monetary union? It may not be necessary for the member countries to achieve complete free trade – a single market in goods and services – although that was the path that Europe took and the one that would fully exploit the efficiency gains conferred by the adoption of a single currency.[76] It would be important, however, to unify the members' financial markets; otherwise, the union's central bank could not conduct a single monetary policy. But the major ASEAN countries are now working on that task and could perhaps achieve enough financial integration in fewer than ten years. Remember,

---

to other Asian countries. Furthermore, there might be political problems if some of the ASEAN countries formed a monetary union that excluded even temporarily the rest of the ten ASEAN countries. (Note that an ASEAN monetary union might well choose to tie its single currency to an external basket, one that might include the renminbi as well as the dollar, euro, and yen.)

[74] This possibility was much discussed in New Zealand a few years ago, and interest in the subject appears to have revived, due perhaps to the sharp depreciation of the New Zealand dollar relative to the Australian dollar. On the issues raised in the earlier discussion, see, e.g., Coleman (2001).

[75] Data from World Bank, *World Development Indicators*; data are converted to U.S. dollars using the World Bank Atlas method and divided by midyear population. Comparable data for Brunei and Myanmar are not available, but the former is thought to be in the neighborhood of $10,000 and the latter in the neighborhood of $800. In the same year, the gap between high and low incomes per capita was smaller in the euro area.

[76] On the possibility of moving to monetary union before moving to free trade, see Shin and Wang (2004).

moreover, that the move to EMU began in 1988 and was not completed for another decade.

It might take much longer, however, to solve the fundamental problem – closing the institutional deficit that stands in the way of deeper economic integration, even among the ASEAN countries. It would not be necessary to create supranational institutions resembling those of the EU. Recall the suggestion made before, that special-purpose entities might be created to take on the various tasks performed by the EU institutions during and after the transition to EMU. It would be necessary, however, to grant them the authority they would need to perform those tasks, and this could take longer than Europe took to move from the Treaty of Rome to the start of EMU. The institutional deficit is deeper in East Asia than it was in Europe fifty years ago. Asia has just begun to develop intergovernmental institutions. It has not even begun to contemplate supranational institutions. Indeed, the whole notion of supranationality is alien to Asian thought and history.[77]

What, then, might be done more quickly? Several authors have suggested that some or all of the East Asian countries adopt the less ambitious option proposed at the start of this section, a common currency basket, until they are ready to move to monetary union. Some favor the use of an internal basket, resembling the ECU.[78] Haruhiko Kuroda has suggested that the principal ASEAN countries start with an external basket but that they be joined later by China, Japan, and Korea (and would then adopt instead an internal basket).[79] Much time would be needed, however, to get to monetary union, even for a subset of the ASEAN countries, and the outcome would assuredly depend on the evolution of relations between Beijing and Tokyo – a matter to which we return at the end of the next chapter.

[77] Eichengreen and Bayoumi (1999, pp. 360–64) make this point with eloquence and elegance.

[78] See, e.g., Kuroda and Kawai (2004), Latter (2005), and Wyplosz (2001).

[79] Kuroda (2004).

7

The Outlook and Implications for
the United States

INTRODUCTION

In this book, we have explored the possibility and evaluated the likelihood of increased regional monetary integration over the next two decades. We have argued that economic and political conditions in most regions are not now conducive to the formation of additional full-fledged monetary unions, even among country groups that have strong trade ties. Obviously, monetary union in Europe is already well-established. However, further expansion of the euro area to include additional new EU members in Central Europe will present some challenges. In addition, there is the possibility of closer regional monetary cooperation in East Asia, even the formation of a monetary union among some or all of the ASEAN countries. In this final chapter, we look at the implications for the United States if the international monetary system evolves as we have predicted.

We begin by reviewing our reasons for believing that we will not see many new monetary unions. Thereafter, we examine what this is likely to mean for the U.S. economy, the international role of the dollar, and the broader issue of U.S. leadership and influence in the international monetary system.

WHY EMU IS NOT READILY REPRODUCIBLE

The birth of EMU in 1999 spawned a flurry of interest in the creation of monetary unions elsewhere in the world, not only among academic economists, but also in official circles and the private sector. This interest has diminished recently, however, for reasons set out in previous chapters.

First, EMU is rightly seen to be part of a larger project, the "ever closer union" of the EU countries, and no other country group has comparable aspirations, not even those defined by comprehensive trade agreements. Furthermore, Europe's commitment was already embodied in supranational institutions, such as the European Commission and European Parliament, and the treaty that looked to the early creation of EMU also broadened the domains of those institutions. Comparable institutions are rarely found elsewhere, even in regions where governments cooperate quite closely.

Second, the European countries were already committed implicitly to pursue a single monetary policy. Their adherence to the rules of the European Monetary System, combined with the growth of capital mobility, had the effect, if not the aim, of forcing their countries' central banks to emulate the Bundesbank's monetary policy. The move to full-fledged monetary union served therefore to formalize those countries' implicit commitments, while introducing new decision-making processes. It introduced a single currency and substituted the single monetary policy of the ECB for the hegemonic monetary policy of the Bundesbank.

Third, bilateral trade within the European Union accounted for a larger share of its members' total trade than is the case elsewhere. No other region, apart from North America, has comparable amounts of intraregional trade relative to its total trade. (See Table 1.1.) Furthermore, the geographic patterns of its members' trade with the outside world did not differ hugely among the EU countries, so they had little cause to fear that changes in the value of the euro *vis-à-vis* the dollar would affect them differently.[1]

---

[1] Although there is little intraregional trade within the CAEMC and WAEMU (the monetary unions of sub-Saharan Africa), much of their members' external trade involves France and other EU countries, and they are likewise safe from idiosyncratic shocks resulting from exchange-rate changes. The countries due to join the WAMZ trade even less with each other, but the geography of their external trade is less homogeneous; Nigeria, for example, is a major oil-exporting country.

Fourth, it is now very clear that participation in a monetary union can be very costly if its members' labor and product markets are not flexible enough to prevent the emergence of large cost differences. The theory of optimum currency areas has not lost its relevance – as we have emphasized repeatedly throughout this book – despite the fact that this theory has not played a decisive role in governments' decisions to form or join a monetary union.[2]

PROSPECTS ELSEWHERE IN THE WORLD

Our survey of various regions in Chapters 5 and 6, when set against our discussion of EMU in Chapter 3, led us to conclude that full-fledged monetary unions are unlikely to emerge in the western hemisphere or East Asia for the foreseeable future. As we discussed in Chapter 4, the West African countries may succeed in creating the WAMZ, and they may even reach their more ambitious goal – merging the WAMZ and WAEMU to create a single West African monetary union. Likewise, the members of the Gulf Cooperation Council may resolve disagreements that have slowed their progress toward monetary union. But EMU will still be the only monetary union of sufficient size to influence the form and functioning of the international monetary system or pose a potential challenge to the preeminent roles of the United States and the U.S. dollar.

In Chapter 5, on the western hemisphere, we argued that the countries of North America are unlikely to form a monetary union for the foreseeable future. Mexico and Canada would not readily agree to a monetary union with the United States on terms acceptable to the latter, and we took the same view with regard to the prospects for monetary union within South America, albeit for different reasons: First, there is insufficient trade integration. Second, there are large cross-country differences

---

[2] Ahearne and Pisani-Ferry (2006) make the same point when warning the new EU members of Central Europe not to join EMU too soon, before their labor and product markets have become more flexible, but the point is equally applicable retrospectively to countries such as Italy, already in EMU. Those countries have experienced large real appreciations *vis-à-vis* their EMU partners, as a result of a combination of high wage growth and low productivity growth.

in the countries' trade patterns with the outside world, and these can cause problems like those that beset Argentina when it tied its currency to the U.S. dollar just when the dollar was appreciating *vis-à-vis* the euro and Brazilian *real*. Finally, the reemergence of populist governments in Latin America may go hand-in-hand with a reluctance to forgo the option of printing money to pay for extravagant populist promises (although, admittedly, some of these countries earn enough foreign exchange from oil and gas exports to forgo that option).

In the interim, we might see more unilateral dollarization by small and medium-sized countries in the region, as well as more unilateral euroization by small Balkan countries and perhaps some Mahgreb countries. But the EU is ambivalent about this possibility. It has taken justifiable pride in the modest but growing international role of the euro, but it has cautioned new and potential EU members against unilateral euroization, because it would usurp the roles of the EU institutions in setting the exchange rates at which those countries will join EMU when they have qualified for membership.

It should likewise be noted that the United States has distanced itself from *de jure* dollarization. Lawrence Summers, when Secretary of the Treasury, warned that the United States would not undertake to supervise commercial banks in dollarizing countries, would not grant them access to the Federal Reserve discount window, and would not broaden the domain of the Federal Reserve System to take explicit account of economic conditions in countries adopting the dollar.[3]

In Chapter 6, we reached similar conclusions regarding East Asia, albeit for reasons unique to that region. Monetary union is unlikely in the near term, and a comprehensive monetary union involving all of the East Asian countries is, at best, a long way off. There is insufficient political cohesion, to say the least. Ancient animosities are compounded by disagreements and distrust. And there is little, if any, taste for the creation of supranational institutions. Nevertheless, some countries in that

---

[3] Summers (1999). Senator Connie Mack of Florida sponsored legislation in 1999 aimed at compensating a dollarizing country for the interest-income loss it would suffer by using its dollar reserves or borrowing dollars in order to redeem its own currency, but that legislation was not adopted. See Box 5.1 for a detailed discussion of this legislation.

region could move to monetary union late in the twenty-year period covered by this book. In the interim, moreover, some East Asian countries may adopt a common exchange-rate regime based on a currency basket.

IMPLICATIONS FOR THE UNITED STATES

What, then, are the implications of our predictions for the United States and for the form and functioning of the international monetary system? To answer this question, we must ask how the formation and functioning of monetary unions affect other countries, such as the United States, and, more important, what further monetary integration of the sort that we are predicting would imply for the dominant role of the U.S. dollar in the world economy.

In Chapter 2, in which we outlined the theory of optimum currency areas, we focused exclusively on the ways in which a monetary union might affect its members, attaching particular importance to the effects on trade and the workings of a single monetary policy like that of EMU. Yet a monetary union among countries of significant economic size could affect outsiders in several ways, even large outsiders like the United States. By creating a single currency, a monetary union banishes exchange rate changes as well as the risk of future exchange rate changes. To this extent, it favors trade among its members at the expense of trade with outsiders. This effect may be small, although evidence cited in Chapter 2 suggests that it is not negligible. It may likewise stimulate foreign direct investment in the monetary union, as foreign firms seek to hedge against exchange-rate risk by substituting goods produced within the monetary union for goods exported from outside.[4]

The unification of capital markets resulting from the introduction of a single currency is likely to attract foreign investors, as the growing depth and breadth of those markets attracts new business from the outside world. The unification of securities markets, especially stock markets has

---

[4] It should nevertheless be noted that the United Kingdom continues to attract large amounts of foreign direct investment, confounding the predictions of those who warned that it would be disadvantaged by not joining EMU.

been accelerating in the European Union, although some of the more prominent alliances involve outsiders as well as securities markets and financial institutions within the EU.

In effect, a monetary union affords preferential treatment to its members' firms – financial as well as industrial – not by raising barriers against foreign competition but rather by uniting its members' economies, affording foreigners relief from exchange-rate risk when they do business inside the monetary union, and integrating the financial sector in the monetary union. The magnitude of these effects is hard to measure, but the mediocre performance of the European economy since the start of EMU suggests that they pose no serious threat to the functioning or prospects of the U.S. economy. The far larger problems of adjustment for the United States arise from the remarkable growth of the East Asian countries – countries without a monetary union. The more serious problems posed by EMU derive from the potential threat to the international role of the U.S. dollar.

THE DOMINANT ROLE OF THE DOLLAR

Despite the many changes in the world economy that have taken place in the last half century, the dollar is still the dominant international currency.

The Many Global Uses of the Dollar

Most industrial countries invoice a large fraction of their exports in their own national currencies, but many also use the dollar, not only in their trade with the United States but with other countries, too. Furthermore, many developing countries, including the East Asian countries and the major oil producers, invoice most of their exports in dollars.[5] The dollar is also used extensively in international capital markets; the bulk of the foreign-currency debt issued by national governments is dollar-denominated, along with much of the corporate debt issued

---

[5] For recent data and research on the invoicing of trade, see Goldberg and Tille (2005) and Kamps (2005).

on international markets. Finally, the dollar plays a unique role in the foreign-exchange market. The most recent triennial survey by the Bank for International Settlements, conducted in 2004, found that the dollar was involved in 89 percent of all foreign-currency trades, of which 28 percent were dollar-euro trades.[6]

The very large role of the dollar in foreign-exchange trading reflects two phenomena: purchases and sales of dollars for commercial and financial purposes, and the so-called vehicle use of the dollar. Here is an example of the latter: A Korean importer wanting to sell Korean won for Mexican pesos will first sell the won for dollars and then sell the dollars for pesos. As the won and peso are traded often for the dollar, but they are rarely traded for each other, the total cost of this two-part transaction is lower than the cost of a single bilateral won-peso trade; that is because foreign-exchange dealers find it hard to match up an occasional offer of won for pesos with an occasional offer of pesos for won.

The Reserve Role of the Dollar

The dominant role of the dollar in foreign-exchange markets gives it another role in the international monetary system. It is the currency used by most countries' central banks when they intervene on foreign-exchange markets to influence the value of their domestic currencies. That is itself one reason why most countries' central banks hold some of their reserves in dollars, but not the only reason. At the end of 2006, foreign official holdings of U.S. government securities totaled $1.4 trillion, accounting for nearly 30 percent of the global total of reserves.[7] And the share of the dollar in total reserves is even larger than that. Some governments hold large dollar claims, including U.S. government securities, *via* intermediaries, and these appear as private holdings, rather than official holdings, in the U.S. data.

Members of the IMF are not obliged to reveal the currency composition of their reserves, and many developing countries have declined to do so. At the end of 2006, however, the dollar reserves of the countries that

---

[6] Bank for International Settlements (2005).
[7] Federal Reserve Bulletin (2007), Table 3.15.

Table 7.1. *U.S. dollar value of foreign exchange reserves*

Category	Billions of U.S. dollars		Percent of subtotal identified	
	1999 Q4	2006 Q4	1999 Q4	2006 Q4
All countries				
Total	1781.7	5036.8	–	–
Identified by currency	1378.6	3331.5	–	
U.S. dollars	978.6	2151.1	71.0	64.6
Euros	247.0	861.6	17.9	25.9
Yen	87.9	108.1	6.4	3.2
All other currencies	65.2	210.6	4.7	6.3
Unidentified	403.0	1705.3	–	–
Industrial countries				
Total	726.1	1394.9	–	–
Identified by currency	721.3	1390.7	–	–
U.S. dollars	528.4	995.7	73.3	71.6
Euros	117.8	288.1	16.3	20.7
Yen	48.0	49.1	6.7	3.5
All other currencies	27.1	57.8	3.8	4.2
Unidentified	4.8	4.3	–	–
Developing countries				
Total	1055.5	3641.8		
Identified by currency	657.3	1940.8	–	
U.S. dollars	450.2	1155.3	68.5	59.5
Euros	129.2	573.6	19.7	29.6
Yen	39.9	59.1	6.1	3.0
All other currencies	38.0	152.8	5.8	7.9
Unidentified	398.2	1701.0	–	–

Source: International Monetary Fund, *Currency Composition of Official Foreign Exchange Reserves* (*COFER Data Base*), June 2007. Detail may not add to total because of rounding.

do disclose their holdings (described hereafter as identified holdings) amounted to 64.6 percent of their total holdings. Holdings of euros came next, accounting for 25.9 percent; see Table 7.1.

Under the Bretton Woods System of quasi-fixed exchange rates, the regime that prevailed from the end of the Second World War until the early 1970s, the role of the dollar was even larger. Some countries still held sterling, a vestige of their membership in the sterling area during and after World War II; others held small quantities of third countries' currencies, most notably the deutschemark and Swiss franc.[8] Under the Bretton Woods System, however, gold was the main alternative to the U.S. dollar, with Britain, France, and other European countries holding very large amounts relative to their reserves. But gold was not especially attractive as a reserve asset. Its price was fixed in U.S. dollars at $35 per ounce, and gold holdings earned no interest. It was also understood that large gold purchases from the United States would erode the net reserve position of the United States; by reducing the gold backing of the dollars held by foreign central banks, such purchases would cast doubt on the long-term viability of the fixed dollar price of gold and of the Bretton Woods System itself.[9]

In August 1971, however, President Nixon closed the U.S. Treasury's gold window, breaking the fixed gold-dollar link, in an effort to achieve an exchange-rate realignment – a devaluation of the dollar *vis-à-vis* the rest of the world's major currencies. Although that effort was successful, it was not long-lived. The pound was allowed to float in mid-1972, and the rest of the world's major currencies were likewise set free to float in early 1973, after the United States attempted unsuccessfully to achieve a second exchange-rate realignment. And that is where we are today, with two important qualifications. The euro has replaced the national currencies of the thirteen EMU members and most of the major Asian currencies (with the exception of the yen) are fairly tightly tied to the U.S. dollar, although their countries' governments profess to have floating rates or, at least, to allow modest flexibility.

The Dollar and the Euro

What, then, is likely to happen hereafter to the dollar's reserve role? The role of the euro has begun to grow. At the end of 1999, soon after the start of EMU, identified euro reserves were one-fourth the size of identified

---

[8] The reserve role of sterling shrank steadily, however, as the wartime controls that had defined the sterling area were gradually dismantled and as Britain's colonies achieved independence. The small reserve roles of the deutschemark and Swiss franc are commonly attributed to the fact that the German and Swiss bond markets were far smaller and less liquid than the markets for U.S. government securities.

[9] For the first warning of this systemic risk, see Triffin (1960).

dollar reserves, and nearly half of the euro reserves were held by near neighbors of EMU, including the countries in Central Europe that had joined the European Union in 2004. By mid-2006, however, identified euro reserves had tripled and were almost one-third as large as identified dollar reserves.[10]

Some say that the euro is destined to remain a regional currency and will not displace the dollar as the most important international currency, let alone the most important reserve currency.[11] However, two economists, Menzie Chinn and Jeffrey Frankel, have produced an econometric model that identifies some of the phenomena that caused the dollar to replace the pound as the dominant reserve currency, and they have then used their model to show how and why the euro might displace the dollar as the principal reserve currency during the next two decades.[12]

Although we are rather skeptical of the results obtained by Chinn and Frankel, we nevertheless believe that there could be significant changes in the relative roles of the dollar and euro during the next several years.

---

[10] Three caveats are in order here: (1) The data published by the IMF are U.S. dollar values, and the dollar value of the euro was higher in 2005 than in 1999. (2) The currency composition of the industrial countries' reserves may not fully reflect their asset preferences, because their choices are constrained. As no country can hold its own currency as a reserve asset, the United States cannot hold dollars, the ECB and euro zone countries cannot hold euros, and Japan cannot hold yen. (3) The unidentified holdings of reserves are, as noted, mainly those of developing countries, and their large size strongly suggests that they include the holdings of China and other East Asian countries. As those countries' reserves have grown hugely in recent years, and it is widely believed that East Asian reserves are invested largely in U.S. dollar assets, the ratio of euro to dollar reserves was probably smaller in 2005 than the figure cited in the text.

[11] See, e.g., Truman (2005), p. 63. Note, moreover, that Truman is writing about the overall role of the euro, not just its reserve-asset role, although the two may go together.

[12] Chinn and Frankel (2007); the likelihood and timing of this result depends on assumptions about the number and economic importance of the countries that join the euro zone in the next two decades and about the speed with which the dollar depreciates *vis-à-vis* the euro in the intervening years; their results also depend importantly on whether the United Kingdom, with its large financial markets, joins the euro zone during the next twenty years. See also Papaioannou, Portes, and Siourounis (2006), who use a mean-variance framework to estimate the optimal shares of the main international currencies in global reserve holdings, as well as their optimal shares in the reserve holdings of four big countries (Brazil, China, India, and Russia), taking account of the currency-composition of those countries' debts and trade. They find that actual dollar holdings are far larger than the optimal holdings predicted by their computations, which leads them to conclude that the euro poses a potential threat to the dominance of the dollar.

Much will depend on the speed with which the East Asian countries build up their reserves and how they choose to manage them.

If China and other East Asian countries allow their currencies to appreciate *vis-à-vis* the dollar, they will suffer losses on their dollar holdings. This possibility may explain a statement made by the State Administration of Foreign Exchange (SAFE), which manages China's reserves. In January 2006, SAFE said that it would seek to improve the operation and management of its foreign exchange reserves by optimizing their currency and asset structure. Soon thereafter, however, a senior official of the People's Bank of China explained that China might add to its holdings of other currencies as its reserves continued to grow but was not likely to reduce its existing dollar holdings.[13] Assuming that China continues to accumulate reserves, even at a slower pace than in recent years, what do these statements foretell? Consider two possibilities.

Suppose that China bought euros instead of dollars, stabilizing the renminbi against the euro rather than the dollar. It would presumably choose a renminbi-euro exchange rate that did not suddenly alter the renminbi-dollar rate. Thereafter, however, the dollar would depreciate against the renminbi, because China would no longer be accumulating dollars, assuming of course that no other participant in the foreign-exchange market stepped in to fill the void. With the dollar depreciating against the renminbi, China would then suffer losses on its existing dollar holdings. The dollar also would depreciate against the euro, because China would be buying euros, raising the global demand for them, and it would not be buying dollars, reducing the global demand for them.

Suppose instead that China continued to use the dollar as its intervention currency; it would buy dollars with renminbi, just as it does now, to prevent the renminbi from rising too fast or too far. It could then reenter the foreign-exchange market to sell some of its newly acquired dollars for euros and other foreign currencies, and these two-stage transactions would minimize the losses that China would suffer on its existing dollar

---

[13] The Chinese statements in the text jibe with the results of a recent survey covering fifty-six central banks. Apart from those that are near neighbors of the euro zone, few of those fifty-six central banks said that they planned to reduce their dollar holdings. Like SAFE itself, however, they said that they are investing in riskier assets, including corporate bonds, to raise the income they earn on their reserve holdings. See Carver et al. (2006).

holdings. China would not suffer large losses on its huge dollar holdings unless it ceased or limited its purchases of dollars before selling the dollars for euros.

Regardless of which scenario the Chinese authorities chose – changing the intervention currency to the euro or continuing with the dollar as the intervention currency but swapping the dollars for euros – these actions would necessarily reduce the Chinese demand for U.S. government securities, because China would accumulate fewer dollars. That would tend to raise U.S. interest rates, although there is much disagreement about the size of the increase. Some say that it would be no larger than fifty basis points. Ultimately, the total effect would depend on the behavior of others, not on China's behavior alone. If other holders of dollars concluded that China was no longer adding to its dollar holdings, they might start reducing their own dollar holdings, not just halt their purchases, and U.S. interest rates could then rise quite steeply.

Furthermore, under both scenarios, the euro would appreciate against the dollar. If that effect were large, it could depress Europe's exports and thus stultify economic growth in Europe. Therefore, the ECB might be compelled to intervene by selling euros for dollars and thus acquiring some of the dollars that China had ceased to accumulate. In effect, the large imbalance in transpacific trade would be offset by a transatlantic financial imbalance; the euro zone would be financing the U.S. current-account deficit with East Asia – a situation that could generate transatlantic tensions without greatly lessening transpacific tensions.

There is another possibility. As the East Asian countries strengthen and integrate their national bond markets, private investors around the world, including U.S. residents, may purchase more Asian securities and fewer American securities, reducing the net inflow of private capital to the United States – an inflow that has financed a significant part of the U.S. current-account deficit. Furthermore, Asian and other central banks wanting to diversify the asset composition of their own reserves may substitute Asian securities for U.S. securities.[14] This would not necessarily

---

[14] Recall the point made in the previous footnote that many countries' central banks are seeking to earn higher yields on their reserve assets and are thus willing to invest in riskier securities. There have, indeed, been reports that China is starting to acquire debt instruments issued by other East Asian countries.

affect the dollar values of the Asian currencies; that would depend on the responses of the Asian central banks to the resulting demand for their countries' currencies. Yet it would necessarily reduce their demand for U.S. government securities, adding to the upward pressure on U.S. interest rates that is certain to occur if China continues to build up its reserves but invests the increments in nondollar currencies.

Outcomes like this are quite likely unless the United States and the East Asian countries make the major policy changes needed to reduce the huge transpacific payments imbalance that is an underlying cause of transpacific tensions.

The Controversy over Sustainability

To discuss the measures required to reduce the huge transpacific imbalance would take us far afield. It is worth dwelling briefly, however, on a related issue – whether that imbalance is sustainable over the medium term or has to be addressed as speedily as possible.

Some economists maintain that the situation is sustainable. Their view derives from the belief that the growth and social stability of China require that country to increase its exports. Otherwise, they say, it cannot create the huge number of jobs needed to absorb its vast rural population, which still lives in poverty. In their view, then, China cannot permit the large appreciation of the renminbi that would be required to limit the growth of its exports and thereby reduce its huge current-account surplus, and it will perforce continue to accumulate reserves in one form or another.[15]

Other economists disagree strongly. The situation, they say, is unsustainable and must be rectified as rapidly as possible. There must be

---

[15] See, e.g., Dooley, Folkerts-Landau, and Garber (2005), in which they collect their previous writings on this subject, and Dooley and Garber (2005) in which they provide an up-to-date summary of their views. They do not claim that the present situation can last indefinitely. But they draw an analogy with the Bretton Woods System and claim that that the world is closer to 1958, when the Bretton Woods System was young, than to 1968, when it was nearing collapse. In one of their papers, moreover, they argue that China's huge dollar reserves serve a further purpose; they are, in effect, collateral against the risks faced by foreign investors in China. See also Cooper (2005) who likewise agrees that the United States can continue to live for a long time with a large current-account deficit, and the *Economic Report of the President* (2006), ch. 6, which takes the same view.

reciprocal policy changes by the principal parties involved – the United States and China – as well as a significant change in the renminbi-dollar exchange rate. Otherwise, they say, the transpacific imbalance may end in a very disorderly way.[16] It will intensify protectionist pressures in the United States and even give rise to a run on the dollar by official as well as private holders. Concerns of this sort were reflected in a recommendation by the Managing Director of the IMF, who proposed that the Fund undertake multilateral consultations with the principal countries involved whenever the policies of those countries pose a serious threat to the stability of the global economy.[17]

It should perhaps be noted, however, that one of our own recommendations, if adopted in East Asia, could perhaps inhibit rectification of the transpacific imbalance. In Chapter 6, we defined two types of currency baskets, an *internal* basket comprising the currencies of the East Asian countries, and an *external* basket comprising the dollar, euro, and yen. We then gave two reasons for favoring the latter.

First, it would limit the size of fluctuations in the value of each East Asian currency, not only against the dollar, euro, and yen, but also against the currencies of the other Asian countries that adopted the same basket. An internal basket, by contrast, would limit fluctuations in intra-Asian exchange rates but would not limit fluctuations against the dollar, euro, and yen. Second, countries adopting an external basket would import to some degree the monetary policies of the major countries whose currencies comprised the external basket, whereas countries adopting an internal basket would have no obvious anchor for their monetary policies.

When viewed from the U.S. standpoint, however, as well as other countries affected by the values of their national currencies in terms of the

---

[16] See, e.g., Roubini and Setser (2004), Blanchard, Giavazzi, and Sa (2005), Edwards (2005), Faruqee et al. (2007), and Obstfeld and Rogoff (2005, 2007). Nevertheless, the members of this group and others who agree with them differ in their views about the amount by which the U.S. current-account deficit must be reduced, as well as the size of the exchange-rate change required for that purpose. Their differences are due in part to different ways of estimating the way that trade flows would respond to exchange-rate changes, but they are also due to different views about the impact of a change in the renminbi-dollar rate on other Asian currencies.

[17] IMF (2006), pp. 3–4.

renminbi and other Asian currencies, an internal basket would be more satisfactory. It would not limit fluctuations between outsiders' currencies and the Asian currencies, taken as a group. In other words, an internal basket would allow the Asian currencies to float more freely against the currencies of all other major countries.[18]

Asia and the IMF

The Asian currency crisis of the late 1990s was, of course, the catalyst for Asian cooperation in monetary and financial matters. For reasons described in the previous chapter, there was deep dissatisfaction with the role played by the IMF during the crisis, as well as criticism of the United States for failing to come to the aid of Thailand. The amounts of financing were deemed to be inadequate, and the policy conditions attached to IMF financing were roundly criticized. The macroeconomic policy conditions were widely blamed, somewhat unfairly, for the dramatic fall in output in the crisis-stricken countries. The very large number of structural reforms required by the IMF were rightly seen by some as being irrelevant to the Asian countries' immediate problems, and they were seen by others as a brazen attempt to replace an indigenous development strategy – one that had been widely praised for fostering rapid economic growth – with a development strategy less appropriate to the Asian context.

The resentments stirred by the Asian crisis had their first formal man-ifestation in the Japanese proposal to establish an Asian Monetary Fund, and though it was rejected in 1997, the idea lives on. The Chiang Mai Initiative, described in Chapter 6, is still tethered to the IMF, but it is seen by some in Asia as the natural precursor to an AMF.[19] The existing link to the IMF – the need for a participant in the CMI to have an IMF agreement

---

[18] Although he did not distinguish between the two types of currency baskets, the U.S. Under Secretary of the Treasury for International Affairs has expressed similar reser-vations about forms of currency cooperation that might limit exchange-rate flexibility in East Asia; see Adams (2006), p. 2. (It would be possible, however, for a group of countries using a common external basket to make periodic changes to the value of that basket *vis-à-vis* the currencies entering the basket. They would have merely to agree on the size of the uniform change in the value of the basket, expressed in terms of their own countries' currencies. What may be simple in principle, however, could be hard in practice.)

[19] See, e.g., the sources cited in Chapter 6, note 26.

before it can draw heavily on the credit limes created by the CMI – is, we said, an artifact of the ASEAN inhibition against intervention in the internal affairs of the ASEAN countries. If that inhibition is overcome, there will be no major obstacle to the creation of an AMF.

There is, moreover, evidence that this inhibition will be overcome. Heretofore, the policy dialogue in East Asia has focused on common threats – problems that all of its members may face – and on containing contagion in the event of a future crisis in an East Asian country. Recently, however, the Asian Development Bank has established an Office of Regional Economic Integration which could, with time, come to resemble a regional department of the IMF. It would be able to offer policy advice to individual Asian countries and, eventually, aid in the formulation of policy conditions analogous to those in the Letter of Intent required by the IMF when a country seeks financing from that institution. Even before that happens, moreover, the participants in the CMI may take two more steps toward an AMF: the multilateralization of the bilateral credit lines of the CMI, and the partial pooling of national reserves to supplement the limited financing available under the CMI and, more important, to reduce the high opportunity cost of holding large reserves.

The creation of regional monetary funds – and there might be more of them if East Asia took the lead – would pose a threat to the primacy of the IMF and would thereby diminish the global influence of the United States.[20] Although the United States does not "run" the Fund, its influence exceeds its large voting power. It would indeed be hard to find a significant number of cases in which the IMF has acted without the explicit or tacit consent of the United States.

The Fund itself has barely begun to respond to the challenge posed by the likely creation of regional rivals – agencies to which governments might turn for larger amounts of financial assistance than those available from the IMF or, more importantly, with fewer or less rigorous policy commitments. It has acknowledged that many developing countries, including some East Asian countries, are underrepresented in the IMF

---

[20] There is already one such fund, the Arab Monetary Fund established in 1976, but it has not played a major role within its own region. In 2004, the most recent year for which data are available, its lending totaled only $180 million.

and has undertaken to address the problem by revising IMF quotas and thus voting power. But a redistribution of voting power is necessarily a zero-sum game, requiring the consent of those who lose as well as those who gain. The Managing Director of the IMF also suggested that the IMF "should be open to supporting regional and other arrangements for pooling reserves," citing the Chiang Mai Initiative and the Fund for Latin American Reserves involving countries, in the Andean Region.[21] Yet he has not explicitly confronted the risk that regional arrangements might undermine the rigor of Fund conditionality or the risk that countries with large reserves might lend directly to their neighbors on terms set unilaterally.

In a thoughtful account of the potential problems posed by regional arrangements, including regional monetary funds, C. Randall Henning has suggested that the Fund adopt criteria to distinguish acceptable regional arrangements from unacceptable ones and that it formulate principles to govern future relations between regional arrangements and the IMF itself. Under those principles, a regional arrangement would be legitimate if and only if it mimicked the practices of the Fund or supplemented Fund financing when, for instance, the small size of a country's quota limited its access to Fund credit. Henning goes on to suggest that his proposals could be introduced in a soft or hard form. A hard form, however, would have to be backed by sanctions and the power to impose them would have to be conferred formally on the IMF by amending its Articles of Agreement. Yet countries contemplating regional arrangements, including the East Asian countries, might unite to block any such amendment.[22]

---

[21] IMF (2006), p. 7. The Managing Director at the time was Rodrigo de Rato.

[22] Henning argues, however, that the adoption of his rules would be beneficial to East Asia. "By defining more clearly the types of facilities that are in and out of bounds, these principles would simplify bargaining within the region over the directions in which the CMI could evolve. They dampen the temptation to experiment with unorthodox arrangements that could lead to mistakes that set back or kill the regional integration process" (Henning, 2006, p. 181). More important, Henning's proposal, even in its strong form, might be attractive to countries such as China and Japan, which are apt to be net lenders *via* an AMF and would therefore want adequate assurance that the net borrowers would repay their debts, including conditionality comparable to that of the IMF.

Most important from the U.S. standpoint, the proliferation of regional funds, even if formally consistent with the rules proposed by Henning, would necessarily diminish the influence of the United States, as it would have no role whatsoever in the decision-making processes of regional funds.

Why We Might Be Wrong about the Future of the Monetary System

It would be foolhardy to look beyond the next two decades – the period we chose for our assessment of the prospects for monetary integration and, in this concluding chapter, the international role of the dollar. You have only to look back twenty years and ask how many of the major events that took place in that period could have been anticipated before it began. The fall of the Berlin Wall occurred at the start of that period and it was unexpected, as was the subsequent disintegration of the Soviet Union itself. The rise of China had begun, but its extraordinary growth and its systemic importance today were not widely foreseen. And when we look ahead, we know that we will be surprised, sometimes unpleasantly.

There are, even now, reasons for concern about the prospects for an orderly resolution of the huge transpacific imbalance. We may well see a revival of U.S. private savings as households are obliged to reduce their debts by higher mortgage interest rates. We are less likely to see a rapid reduction of the U.S. budget deficit, regardless of the outcome of the 2008 election. And we are likewise unlikely to see the substantial fall in Asian saving needed to offset any increase of U.S. private saving, nor a large but orderly appreciation of the Asian currencies that must accompany the reciprocal changes in saving needed to reduce the U.S. current-account deficit.

Does this mean that the dollar will cease to be the dominant currency in the international monetary system? Probably not, although we may have to pay a high price in terms of capital losses on real and financial assets, as well as output losses, on the way to a new equilibrium in international payments.

What about our answer to the main question raised in this book? Could we see more monetary unions than we now anticipate?

We can conceive of one such outcome. If Canada becomes a major oil exporter during the next decade, thanks to the exploitation of Alberta's vast tar sands, the Canadian dollar is apt to appreciate by more than it has recently, and Canadian industry will be severely handicapped in its main export markets. Ontario might then favor a monetary union with the United States, even on U.S. terms – a union dominated by the United States – and the outcome might then be decided by interprovincial bargaining over the domestic distribution of Alberta's future wealth.

What about Latin America? A monetary union with the United States would be anathema to the neopopulists who govern some countries now and could govern a few more, and a monetary union *within* South America is not apt to appeal to them or their followers either, nor would it make much economic sense given the fairly low levels of trade within much of the region. There is, of course, the possibility of *de jure* dollarization by more countries in Central America, and even in South America, but that would not be an attractive option for those who have come to power or prominence by riding the current wave of anti-American sentiment. It would be hard, even for a demagogue, to exploit anti-American sentiment and, at the same time, adopt the U.S. dollar.

Turning finally to East Asia, where we have seen some signs of interest in monetary integration, we must again emphasize the primacy of politics. There may well be a significant improvement in relations among the three large countries of North East Asia, but there may be new divisions within South East Asia. The influence of militant Islam may grow in Indonesia and Malaysia, shattering the fragile cohesion of ASEAN and precluding the possibility raised in Chapter 6 of a full-fledged monetary union of the ASEAN countries.

Economics and demography matter too, however, and they point to a major change in the relative roles of China and Japan. Thus far, Japan has sought to lead in fostering monetary cooperation among the East Asian countries. It has exercised its influence directly and *via* the ADB in a defensive attempt to shape the institutional framework for monetary cooperation before China is ready to claim that role. Yet leadership may pass to China even if China does not seek to claim it. If its economy continues to grow at or near the rapid rates achieved in recent years and the Chinese authorities are able to maintain domestic political stability, the ASEAN countries will have to defer to China even if it does not seek to exercise leadership in regional monetary matters.

The most likely outcome in our view is the one suggested in Chapter 6, the use of a currency basket by the ASEAN countries, but we should not rule out a radically different result – a decision by some of the ASEAN countries to peg their currencies exclusively to the renminbi once it has become fully convertible. The renminbi is not likely to become a full-fledged reserve currency, even for the ASEAN countries. It cannot do that unless China undertakes wide-ranging financial reforms aimed at making its currency and bond markets deeper and more liquid. But the renminbi could perhaps replace the dollar as the principal currency in which intra-Asian trade is invoiced, not only trade with China itself but between the ASEAN countries.

Although monetary union began in Europe, monetary innovation is bound to take place elsewhere, and it may take forms we cannot now anticipate.

References

Adams, Timothy D. (2006), "Remarks at the World Economic Forum – East Asia; Panel on Asia's Financial Integration." Washington, DC: U.S. Treasury.

Ahearne, Alan, and Jean Pisani-Ferry (2006), "The Euro: Only for the Agile," Policy Brief 1. Brussels: Bruegel.

Al-Bassam, Khalid (2003), "The Gulf Cooperation Council Monetary Union: A Bahraini Perspective," in J. Hawkins and P. Masson, eds., *Regional Currency Areas and the Use of Foreign Currencies*, Paper 17. Basel: Bank for International Settlements.

Alesina, Alberto, and Robert J. Barro (2002), "Currency Unions," *Quarterly Journal of Economics, CXVII*, pp. 409–36.

Alesina, Alberto, Robert J. Barro, and Silvana Tenreyro (2003), "Optimal Currency Areas," in M. Gertler and K. Rogoff, eds., *NBER Macroeconomics Annual 2002*. Cambridge, MA: MIT Press, pp. 301–45.

Al-Falasi, Mohammed Ali Bin Zayed (2003), "Concrete Steps Towards the Establishment of a Monetary Union for the Gulf Cooperation Council Countries," in J. Hawkins and P. Masson, eds., *Regional Currency Areas and the Use of Foreign Currencies*, Paper 17. Basel: Bank for International Settlements.

Al-Jasser, Muhammad, and Abdulrahman Al-Hamidy (2003), "A Common Currency Area for the Gulf Region," in J. Hawkins and P. Masson, eds., *Regional Currency Areas and the Use of Foreign Currencies*, Paper 17. Basel: Bank for International Settlements.

Allington, Nigel F. B., Paul A. Kattuman, and Florian A. Waldmann (2005), "One Market, One Money, One Price?" *International Journal of Central Banking, 1*, pp. 73–115.

Amano, Robert, and Simon van Norden (1995), "Terms of Trade and Real Exchange Rates: The Canadian Evidence," *Journal of International Money and Finance, 14*, pp. 83–104.

Amyx, Jennifer (2005), "What Motivates Regional Financial Cooperation in East Asia Today?" *Asia Pacific Issues, 76.* Honolulu: East-West Center.

Andrews, David M. (2003), "The Committee of Central Bank Governors as a Source of Rules," *Journal of European Public Policy, X*, pp. 956–73.

Angeloni, Ignazio (2004), "Unilateral and Multilateral Currency Unions: Thoughts from an EMU Perspective," in V. Alexander, J. Mélitz, and G. M. von Furstenberg, eds., *Monetary Unions and Hard Pegs*. Oxford: Oxford University Press, pp. 41–49.

Angeloni, Ignazio, and Michael Ehrmann (2003), "Monetary Transmission in the Euro Area: Early Evidence," *Economic Policy, XXXVII*, pp. 469–501.

Angeloni, Ignazio, and Michael Ehrmann (2004), "Euro Area Inflation Differentials," Working Paper 388. Frankfurt: European Central Bank.

Angeloni, Ignazio, Anil K. Kashyap, Benoît Mojon, and Daniele Terlizzese (2003a), "Monetary Transmission in the Euro Area: Does the Interest Rate Channel Explain All?" Working Paper 9984. Cambridge, MA: National Bureau of Economic Research.

Angeloni, Ignazio, Anil K. Kashyap, Benoît Mojon, and Daniele Terlizzese (2003b), "The Output Composition Puzzle: A Difference in the Monetary Transmission Mechanism in the Euro Area and U.S." Working Paper 9985. Cambridge, MA: National Bureau of Economic Research.

Arroyo, Heliodoro Temprano (2002), "Latin America's Integration Processes in Light of the EU's Experience with EMU," Economic Papers 173. Brussels: European Commission.

Asian Development Bank (2002a), "Study on Monetary and Financial Cooperation in East Asia (Summary Report)." Paper Prepared for the Kobe Research Project Sponsored by the ASEM (Asia-Europe Meeting) of Finance Ministers.

Asian Development Bank (2002b), "A Regional Early Warning System Prototype for East Asia." Paper Prepared for the Kobe Research Project Sponsored by the ASEM (Asia-Europe Meeting) of Finance Ministers.

Associated Press (2006), "Chávez Marks Mercosur Entry With Summit," July 5.

Baele, Lieven, Annalisa Ferrando, Peter Hördahl, Elizaveta Krylova, and Cyril Monnet (2004), "Measuring Financial Integration in the Euro Area," Occasional Paper 14. Frankfurt: European Central Bank.

Bailliu, Jeannine, Robert Lafrance, and Jean-François Perrault (2003), "Does Exchange Rate Policy Matter for Growth," *International Finance, 6*, pp. 381–414.

Baliño, Tomás J. T., and Charles Enoch (1997), *Currency Board Arrangements: Issues and Experiences*, Occasional Paper 151. Washington, DC: International Monetary Fund.

Baliño, Tomás J. T., Adam Bennett, and Eduardo Borensztein (1999), *Monetary Policy in Dollarized Economies*, Occasional Paper 171. Washington, DC: International Monetary Fund.

Bank for International Settlements (2005), "Triennial Central Bank Survey: Foreign Exchange and Derivative Market Activity in 2004." Basel: Bank for International Settlements.

Barro, Robert J. (1999), "Let the Dollar Reign Supreme from Seattle to Santiago," *The Wall Street Journal*, March 8.

Barro, Robert J. (2004), "Currency Unions for the World," in Asian Development Bank, *Monetary and Financial Integration in East Asia: The Way Ahead*, vol 2. Basingstoke: Palgrave, pp. 1–47.

Barro, Robert J., and David B. Gordon (1983), "Rules, Discretion, and Reputation in a Model of Monetary Policy," *Journal of Monetary Economics, XII*, pp. 101–121.

Bartolini, Leonardo, and Alessandro Prati (2003), "The execution of monetary policy: a tale of two central banks," *Economic Policy, XXXVII*, pp. 435–67.

Bayoumi, Tamim, and Barry Eichengreen (1994a), "Monetary and Exchange Rate Arrangements for NAFTA," *Journal of Development Economics, 43*, pp. 125–65.

Bayoumi, Tamim, and Barry Eichengreen (1994b), "One Money or Many? Analyzing the Prospects for Monetary Unification in Various Parts of the World," *Princeton Studies in International Finance 78*. Princeton, NJ: Princeton University International Finance Section.

Bayoumi, Tamim, and Barry Eichengreen (1998), "Exchange Rate Volatility and Intervention: Implications of the Theory of Optimum Currency Areas," Discussion Paper 1982. London: Centre for Economic Policy Research.

Bayoumi, Tamim, and Barry Eichengreen (1999), "Operationalizing the Theory of Optimum Currency Areas," in R. E. Baldwin, D. Cohen, A. Sapir, and A. J. Venables, eds., *Market Integration, Regionalism, and the Global Economy*. Cambridge: Cambridge University Press, pp. 187–216.

Bayoumi, Tamim, and Paolo Mauro (1999), "The Suitability of ASEAN for a Regional Currency Arrangement," Working Paper 99/162. Washington, DC: International Monetary Fund.

Bayoumi, Tamim, Barry Eichengreen, and Paolo Mauro (2000), "On Regional Monetary Arrangements for ASEAN," *Journal of the Japanese and International Economies, 14*, pp. 121–48.

Beetsma, Roel M. W. J., and Xavier Debrun (2004), "Reconciling Stability and Growth: Smart Pacts and Structural Reforms," *IMF Staff Papers, 51*, pp. 431–56.

Begg, David, Francesco Giavazzi, Luigi Spaventa, and Charles Wyplosz (1991), "European Monetary Union – the Macro Issues," in *Monitoring European Integration: The Making of Monetary Union*. London: Centre for Economic Policy Research, pp. 1–66.

Begg, David, Fabio Canova, Paul de Grauwe, Antonio Fatás, and Phillip R. Lane (2002), "Surviving the Slowdown," *Monitoring the European Central Bank 4*. London: Centre for Economic Policy Research.

Beine, Michel, and Serge Coulombe (2003), "Regional Perspectives on Dollarization in Canada," *Journal of Regional Science, 43*, pp. 541–69.

Belke, Ansgar, and Daniel Gros (2002), "Monetary Integration in the Southern Cone: Mercosur Is Not Like the EU?" Working Paper 188. Santiago: Central Bank of Chile.

Berg, Andrew, and Eduardo R. Borensztein (2003), "The Pros and Cons of Full Dollarization," in D. Salvatore, J. W. Dean, and T. D. Willett, eds., *The Dollarization Debate*. Oxford: Oxford University Press, pp. 72–101.

Berger, Helge (2002), "The ECB and Euro-Area Enlargement," Working Paper 02/175. Washington, DC: International Monetary Fund.

Bergsten, C. Fred, and Yung Chul Park (2002), "Toward Creating a Regional Monetary Arrangement in East Asia," Research Paper 50. Tokyo: ADB Institute.

Bhagwati, Jagdish, and Arvin Panagariya (1996), "Preferential Trading Arrangements and Multilateralism: Strangers, Friends or Foes?" Working Paper 22. College Park, MD: University of Maryland Center for International Economics.

Bini Smaghi, Lorenzo, and Silvia Vori (1992), "Rating the EC as an Optimal Currency Area," in R. O'Brien, ed., *Finance and the International Economy* 6. Oxford: Oxford University Press for the Amex Bank Review, pp. 78–104.

Bird, Graham, and Ramkishen S. Rajan (2002), "The Evolving East Asian Financial Architecture," *Essays in International Economics* 226. Princeton, NJ: Princeton University International Economics Section.

Blanchard, Olivier, Francesco Giavazzi, and Filia Sa (2005), "International Investors, the U.S. Current Account, and the Dollar," *Brookings Papers on Economic Activity, 1*, pp. 1–49.

Blanchard, Olivier J., and Lawrence F. Katz (1992), "Regional Evolutions," *Brookings Papers on Economic Activity, 1*, pp. 1–75.

Blanchard, Olivier J., and Danny Quah (1989), "The Dynamic Effects of Aggregate Supply and Demand Disturbances," *American Economic Review, LXXIX*, pp. 655–673.

Blinder, Alan, Charles Goodhart, Philip Hildebrand, David Lipton, and Charles Wyplosz (2001), "How Do Central Banks Talk?" *Geneva Report on the World Economy IV*. London: Centre for Economic Policy Research.

Bogetić, Željko (2000), "Official Dollarization: Current Experiences and Issues," *Cato Journal, 20:2*, pp. 179–213.

Bordo, Michael D., and Lars Jonung (2003), "The Future of EMU: What Does the History of Monetary Unions Tell Us?" in F. H. Capie and G. E. Wood, eds., *Monetary Unions: Theory, History, Public Choice*. London: Routledge, pp. 42–69.

Boughton, James M. (1993), "The Economics of the CFA Franc Zone," in P. R. Masson and M. P. Taylor, eds., *Policy Issues in the Operation of Currency Unions*. New York: Cambridge University Press, pp. 96–107.

Brandão de Brito, José (2004), "Monetary Integration in East Asia: An Empirical Approach," *Journal of Economic Integration, 18*, pp. 536–67.

Bubula, Andrea, and Inci Ötker-Robe (2002), "The Evolution of Exchange Rate Regimes since 1990: Evidence from De Facto Policies," Working Paper 02/155. Washington, DC: International Monetary Fund.

Buiter, Willem H. (1999), "The EMU and the NAMU: What is the Case for North American Monetary Union?" *Canadian Public Policy – Analyse de Politiques, XXV*, pp. 285–305.

Buiter, Willem H., Giancarlo Corsetti, and Nouriel Roubini (1993), "Excessive deficits: sense and nonsense in the Treaty of Maastricht," *Economic Policy, XVI*, pp. 57–100.

"Business and Policy Views on the Monetary Integration of North America" (2003), Thematic Issue, *International Management, 8*.

Buti, Marco (2006), "Will the New Stability and Growth Pact Succeed? An Economic and Political Perspective," Economic Papers 241. Brussels: European Commission.

Buti, Marco, Sylvester Eijffinger, and Daniele Franco (2003), "Revisiting the Stability and Growth Pact: Grand Design or Internal Adjustment?" Discussion Papers 3692. London: Centre for Economic Policy Research.

Calvo, Guillermo A. (1999), "On Dollarization." College Park, MD: University of Maryland, http://www/bsos.umd.edu/econ/ciepn5.pdf.

Calvo, Guillermo A., and Carmen M. Reinhart (2002), "Fear of Floating," *Quarterly Journal of Economics, CXVII*, pp. 379–408.

Carr, Jack, Thomas J. Courchene, John W. Crow, Herbert Grubel, and Bernard Wolf (1999), "Round Table on a North American Currency," *Canadian Parliamentary Review, 22:2*, pp. 5–13.

Carver, Nick (2006), "Trends in reserve management: 2006 survey results" in *RBS Reserve Management Trends 2006*. London: Central Banking Publications.

Castellano, Marc (2000), "East Asian Monetary Union: More Than Just Talk?" *JEI Report 12*. Tokyo: Japan Economic Institute.

Cavoli, Tony, and Ramkishen S. Rajan (2007), "Managing in the Middle: Characterizing Singapore's Exchange Rate Policy," *Asian Economic Journal* (forthcoming).

Cecchetti, Stephen, and Mark Wynne (2003), "Inflation measurement and the ECB's pursuit of price stability: a first assessment," *Economic Policy, XXXVII*, pp. 395–434.

Chang, Li Lin, and Ramkrishen Rajan (2001), "The Economics and Politics of Monetary Regionalism in Asia" *ASEAN Economic Bulletin, 18*, pp 103–18.

Chappell, Henry W., Jr., Rob Roy McGregor, and Todd Vermilyea (2006), "Regional Economic Conditions and Monetary Policy" (unpublished manuscript).

Cheung, Yin-Wong, and Jude Yuen (2005), An Output Perspective on a Northeast Asian Currency Union," in P. de Grauwe and J. Mélitz, eds., *Prospects for Monetary Unions after the Euro*. Cambridge, MA: MIT Press, pp. 290–317.

Chinn, Menzie, and Jeffrey Frankel (2007), "Will the Euro Eventually Surpass the Dollar as Leading International Reserve Currency?" in R. H. Clarida, ed., *G7 Current Account Imbalances: Sustainability and Adjustment*. Chicago: University of Chicago Press, pp. 283–322.

Chriszt, Michael (2000), "Perspectives on a Potential North American Monetary Union," *Economic Review, 85: 4*. Atlanta: Federal Reserve Bank of Atlanta, pp. 29–38.

Clarida, Richard, and Jordi Gali (1994), "Sources of Real Exchange Rate Fluctuations: How Important Are Nominal Shocks?" *Carnegie-Rochester Conference Series on Public Policy, 41*, pp. 1–56.

Cohen, Benjamin J. (1993), "Beyond EMU: The Problem of Sustainability," *Economics and Politics, 5*, pp. 187–203.

Cohen, Benjamin J. (1998), *The Geography of Money*. Ithaca, NY: Cornell University Press.

Cohen, Benjamin J. (2003a), "Are Monetary Unions Inevitable?" *International Studies Perspectives, 4*, pp. 275–92.

Cohen, Benjamin J. (2003b), "Monetary Unions," EH.Net Encyclopedia, http://eh.net/encyclopedia.

Cohen, Benjamin J. (2004a), *The Future of Money*. Princeton, NJ: Princeton University Press.

Cohen, Benjamin J. (2004b), "America's Interest in Dollarization," in V. Alexander, J. Mélitz, and G. M. von Furtstenberg, eds., *Monetary Unions and Hard Pegs*. Oxford: Oxford University Press, pp. 289–301.

Cohen, Benjamin J. (2006), "North American Monetary Union: A United States Perspective," *Current Politics and Economics of Europe* 17, pp. 219–39.

Coleman, Andrew (2001), "Three Perspectives on an Australasian Monetary Union." *Conference Volume on Future Directions for Monetary Policy in East Asia*. Sydney: Reserve Bank of Australia, pp. 156–88.

Collignon, Stefan, and Daniela Schwarzer (2003), *Private Sector Involvement in the Euro: The Power of Ideas*. London and New York: Routledge.

Committee for the Study of Economic and Monetary Union (1989), *Report*. Luxembourg: Office for Official Publications of the European Communities [cited as Delors Report (1989)].

Cooper, Richard N. (2005), "Living with Global Imbalances: A Contrarian View," *Policy Briefs in International Economics 05-3*. Washington, DC: Peterson Institute for International Economics.

Courchene, Thomas J., and Richard G. Harris (1999), "From Fixing to Monetary Union: Options for North American Currency Integration," C. D. Howe Institute Commentary 127, Toronto: C. D. Howe Institute.

Courchene, Thomas J., and Richard G. Harris (2003), "North American Currency Integration: A Canadian Perspective," in D. Salvatore, J. W. Dean, and T. D. Willett, eds., *The Dollarization Debate*. Oxford: Oxford University Press, pp. 299–317.

Cowan, Kevin, Erwin Hansen, and Luis O. Herrera (2005), "Currency Mismatches, Balance Sheet Effects and Hedging in Chilean Non-Financial Corporations," in R. Caballero, C. Calderon, and L. F. Cespedes, eds., *External Vulnerability and Preventive Policies*. Chile: Central Bank of Chile.

Crowe, Christopher, and Ellen E. Meade (2007), "Central Bank Governance: What Is It and Does It Matter?" *Journal of Economic Perspectives* (forthcoming).

Cuevas, Alfredo, and Alejandro Werner (2003), "Mexico's Experience with a Flexible Exchange Rate Regime," *International Management, 8*, pp. 29–49.

Da Motta Veiga, Pedro (2004), "MERCOSUR: In Search of a New Agenda," Integration and Trade Paper 6, Washington, DC: Inter-American Development Bank.

Debelle, Guy, and Stanley Fischer (2004), "How Independent Should a Central Bank Be?" in J. C. Fuhrer, ed., *Goals, Guidelines, and Constraints for Monetary Policy Makers*. Federal Reserve Bank of Boston Conference Series 38, pp. 195–225.

de Brouwer, Gordon (2002), "Does a Formal Common-Basket Peg in East Asia Make Economic Sense?" in G. de Brouwer, ed., *Financial Markets and Policies in East Asia*. London: Routledge, pp. 286–314.

de Brouwer, Gordon (2004a), "Institutions to Promote Financial Stability: Reflections on East Asia and an Asian Monetary Fund," http://www.weforum.org/pdf/initiatives/MPC/Brouwer.pdf.

de Brouwer, Gordon (2004b), "IMF and ADB Perspectives on Regional Surveillance in East Asia," in G. de Brouwer and Y. Wang, eds., *Financial Governance in East Asia: Policy Dialogue, Surveillance and Cooperation*. London: Routledge, pp. 38–49.

de Cecco, Marcello (1992), "European Monetary and Financial Cooperation before the First World War," *Rivista di Storia Economica, 9: 1–2*, pp. 55–76.

de Vanssay, Xavier (2002), "Monetary Unions: A Historical Perspective," in P. M. Crowley, ed., *Before and Beyond EMU*. London: Routledge, pp. 26–41.

Dodge, David (2001), "Canada's Monetary Policy Approach: It Works for Canadians," Speech to the Edmonton Chamber of Commerce (June).

Dooley, Michael, David Folkerts-Landau, and Peter Garber (2005), *International Financial Stability: Asia, Interest Rates and the Dollar*. London: Deutsche Bank Global Research.

Dooley, Michael, and Peter Garber (2005), "Is It 1958 or 1968? Three Notes on the Longevity of the Revived Bretton Woods System," *Brookings Papers on Economic Activity, 1*, pp. 148–188.

Dornbusch, Rudiger (1990), "Two-Track EMU, Now!" in R. Layard, ed., *Britain and EMU*. London: Centre for Economic Performance, pp. 103–111.

Dornbusch, Rudiger, and Yung Chul Park (1999), "Flexibility or Nominal Anchors," in S. Collignon, J. Pisani-Ferry, and Y. C. Park, eds., *Exchange Rate Policies in Emerging Asian Countries*. London: Routledge, pp. 3–34.

Dwyer, Gerald P., Jr., and James R. Lothian (2004), "International Money and Common Currencies in Historical Perspective," in V. Alexander, J. Mélitz, and G. M. von Furstenberg, eds., *Monetary Unions and Hard Pegs*. Oxford: Oxford University Press, pp. 51–66.

Dyson, Kenneth, and Kevin Featherstone (1999), *The Road to Maastricht*. Oxford: Oxford University Press.

Economic Report of the President (2006). Washington, DC: U.S. Government Printing Office.

Edwards, Sebastian (2002), "The Great Exchange Rate Debate after Argentina," Working Paper 9257. Cambridge, MA: National Bureau of Economic Research.

Edwards, Sebastian (2003), "Dollarization: Myths and Realities," in D. Salvatore, J. W. Dean, and T. D. Willett, eds., *The Dollarization Debate*. Oxford: Oxford University Press, pp. 111–28.

Edwards, Sebastian (2005), "Is the U.S. Current Account Deficit Sustainable? If Not, How Costly Is Adjustment Likely to Be?" *Brookings Papers on Economic Activity, 1*, pp. 211–72.

Edwards, Sebastian, and Igal Magendzo (2003), "A Currency of One's Own? An Empirical Investigation on Dollarization and Independent Currency Unions," Working Paper 9514. Cambridge, MA: National Bureau of Economic Research.

Eichengreen, Barry (1994), *International Monetary Arrangements for the 21st Century*. Washington, DC: The Brookings Institution.

Eichengreen, Barry (1998), "Does MERCOSUR Need a Single Currency?" Working Paper 6821. Cambridge, MA: National Bureau of Economic Research.

Eichengreen, Barry (2001a), "What Problems Can Dollarization Solve?" *Journal of Policy Modeling, XXIII*, pp. 267–277.

Eichengreen, Barry (2001b), "Hanging Together? On Monetary and Financial Cooperation in Asia," emlab.berkeley.edu/users/eichengreen/research/eastasiashadid2.pdf.

Eichengreen, Barry (2002), "What to Do with the Chiang Mai Initiative," *Asian Economic Papers, 2*, pp. 1–52.

Eichengreen, Barry (2004), "The Case for Floating Exchange Rates in Asia," in Asian Development Bank, *Monetary and Financial Integration in East Asia: The Way Ahead*, vol. 2. Basingstoke: Palgrave, pp. 490–89.

Eichengreen, Barry (2005), "Real and Pseudo Preconditions for an Asian Monetary Union," in *Asian Economic Cooperation and Integration: Prospects, Prospects, and Challenges.* Manila: Asian Development Bank, pp. 197–212.

Eichengreen, Barry (2006), "The Parallel Currency Approach to Asian Monetary Integration," *American Economic Review, 96: 2*, pp. 432–36.

Eichengreen, Barry, and Tamim Bayoumi (1999), "Is Asia an Optimum Currency Area? Can It Become One?" in S. Collignon, J. Pisani-Ferry, and Y. C. Park, eds., *Exchange Rate Policies in Emerging Asian Countries.* London: Routledge, pp. 347–66.

Eichengreen, Barry, and Ricardo Hausmann (1999), "Exchange Rates and Financial Fragility," *Proceedings: New Challenges for Monetary Policy.* Kansas City, MO: Federal Reserve Bank of Kansas City, pp. 329–68.

Eichengreen, Barry, and Pipat Luengnaruemitchai (2004), "What Doesn't Asia Have Bigger Bond Markets?" Working Paper 10576. Cambridge, MA: National Bureau of Economic Research.

Eichengreen, Barry, and Yung Chul Park (2005), "Why Has There Been Less Financial Integration in Asia than in Europe?" in T. Ito, Y. C. Park, and Y. C. Jong, eds., *A New Financial Market Structure for East Asia.* Northampton, MA: Edward Elgar.

Engel, Charles, and John Rogers (2004), "European product market integration after the euro," *Economic Policy, 19*, pp. 347–84.

Estevadeordal, Antoni, Junichi Goto, and Raul Saez (2000), "The New Regionalism in the Americas: The Case of MERCOSUR," Integration and Trade Paper 5. Washington, DC: Inter-American Development Bank.

European Central Bank (1999), "The stability-oriented monetary policy strategy of the Eurosystem," *Monthly Bulletin*, pp. 39–50 (January).

European Central Bank (2000a), "EMU and banking supervision," *Monthly Bulletin*, pp. 49–64 (April).

European Central Bank (2000b), "The two pillars of the ECB's monetary policy strategy," *Monthly Bulletin*, pp. 37–48 (November).

European Central Bank (2003), "The outcome of the ECB's evaluation of its monetary policy strategy," *Monthly Bulletin*, pp. 79–92 (June).

European Central Bank (2004), *Target Annual Report 2003.*

European Central Bank (2005a), *The Implementation of Monetary Policy in the Euro Area.*

European Central Bank (2005b), "Monetary policy and inflation differentials in a heterogeneous currency area," *Monthly Bulletin* (May).

European Commission (1990), "One Market, One Money," *European Economy, XLIV.*

European Commission (2004a), "EMU after 5 Years," *European Economy Special Report 1.*

European Commission (2004b), "Strengthening Economic Governance and Clarifying the Implementation of the Stability and Growth Pact." Communication from the Commission to the Council and the European Parliament [COM(2004) 581].

European Council (2005), Presidency Conclusions, March 22–23.

Faruqee, Hamid, Douglas Laxton, Dirk Muir, and Paolo A. Pesenti (2007), "Smooth Landing or Crash? Model-Based Scenarios of Global Current Account Rebalancing," in R. H. Clarida, ed., *G7 Current Account Imbalances: Sustainability and Adjustment.* Chicago: University of Chicago Press, pp. 377–451.

Fasano, Ugo, Rina Bhattacharya, and Andrea Schaechter (2003), *Monetary Union among Member Countries of the Gulf Cooperation Council,* Occasional Paper 223. Washington, DC: International Monetary Fund.

Fatàs, Antonio, Andrew Hughes Hallet, Anne Sibert, Rolf R. Strauch, and Jürgen von Hagen (2003), *Stability and Growth in Europe: Towards a Better Pact. Monitoring European Integration XIII.* London: Centre for Economic Policy Research.

Federal Reserve Bulletin (2007), Washington, DC: Board of Governors of the Federal Reserve System (May).

Feldstein, Martin (1997), "EMU and International Conflict," *Foreign Affairs, LXXVI:* 6, pp. 60–73.

Fernández-Arias, Eduardo, Ugo Panizza, and Ernesto Stein (2004), "Trade Agreements, Exchange Rate Disagreements," in V. Alexander, J. Mélitz, and G. M. von Furstenberg, eds., *Monetary Unions and Hard Pegs.* Oxford: Oxford University Press, pp. 135–150.

Fischer, Stanley (2001), "Exchange Rate Regimes: Is the Bi-Polar View Correct?" *Journal of Economic Perspectives, XV,* pp. 3–24.

Flandreau, Marc (2003), "The Bank, the States, and the Market: An Austro-Hungarian Tale for Euroland, 1867–1914," in F. H. Capie and G. E. Wood, eds., *Monetary Unions: Theory, History, Public Choice.* London: Routledge, pp. 111–41.

Frankel, Jeffrey A. (2003), "Experience of and Lessons from Exchange Rate Regimes in Emerging Economies," Working Paper 10032. Cambridge, MA: National Bureau of Economic Research.

Frankel, Jeffrey A., and Andrew K. Rose (1998), "The Endogeneity of the Optimum Currency Area Criteria," *Economic Journal, CVIII,* pp. 1009–24.

Frankel, Jeffrey A., and Andrew K. Rose (2002), "An Estimate of the Effect of Common Currencies on Trade and Income," *Quarterly Journal of Economics, 117,* pp. 437–66.

Frankel, Jeffrey A., and Shang-Jin Wei (1994), "Yen Bloc or Dollar Bloc? Exchange Rate Policies in East Asian Economies," in T. Ito and A. O. Krueger, eds., *Macroeconomic Linkages: Savings, Exchange Rates, and Capital Flows.* Chicago: University of Chicago Press, pp. 295–329.

Fratianni, Michele, and Jürgen von Hagen (1992), *The European Monetary System and European Monetary Union.* Boulder, CO: Westview.

Fuchs, William, and Francesco Lippi (2006), "Monetary Union with Voluntary Participation," *Review of Economic Studies, 73,* pp.437–57.

Galí, Jordi, and Roberto Perotti (2003), "Fiscal policy and monetary integration in Europe," *Economic Policy, XXXVII*, pp. 533–72.

Galí, Jordi, Stefan Gerlach, Julio Rotemberg, Harald Uhlig, and Michael Woodford (2004), "The Monetary Policy Strategy of the ECB Reconsidered," *Monitoring the European Central Bank V*. London: Centre for Economic Policy Research.

Gandolfo, Giancarlo (1992), "Monetary Unions," in P. Newman, M. Milgate, and J. Eatwell, eds., *The New Palgrave Dictionary of Money and Finance*. London: Palgrave.

Gaspar, Vítor, and Philipp Hartmann (2005), "The Euro and Money Markets: Lessons for European Financial Integration," in A. S. Posen, ed., *The Euro at Five: Ready for a Global Role?* Washington, DC: Peterson Institute for International Economics, pp. 87–98.

Genberg, Hans (2006), "Exchange-Rate Arrangements and Financial Integration in East Asia: On a Collision Course?" Hong Kong: Hong Kong Monetary Authority.

Genberg, Hans, Robert McCauley, Young Chul Park, and Avinash Persaud (2005), *Official Reserves and Currency Management in Asia: Myth, Reality and the Future*, 7th Geneva Report on the World Economy. Geneva: International Center for Monetary and Banking Studies.

Ghosh, Atish R., Anne-Marie Gulde, and Holger C. Wolf (2000), "Currency boards: more than a quick fix?" *Economic Policy, XXXI*, pp. 271–334.

Ghosh, Atish R., Anne-Marie Gulde, and Holger C. Wolf (2002), *Exchange Rate Regimes: Choices and Consequences*. Cambridge, MA: MIT Press.

Giambiagi, Fabio (1999), "MERCOSUR: Why Does Monetary Union Make Sense in the Long Run?" Integration and Trade Paper 9. Washington, DC: Inter-American Development Bank.

Giavazzi, Francesco, and Charles Wyplosz (2006), "Selection of the Central Bank Board Is a Fait Accompli," *Financial Times*, February 10.

Girardin, Eric (2004), "Information Exchange, Surveillance Systems, and Regional Institutions in East Asia," in Asian Development Bank, *Monetary and Financial Integration in East Asia: The Way Ahead*, vol. 1. Basingstoke: Palgrave, pp. 53–95.

Glick, Reuven, and Andrew Rose (2002), "Does a Currency Union Affect Trade? The Time Series Evidence," *European Economic Review, XLVI*, pp. 1125–51.

Goldberg, Linda S., and Cedric Tille (2005), "Vehicle Currency Use in International Trade," Working Paper 11127. Cambridge, MA: National Bureau of Economic Research.

Goldberg, Pinelopi Koujianou, and Frank Verboven (2004), "Cross-country price dispersion in the euro area: a case study of the European car market," *Economic Policy, XL*, pp. 485–521.

Goldstein, Morris (2002), "Managed Floating Plus," *Policy Analyses in International Economics 66*. Washington, DC: Peterson Institute for International Economics.

Goldstein, Morris, and Philip Turner (2004), *Controlling Currency Mismatches in Emerging Markets*. Washington, DC: Peterson Institute for International Economics.

González-Páramo, José Manuel (2005), "Regional Divergence in the Euro Area," www.ecb.int/press/key/date2005/html/sp050919.en.html.

Goodhart, Charles (2002), "Myths about the Lender of Last Resort," in C. Goodhart and G. Illing, eds., *Financial Crises, Contagion, and the Lender of Last Resort.* Oxford: Oxford University Press, pp. 227–45.

Goodhart, Charles, and Lu Dai (2003), *Intervention to Save Hong Kong: The Authorities' Counter-Speculation in Financial Markets.* Oxford: Oxford University Press.

Graboyes, Robert F. (1990), "The EMU: Forerunners and Durability," *Federal Reserve Bank of Richmond Economic Review, 76*, pp. 8–17.

Grenville, Stephen (2004), "Policy Dialogue in East Asia: Principles for Success," in G. de Brouwer and Y. Wang, eds., *Financial Governance in East Asia; Policy Dialogue, Surveillance and Cooperation.* London: Routledge, pp. 16–37.

Gros, Daniel, and Niels Thygesen (1999), *European Monetary Integration.* London: Addison Wesley Longmans.

Grubel, Herbert G. (1999), "The Case for the Amero: The Merits of Creating a North American Monetary Union," *Critical Issues Bulletin.* Vancouver: Frazer Institute.

Grubel, Herbert G. (2003), "The Merit of a North American Monetary Union," in D. Salvatore, J. W. Dean, and T. D. Willett, eds., *The Dollarization Debate.* Oxford: Oxford University Press, pp. 318–40.

G-7 (1999), *Strengthening the International Financial Architecture: Report from the G-7 Finance Ministers to the Köln Economic Summit.*

Gulde, Anne-Marie, David Hoelscher, Alain Ize, David Marston, and Gianni De Nicoló (2004), *Financial Stability in Dollarized Economies*, Occasional Paper 230. Washington, DC: International Monetary Fund.

Hamilton-Hart, Natasha (2000), "Regional Capital and Cooperation in Asia," in P. J. Katzenstein, N. Hamilton-Hart, K. Kato, and M. Yue, eds., *Asian Regionalism.* Ithaca, NY: Cornell University East Asia Series, pp. 115–69.

Hanke, Steve H. (2002), "On Dollarization and Currency Boards: Errors and Deception," *Journal of Policy Reform, V*, pp. 203–22.

Hanke, Steve H., Lars Jonung, and Kurt Schuler (1993), *Russian Currency and Finance: A Currency Board Approach to Reform.* London: Routledge.

Hartmann, Philipp, Angela Maddaloni, and Simone Manganelli (2003), "The Euro-Area Financial System: Structure, Integration, and Policy Initiatives," *Oxford Review of Economic Policy, XIX:1*, pp. 180–213.

Hawkins, John, and Paul Masson, eds. (2003), *Economic Aspects of Regional Currency Areas and the Use of Foreign Currencies*, Paper 17. Basel: Bank for International Settlements.

Hefeker, Casten, and Andreas Nabor (2005), "China's Role in East-Asian Monetary Integration," *International Journal of Finance and Economics, 10*, pp. 157–166.

Helleiner, Eric (2006), *Towards North American Monetary Union? The Politics and History of Canada's Exchange Rate Regime.* Montreal: McGill-Queen's University Press.

Helliwell, John F., and Ross McKitrick (1998), "Comparing Capital Mobility across Provincial and National Borders," Working Paper 6624. Cambridge, MA: National Bureau of Economic Research.

Henning, C. Randall (1998), "Systemic Conflict and Regional Monetary Integration: The Case of Europe," *International Organization, 52*, pp. 537–73.

Henning, C. Randall (2002), "East Asian Financial Cooperation," *Policy Analyses in International Economics, 68.* Washington, DC: Peterson Institute for International Economics.

Henning, C. Randall (2004), "East Asian Financial Cooperation and Global Adjustment: Building on the Chiang Mai Initiative" (unpublished manuscript).

Henning, C. Randall (2005), "Systemic Contextualism and Financial Regionalism: The Case of East Asia." Washington, DC: American University, www.hwwa.de/ Forschung/Handel_&_Entwicklung/docs/2006/Publikationen/Volz_FOX01.pdf.

Henning, C. Randall (2006), "Regional Arrangements and the International Monetary Fund," in E. M. Truman, ed., *Reforming the IMF for the 21st Century*, Special Report 19. Washington, DC: Peterson Institute for International Economics, pp. 171–83.

Hinds, Manuel (2004), "Is Dollarization a Worthwhile Option for Developing Countries?" *International Finance, 7:2*, pp. 287–309.

Hinds, Manuel (2006), *Playing Monopoly with the Devil: Dollarization and Domestic Currencies in Developing Countries.* New Haven, CT: Yale University Press.

Ho, Corrinne, Guonan Ma, and Robert N. McCauley (2005), "Trading Asian Currencies," *BIS Quarterly Review*, pp. 49–58 (March).

Honohan, Patrick, and Philip R. Lane (2000), "Will the Euro Trigger More Monetary Unions in Africa?" Working Paper WPS-2393. Washington, DC: World Bank.

Honohan, Patrick, and Philip R. Lane (2003), "Divergent inflation rates in EMU," *Economic Policy, XXXVII*, pp. 359–394.

Honohan, Patrick, and Philip R. Lane (2004), "Exchange Rates and Inflation under EMU: An Update," Discussion Paper 4583. London: Centre for Economic Policy Research.

House of Lords (2002–03), "Is the European Central Bank Working?" Paper 170, Select Committee on the European Union. London: The Stationary Office.

Humphrey, Thomas M. (1992), "Lender of Last Resort," in P. Newman, M. Milgate, and J. Eatwell, eds., *The New Palgrave Dictionary of Money and Finance.* London: Macmillan, pp. 571–73.

Independent Evaluation Office of the International Monetary Fund (2002), *Evaluation of Prolonged Use of IMF Resources.* Washington, DC: International Monetary Fund.

Independent Evaluation Office of the International Monetary Fund (2003), *The IMF and Recent Capital Account Crises: Indonesia, Korea, Brazil.* Washington, DC: International Monetary Fund.

Independent Evaluation Office of the International Monetary Fund (2004), *Evaluation of the Role of the IMF in Argentina, 1991–2001.* Washington, DC: International Monetary Fund.

Ingram, James C. (1959), "State and Regional Payments Mechanisms," *Quarterly Journal of Economics, LXXIII*, pp. 619–632.

International Monetary Fund (1999), "Exchange Arrangements and Currency Convertibility: Developments and Issues," *World Economic and Financial Surveys.* Washington, DC: International Monetary Fund.

International Monetary Fund (2005a), *Annual Report on Exchange Arrangements and Exchange Restrictions*. Washington, DC: International Monetary Fund.

International Monetary Fund (2005b), *World Economic Outlook,* (September). Washington, DC: International Monetary Fund.

International Monetary Fund (2006), "The Managing Director's Report on Implementing the Fund's Medium-Term Strategy." Washington, DC: International Monetary Fund.

Issa, Ramzi, Robert Lafrance, and John Murray (2006), "The Turning Black Tide: Energy Prices and the Canadian Dollar," Working Paper 2006–29. Ottawa: Bank of Canada.

Issing, Otmar (2005), "The ECB and the Euro – The First 6 Years: A View from the ECB," *Journal of Policy Modeling, 27*, pp. 405–20.

Issing, Otmar, Vitor Gaspar, Ignazio Angeloni, and Oreste Tristani (2001), *Monetary Policy in the Euro Area: Strategy and Decision Making at the European Central Bank.* Cambridge: Cambridge University Press.

Italianer, Alexander (1993), "Mastering Maastricht: EMU Issues and How They Were Settled," in G. Gretschmann, ed., *Economic and Monetary Union: Implications for National Policy-Makers.* Amsterdam: European Institute of Public Administration, pp. 51–113.

Ito, Takatoshi (2002), "A Case for a Coordinated Basket for Asian Countries." Paper Prepared for the Kobe Research Project Sponsored by the ASEM (Asia-Europe Meeting) of Finance Ministers.

Ito, Takatoshi (2004), "Inflation Targeting in Asia," Occasional Paper 1. Hong Kong: Hong Kong Institute for Monetary Research.

Ito, Takatoshi, Eiji Ogawa, and Yuri Sasaki (1998), "How Did the Dollar Peg Fail in Asia?" *Journal of the Japanese and International Economies, 12*, pp. 256–304.

Ito, Takatoshi, and Yung Chul Park (2004), "Exchange Rate Regimes in East Asia," in Asian Development Bank, *Monetary and Financial Integration in East Asia: The Way Ahead*, vol. 1. Basingstoke: Palgrave, pp. 148–88.

Jaeger, Albert (2003), "The ECB's Money Pillar: An Assessment," Working Paper 03/82. Washington, DC: International Monetary Fund.

Judson, Ruth A., and Richard Porter (1996), "The Location of U.S. Currency: How Much Is Abroad?" *Federal Reserve Bulletin, 82*, pp. 883–903.

Kahler, Miles (2000), "Legalization as Strategy: The Asia-Pacific Case," *International Organization, 54*, pp. 549–71.

Kalemli-Ozcan, Sebnem, Bent E. Sørenson, and Oved Yosha (1999), "Risk-Sharing and Industrial Specialization," Discussion Paper 2295. London: Centre for Economic Policy Research.

Kalemli-Ozcan, Sebnem, Bent E. Sørenson, and Oved Yosha (2004), "Asymmetric Shocks and Risk Sharing in a Monetary Union: Updated Evidence and Policy Implications for Europe," Discussion Paper 4463. London: Centre for Economic Policy Research.

Kamil, Herman (2006), "Does Moving to a Flexible Exchange Rate Regime Reduce Currency Mismatches in Firms' Balance Sheets?" Conference Paper. Washington, DC: International Monetary Fund.

Kamps, Annette (2005), "The Determinants of Currency Invoicing in International Trade." Kiel: Institute for World Economics (unpublished manuscript).

Katzenstein, Peter J. (2005), *A World of Regions*. Ithaca, NY: Cornell University Press.

Kawai, Masahiro (2004), "The Case for a Tri-polar Currency Basket for Emerging East Asia," in G. de Brouwer and M. Kawai, eds., *Economic Linkages and Implications for Exchange Rate Regimes in East Asia*. London: Routledge, pp. 360–84.

Kawai, Masahiro, and Shiguru Akiyama (2000), "Implications of the Currency Crisis for Exchange Rate Arrangements in Emerging East Asia," Working Paper 2502. Washington, DC: World Bank.

Kawai, Masahiro, and Taizo Motonishi (2005), "Macroeconomic Interdependence in East Asia: Empirical Evidence and Issues," in *Asian Economic Cooperation and Integration: Progress, Prospects and Issues*. Manila: Asian Development Bank, pp. 213–68.

Kawai, Masahiro, and Shinji Takagi (2005), "Strategy for a Regional Exchange Rate Arrangement in East Asia: Analysis, Review and Proposal," *Global Economic Review, 34*, pp. 22–65.

Keijzer, Cornelia (2001), "Japan and Asian Regional Integration," Research Report 1. Tokyo: Institute for International Monetary Affairs.

Kenen, Peter B. (1969), "The Theory of Optimum Currency Areas: An Eclectic View," in R. A. Mundell and A. K Swoboda, eds., *Monetary Problems of the International Economy*. Chicago: University of Chicago Press, pp. 41–60.

Kenen, Peter B. (1995), *Economic and Monetary Union in Europe: Moving Beyond Maastricht*. Cambridge: Cambridge University Press.

Kenen, Peter B. (2001), *The International Financial Architecture: What's New? What's Missing?* Washington, DC: Peterson Institute for International Economics.

Kenen, Peter B. (2002), "Currency Unions and Policy Domains," in D. A. Andrews, C. R Henning, and L. W. Pauly, eds., *Governing the World's Money*. Ithaca, NY: Cornell University Press, pp. 78–104.

Kenen, Peter B., and Ellen E. Meade (2004), "EU Accession and the Euro: Close Together or Far Apart?" in R. Pringle and N. Carver, eds., *EU Enlargement and the Future of the Euro*. London: Central Banking Publications, pp. 79–98.

Kenen, Peter B., Jeffrey R. Shafer, Nigel L. Wicks, and Charles Wyplosz (2004), *International Economic and Financial Cooperation: New Issues, New Actors, New Responses*. Geneva and London: International Center for Monetary and Banking Studies and Centre for Economic Policy Research.

Khor, Hoe Ee, Edward Robinson, and Jason Lee (2004), "Managed Floating and Intermediate Exchange Rate Systems: The Singapore Experience," MAS Staff Paper 37. Singapore: Monetary Authority of Singapore.

Kim, Jun Il, and Laura Papi (2005), "Regional Integration and Exchange Rate Arrangements," in M. Rodlauer and A. Schipke, eds., *Central America: Global Integration and Regional Cooperation*, Occasional Paper 243. Washington, DC: International Monetary Fund, pp. 69–98.

Kohl, Helmut (1997), "The Future of a Unified Europe," Address at the Eighth Sinclair-House Discussion of the Herbert Quandt Foundation, April 25.

Kole, Linda S., and Ellen E. Meade (1995), "German Monetary Targeting: A Retrospective View," *Federal Reserve Bulletin, LXXXI*, pp. 917–931.

Krugman, Paul (1993), "Lessons of Massachusetts for EMU," in F. Torres and F. Giavazzi, eds., *Adjustment and Growth in the European Monetary Union*. Cambridge: Cambridge University Press, pp. 241–61.

Kuroda, Haruhiko (2004), "Transitional Steps in the Road to a Single Currency in East Asia." Statement to the Seminar on a Single Currency for East Asia at the Annual Meeting of the Asian Development Bank.

Kuroda, Haruhiko, and Masahiro Kawai (2004), "Strengthening Regional Financial Cooperation in East Asia," in G. de Brouwer and Y. Wang, eds., *Financial Governance in East Asia: Policy Dialogue, Surveillance and Cooperation*. London: Routledge, pp. 136–66.

Kwan, Chi Hung (2001), *Yen Bloc: Toward Economic Integration in Asia*. Washington, DC: The Brookings Institution.

Kydland, Finn, and Edward Prescott (1977), "Rules Rather than Discretion: The Inconsistency of Optimal Plans," *Journal of Political Economy, 85*, pp. 473–90.

Lafrance, Robert, and Lawrence L. Schembri (2000), "The Exchange Rate, Productivity, and the Standard of Living," *Bank of Canada Review*, pp. 17–28.

Laidler, David (1999), "What Do the Fixers Want to Fix? The Debate about Canada's Exchange Rate Regime," C.D. Howe Institute Commentary 131. Toronto: C.D. Howe Institute.

Laidler, David (2002), "Inflation Targets Versus International Monetary Integration: A Canadian Perspective," Working Paper 3, University of Western Ontario.

Laidler, David, and Finn Poschmann (2000), "Leaving Well Enough Alone: Canada's Monetary Order in a Changing International Environment," C.D. Howe Institute Commentary 142. Toronto: C.D. Howe Institute.

Lane, Philip R. (2006), "The Real Effects of EMU," Discussion Paper 5536. London: Centre for Economic Policy Research.

Latter, Tony (2005), "Asian Monetary Union–Where Do We Go from Here?" Occasional Paper 2. Hong Kong: Hong Kong Institute for Monetary Research.

Lee, Jong-Wha, Yyung Chul Park, and Kwanho Shin (2004), "A Currency Union for East Asia," in Asian Development Bank, *Monetary and Financial Integration in East Asia: The Road Ahead*, vol. 2. Basingstoke: Palgrave, pp. 139–175.

Levy-Yeyati, Eduardo, and Federico Sturzenegger (2000), "Is Emu a Blueprint for Mercosur? *Cuadernos de Economia, 37*, pp. 63–99.

Levy-Yeyati, Eduardo, and Federico Sturzenegger (2001), "Exchange Rate Regimes and Economic Performance," *IMF Staff Papers, 47*, pp. 62–98.

Levy-Yeyati, Eduardo, and Federico Sturzenegger (2003), "To Float or to Fix: Evidence on the Impact of Exchange Rate Regimes on Growth," *American Economic Review, 93*, pp. 1173–93.

Levy-Yeyati, Eduardo, and Federico Sturzenegger (2005), "Classifying Exchange Rate Regimes: Deeds vs. Words," *European Economic Review, 49*, pp. 2079–105.

Lincoln, Edward (2004), *East Asian Economic Regionalism*. Washington, DC: The Brookings Institution.

Ludlow, Peter (1982), *The Making of the EMS*. London: Butterworth.

Ma, Guonan, and Eli M. Remolona (2005), "Opening Markets Through a Regional Bond Fund: Lessons from ABF2," *BIS Quarterly Review* (June), pp. 81–92.

Manzano, George (2000), "Is There Any Value-Added in the ASEAN Surveillance Process?" *ASEAN Economic Bulletin, 18*, pp. 94–102.

Martinez, Lorenza, and Alejandro Werner (2002), "The Exchange Rate Regime and the Currency Composition of Corporate Debt: The Mexican Experience," *Journal of Development Economics, 69*, pp. 315–34.

Massmann, Michael, and James Mitchell (2003), "Reconsidering the Evidence: Are Eurozone Business Cycles Converging?" Working Paper, Bonn: Centre for European Integration Studies.

Masson, Paul R., and Catherine Pattillo (2001), *Monetary Union in West Africa (ECOWAS)*, Occasional Paper 204. Washington, DC: International Monetary Fund.

Masson, Paul R., and Catherine Pattillo (2005), *The Monetary Geography of Africa*. Washington, DC: The Brookings Institution.

McCallum, John (1998), "Government Debt and the Canadian Dollar," *Current Analysis 2*, Royal Bank of Canada.

McKinnon, Ronald I. (1998), "Exchange Rate Coordination for Surmounting the East Asian Currency Crisis," *Asian Economic Journal, 12*, pp. 317–29.

McKinnon, Ronald I. (2000a), "After the Crisis, the East Asian Dollar Standard Resurrected: An Interpretation of High-Frequency Exchange-Rate Pegging." Stanford, CA: Stanford University, www-econ.stanford/edu/faculty/workp/swp00013 .pdf.

McKinnon, Ronald I. (2000b), "The East Asian Dollar Standard, Life after Death?" Banca Monte dei Paschi di Siena, *Economic Notes, 29*, pp. 31–82.

McKinnon, Ronald I. (2004), "The East Asian Exchange Rate Dilemma and the World Dollar Standard," in Asian Development Bank, *Monetary and Financial Integration in East Asia: The Way Ahead*, vol. 2. Basingstoke: Palgrave, pp. 177–208.

McKinnon, Ronald I. (2005), *Exchange Rates under the East Asian Dollar Standard: Living with Conflicted Virtue*. Cambridge, MA: MIT Press.

McNamara, Kathleen R. (1998), *The Currency of Ideas: Monetary Politics in the European Union*. Ithaca, NY: Cornell University Press.

McSheehy, Will (2005), "Economists Fear Plan for Monetary Union among Gulf States Is Losing Momentum," *Financial Times*, September 23.

Meade, Ellen E. (2003), "A (Critical) Appraisal of the ECB's Voting Reform," *Intereconomics – Review of European Economic Policy, XXXVII:3*, pp. 129–31.

Meade, Ellen E., and D. Nathan Sheets (2005a), "Regional Influences on FOMC Voting Patterns," *Journal of Money, Credit and Banking, XXXVII:4*, pp. 661–77.

Meade, Ellen E., and D. Nathan Sheets (2005b), "Documenting FOMC Voting Patterns," Conference Paper, National Bank of Austria.

Mélitz, Jacques (2004), "Risk Sharing and EMU," Discussion Paper 4460. London: Centre for Economic Policy Research.

Micco, Alejandro, Ernesto Stein, and Guillermo Ordoñez (2003), "The currency union effect on trade: early evidence from EMU," *Economic Policy, XXXVII*, pp. 317–56.

Midelfart-Knarvik, Karen Helene, Henry G. Overman, Stephen Redding, and Tony Venables (2000), *The Location of European Industry*. Brussels: European Commission.

Montiel, Peter J. (2004), "An Overview of Monetary and Financial Integration in East Asia," in Asian Development Bank, *Monetary and Financial Integration in East Asia: The Way Ahead*, vol. 1. Basingstoke: Palgrave, pp. 1–52.

Morales, R. Armando, and Alfred Schipke (2005), "Regional Integration and Financial System Issues," in M. Rodlauer and A. Schipke, eds., *Central America: Global Integration and Regional Cooperation*, Occasional Paper 243. Washington, DC: International Monetary Fund, pp. 99–111.

Mundell, Robert A. (1961), "The Theory of Optimum Currency Areas," *American Economic Review, LI*, pp. 657–65.

Mundell, Robert (2002), "Does Asia Need a Common Currency?" *Pacific Economic Review, 7*, pp. 3–12.

Mundell, Robert (2003), "Prospects for an Asian Currency Area," *Journal of Asian Economics, 14*, pp. 1–10.

Murray, John D. (2003), "Why Canada Needs a Flexible Exchange Rate," in D. Salvatore, J. W. Dean, and T. D. Willett, eds., *The Dollarization Debate*. Oxford: Oxford University Press, pp. 341–62.

Murray, John D., and James Powell (2003), "Dollarization in Canada: Where Does the Buck Stop?" *North American Journal of Economics and Finance, 14*, pp. 145–72.

Murray, John D., Lawrence Schembri, and Pierre St-Amant (2003), "Revisiting the Case for Flexible Exchange Rates in North America," *North American Journal of Economics and Finance, 14*, pp. 207–40.

National Bank of Austria (2005), "About the OeNB, 1878–1922: The Austro-Hungarian Bank," http://www.ocnb.at/en/ueber_die_oenb/bankh_archiv/geschichte_der_oenb/1878_bis_1922/18781922.jsp.

Nemoto, Yoichi (2003), "An Unexpected Outcome of the Asian Financial Crisis: Is ASEAN+3 (China, Japan, and South Korea) a Promising Vehicle for East Asian Monetary Cooperation?" Princeton, NJ: Princeton University Institute for International and Regional Studies.

Ngiam, Kee Jin, and Hazel Yuen (2001), "Monetary Cooperation in East Asia: A Way Forward," *Singapore Economic Review, 46*, pp. 211–46.

Nitsch, Volker (2005), "Have a Break, Have a . . . National Currency: When Do Monetary Unions Fall Apart?" in P. de Grauwe and J. Mélitz, eds., *Prospects for Monetary Unions after the Euro*. Cambridge, MA: MIT Press, pp. 319–45.

Nölling, Wilhelm (1993), *Monetary Policy in Europe after Maastricht*. London: Macmillan.

Obstfeld, Maurice, and Kenneth Rogoff (2005), "Global Current Account Imbalances and Exchange Rate Adjustments," *Brookings Papers on Economic Activity, 1*, pp. 67–123.

Obstfeld, Maurice, and Kenneth Rogoff (2007), "The Unsustainable U.S. Current Account Position Revisited," in R. H. Clarida, ed., *G7 Current Account Imbalances: Sustainability and Adjustment*. Chicago: University of Chicago Press, pp. 339–66.

Ogawa, Eiji, and Takatoshi Ito (2002), "On the Desirability of a Regional Basket Currency Arrangement," *Journal of the Japanese and International Economies, 16,* pp. 317–34.

Ogawa, Eiiji, Takatoshi Ito, and Yuri Nagataki Sasaki (2004), "Costs, Benefits, and Constraints of the Currency Basket Regime for East Asia," in Asian Development Bank, *Monetary and Financial Integration in East Asia: The Way Ahead,*" vol. 2. Basingstoke: Palgrave, pp. 209–37.

Ogawa, Eiji, and Junko Shimizu (2006), "Stabilization of Effective Exchange Rates under Common Currency Basket Systems," Working Paper 12198. Cambridge, MA: National Bureau of Economic Research.

Ojo, Michael (2003), "Regional Currency Areas and the Use of Foreign Currencies: The Experience of West Africa," in J. Hawkins and P. Masson, eds., *Regional Currency Areas and the Use of Foreign Currencies,* Paper 17. Basel: Bank for International Settlements.

Organisation for Economic Cooperation and Development (2005), *Economic Survey of China.* Paris: Organisation for Economic Cooperation and Development.

Padoa-Schioppa, Tommaso (1988), "The European Monetary System: A Long-Term View," in F. Giavazzi, S. Micossi, and M. Miller, eds., *The European Monetary System.* Cambridge: Cambridge University Press, pp. 369–84.

Padoa-Schioppa, Tommaso (2004a), *The Euro and Its Central Bank.* Cambridge, MA: MIT Press.

Padoa-Schioppa, Tommaso (2004b), "East Asian Monetary Arrangements: A European Perspective," *International Finance, 7,* pp. 311–23.

Padoan, Pier Carlo (2002), "EMU as an Evolutionary Process," in D. A. Andrews, C. R. Henning, and L. W. Pauly, eds., *Governing the World's Money.* Ithaca, NY: Cornell University Press, pp. 105–27.

Pagano, Marco, and Ernst-Ludwig von Thadden (2004), "The European Bond Markets under EMU," Discussion Paper 4779. London: Centre for Economic Policy Research.

Papaioannou, Elias, Richard Portes, and Gregorios Siourounis (2006), "Optimal Currency Shares in International Reserves: The Impact of the Euro and the Prospects for the Dollar, Working Paper 12333. Cambridge, MA: National Bureau of Economic Research.

Pastor, Robert A. (2001), *Toward a North American Community: Lessons from the Old World for the New.* Washington, DC: Peterson Institute for International Economics.

Patrick, Hugh (2005), "Japan, APEC, and East Asian Cooperation: Prime Minister Ohira's Legacy," New York: Columbia University APEC Study Center.

Plummer, Michael G., and Reid W. Click (2005), "Bond Market Developments and Integration in ASEAN," *International Journal of Finance and Economics, 10,* pp. 133–42.

Purposes and Functions (2005), Washington, DC: Board of Governors of the Federal Reserve System.

Rajan, Ramkishen (2002), "Exchange Rate Policy Options for Southeast Asia: Is There a Case for Currency Baskets? *The World Economy, 25,* pp. 137–63.

Rajan, Ramkishen, and Reza Sirigar (2004), "Centralized Reserve Pooling for the ASEAN+3 Countries," in Asian Development Bank, *Monetary and Financial Integration in East Asia: The Way Ahead*, vol. 2. Basingstoke: Palgrave, pp. 283–329.

Reinhart, Carmen M., Kenneth S. Rogoff, and Miguel A. Savastano (2003), "Addicted to Dollars," Working Paper 10015. Cambridge, MA: National Bureau of Economic Research.

Reinhart, Carmen M., and Kenneth S. Rogoff (2004), "The Modern History of Exchange Rate Arrangements: A Reinterpretation," *Quarterly Journal of Economics, CXIX*, pp. 1–48.

Ritschl, Albrecht, and Nikolaus Wolf (2003), "Endogeneity of Currency Areas and Trade Blocs: Evidence from the Inter-War Period," Discussion Paper 4112. London: Centre for Economic Policy Research.

Robson, William B. P., and David Laidler (2002), *No Small Change: The Awkward Economics and Politics of North American Monetary Integration*. Toronto: C.D. Howe Institute.

Rogoff, Kenneth (2001), "Why Not a Global Currency," *American Economic Review, XCI*, pp. 243–47.

Rogoff, Kenneth S., Aasim M. Husain, Ashoka Mody, Robin Brooks, and Nienke Oomes (2004), *Evolution and Performance of Exchange Rate Regimes*, Occasional Paper 229. Washington, DC: International Monetary Fund.

Rose, Andrew (2000), "One money, one market: estimating the effects of common currencies on trade," *Economic Policy, XXX*, pp. 9–33.

Rose, Andrew (2004), "The Effect of Common Currencies on International Trade: A Meta-analysis," in V. Alexander, G. M. von Furstenberg, and J. Mélitz, eds., *Monetary Unions and Hard Pegs*. Oxford: Oxford University Press, pp. 101–11.

Roubini, Nuriel, and Brad Setser (2004), "The U.S. as a Net Debtor: The Sustainability of the U.S. External Imbalance." New York and Oxford: Stern School of Business and Global Economic Governance Program.

Rubin, Robert E., and Jacob Weisberg (2003), *In an Uncertain World*. New York: Random House.

Sakakibara, Eisuke, and Sharon Yamakawa (2003), "Regional Integration in East Asia: Challenges and Opportunities – Part 1: History and Institutions," Working Paper WPS – 3078. Washington, DC: World Bank.

Sala-i-Martin, Xavier, and Jeffrey D. Sachs (1992), "Fiscal Federalism and Optimum Currency Areas: Evidence for Europe from the United States," in M. B. Canzoneri, V. Grilli, and P. R. Masson, eds., *Establishing a Central Bank: Issues in Europe and Lessons from the US*. Cambridge: Cambridge University Press, pp. 195–219.

Salvatore, Dominick (2003), "Which Countries in the Americas Should Dollarize?" in D. Salvatore, J. W. Dean, and T. D. Willett, eds., *The Dollarization Debate*. Oxford: Oxford University Press, pp. 196–205.

Salvatore, Dominick (2006), "Can NAFTA Be a Stepping Stone to Monetary Integration in North America?" *Economie Internationale, 107*, pp. 135–48.

Schinasi, Garry (2003), "Responsibility of Central Banks for Stability in Financial Markets," Working Paper 03/121. Washington, DC: International Monetary Fund.

Schinasi, Garry (2006), *Safeguarding Financial Stability: Theory and Practice.* Washington, DC: International Monetary Fund.

Schuler, Kurt, and Robert Stein (2000), "The Mack Dollarization Plan: An Analysis," Conference Paper, Federal Reserve Bank of Dallas (March).

Shin, Kwanho, and Yungjong Wang (2004), "Sequencing Monetary and Trade Integration," in G. de Brouwer and M. Kawai, eds., *Exchange Rate Regimes in East Asia.* London: Routledge, pp. 433–54.

Singh, Anoop, Agns Belaisch, Charles Collyns, Paula De Masi, Reva Krieger, Guy Meredith, and Robert Rennhack (2005), "Stabilization and Reform in Latin America: A Macroeconomic Perspective on the Experience Since the Early 1990s – Chapter VII: External Vulnerabilities," Occasional Paper 238. Washington, DC: International Monetary Fund.

Sørensen, Bent E., and Oved Yosha (1998), "International Risk Sharing and European Monetary Unification," *Journal of International Economics, XLV*, pp. 211–38.

Stasavage, David (2000), "The Franc Zone as an Agency of Restraint," in P. Collier and C. Patillo, eds., *Risk and Investment in Africa.* Basingstoke: Macmillan.

Stasavage, David, and Dominique Guillaume (2002), "When Are Monetary Commitments Credible? Parallel Agreements and the Sustainability of Currency Unions," *British Journal of Political Science, 32*, 119–46.

Steil, Benn, and Robert Litan (2006), *Financial Statecraft.* New Haven, CT: Yale University Press.

Sturm, Michael, and Nikolaus Siegfried (2005), "Regional Monetary Integration in the Member States of the Gulf Cooperation Council," Occasional Paper 31. Frankfurt: European Central Bank.

Summers, Lawrence H. (1999), "Statement before the Subcommittee on International Trade and Finance of the Senate Finance Committee" (April 22). Washington, DC: U.S. Treasury.

Svensson, Lars E. O. (1997), "Inflation Targeting in an Open Economy: Strict or Flexible Inflation Targeting?" Public Lecture, Victoria University of Wellington, New Zealand (November).

Svensson, Lars E. O. (2002a), "A Reform of the Eurosystem's Monetary-Policy Strategy is Increasingly Urgent," Briefing Paper for the Committee on Economic and Monetary Affairs of the European Parliament (May).

Svensson, Lars E. O. (2002b), "A Good Thing Could Happen to the ECB: An Improvement of the Eurosystem's Definition of Price Stability," Briefing Paper for the Committee on Economic and Monetary Affairs of the European Parliament (September).

Svensson, Lars E. O. (2003a), "How Should the Eurosystem Reform Its Monetary Strategy?" Briefing Paper for the Committee on Economic and Monetary Affairs of the European Parliament (February).

Svensson, Lars E. O. (2003b), "In the Right Direction, but Not Enough: The Modification of the Monetary-Policy Strategy of the ECB," Briefing Paper for the Committee on Economic and Monetary Affairs of the European Parliament (May).

Swoboda, Alexander K. (1991), *The Road to European Monetary Union: Lessons from the Bretton Woods Regime*, The 1991 Per Jacobsson Lecture. Washington: The Per Jacobsson Foundation, International Monetary Fund.

Tan, Kim Song, and Khor Hoe Ee (2005), "China's Changing Economic Structures and Its Implications for Regional Patterns of Trade Production and Integration," Working Paper 23–2005. Singapore: Singapore Management University.

Tenreyro, Silvana, and Robert J. Barro (2003), "Economic Effects of Currency Unions," Working Paper 9435. Cambridge, MA: National Bureau of Economic Research.

Thiessen, Gordon (1999), "The Euro: Its Economic Implications and Its Lessons for Canada," Speech to the Canadian Club of Ottawa (January).

Triffin, Robert (1960), *Gold and the Dollar Crisis: The Future of Convertibility*. New Haven, CT: Yale University Press.

Truman, Edwin M. (2003a), *Inflation Targeting*. Washington, DC: Peterson Institute for International Economics.

Truman, Edwin M. (2003b), "North American Monetary and Financial Integration: Notes on the US Perspective," *International Management, 8*, pp. 75–79.

Truman, Edwin M. (2005), "The Euro and Prospects for Policy Coordination," in A. S. Posen, ed., *The Euro at Five: Ready for a Global Role?* Washington, DC: Peterson Institute for International Economics, pp. 47–77.

Truman, Edwin M. (2006), "North American Monetary Union – Getting from Here to There," Unpublished Remarks, GEC Seminar Series in International Finance. New York: Council on Foreign Relations.

U.S. Senate (1999a), "Hearing on Official Dollarization in Emerging-Market Countries," Committee on Banking, Housing, and Urban Affairs, April 22.

U.S. Senate (1999b), "Hearing on Official Dollarization in Latin America," Committee on Banking, Housing, and Urban Affairs, July 15.

U.S. Senate (2000), "Hearing on S. 1879 – 'The International Monetary Stability Act,'" Committee on Banking, Housing, and Urban Affairs, February 8.

van Beek, Frits, José Roberto Rosales, Mayra Zermeño, Ruby Randall, and Jorge Sherpherd (2000), "The Eastern Caribbean Currency Union: Institutions, Performance, and Policy Issues," Occasional Paper 195. Washington, DC: International Monetary Fund.

van Zyl, Lamburtus (2003), "South Africa's Experience of Regional Currency Areas and the Use of Foreign Currencies," in J. Hawkins and P. Masson, eds., *Regional Currency Areas and the Use of Foreign Currencies*, Paper 17. Basel: Bank for International Settlements.

von Hagen, Jürgen (1992), "Fiscal Arrangements in a Monetary Union: Evidence from the U.S.," in D. E. Fair and C. de Boissieu, eds., *Fiscal Policy, Taxation, and the Financial System in an Increasingly Integrated Europe*. Deventer: Kluwer, pp. 337–59.

von Hagen, Jürgen (2003), "Fiscal Discipline and Growth in Euroland: Experiences with the Stability and Growth Pact." Bonn: Center for European Integration Studies.

Wang, Yunjong (2002), "Monetary and Financial Cooperation in East Asia: Future Directions for Institutional Arrangements of Monitoring and Surveillance." Seoul: Korea Institute for International Economic Policy.

Wang, Yunjong (2004), "Instruments and Techniques for Financial Cooperation," in G. de Brouwer and Y. Wang, eds., *Financial Governance in East Asia: Policy Dialogue, Surveillance and Cooperation*. London: Routledge, pp. 189–215.

Wang, Yunjong, and Wing Thye Woo (2004), "A Timely Information Exchange Mechanism, an Effective Surveillance System, and an Improved Financial Architecture for East Asia," in Asian Development Bank, *Monetary and Financial Integration in East Asia: The Way Ahead*, vol. 2. Basingstoke: Palgrave, pp. 425–58.

Wei, Shang-Jin (1998), "Currency Hedging and Goods Trade," Working Paper 6742. Cambridge, MA: National Bureau of Economic Research.

Williamson, John (1999), "The Case for a Common Basket Peg for East Asian Currencies," in S. Collignon, J. Pisani-Ferry, and Y. C. Park, eds., *Exchange Rate Policies for Emerging Asian Countries*. London: Routledge, pp. 327–43.

Williamson, John (2000), "Exchange Rate Regimes for Emerging Markets: Reviving the Intermediate Option," *Policy Analyses in International Economics 60*. Washington, DC: Peterson Institute for International Economics.

Williamson, John (2001), "The Case for a Basket, Band and Crawl (BBC) Regime for East Asia," in Reserve Bank of Australia, *RBA Annual Conference Volume*. Sydney: Reserve Bank of Australia, pp. 97–111.

Williamson, John (2003), "Dollarization Does Not Make Sense Everywhere," in D. Salvatore, J. W. Dean, and T. D. Willett, eds., *The Dollarization Debate*. Oxford: Oxford University Press, pp. 172–76.

Williamson, John (2005), "A Currency Basket for East Asia, Not Just China," Policy Briefs in International Economics PB05–1. Washington, DC: Peterson Institute for International Economics.

Wyplosz, Charles (1991), "Monetary Union and Fiscal Policy Discipline," in "The Economics of EMU," *European Economy*, Special Edition 1, pp. 165–84.

Wyplosz, Charles (2001), "A Monetary Union in Asia? Some European Lessons," in Reserve Bank of Australia, *RBA Annual Conference Volume*. Sydney: Reserve Bank of Australia, pp. 124–55.

Wyplosz, Charles (2004), "Regional Exchange Rate Arrangements: Lessons from Europe for Far East," in Asian Development Bank, *Monetary and Financial Integration in East Asia: The Way Ahead*, vol. 2. Basingstoke: Palgrave, pp. 241–84.

Yeats, Alexander (1998), "What Can Be Expected from African Regional Trade Arrangements?" Policy Research Working Paper 2004. Washington, DC: The World Bank.

Yoshino, Naoyuki, Sahoko Kaji, and Ayoko Suzuki (2002), "The Comparative Analysis of Exchange Rate Regimes." Paper Prepared for the Kobe Research Project Sponsored by the ASEM (Asia-Europe Meeting) of Finance Ministers.

Index